The Pursuit of Significance

Strategies for
Managerial Success in
Public Organizations

The Pursuit of Significance

Strategies for Managerial Success in Public Organizations

Robert B. Denhardt

WAVELAND

PRESS, INC.

Prospect Heights, Illinois

For information about this book, contact:
Waveland Press, Inc.
P.O. Box 400
Prospect Heights, Illinois 60070
(847) 634-0081
www.waveland.com

ABOUT THE AUTHOR

Robert B. Denhardt is Professor of Public Affairs at Arizona State University and Distinguished Visiting Scholar at the University of Delaware. He is a Past President of the American Society for Public Administration, a nationwide organization of academics and practitioners in the field of public administration at all levels of government. He was the founder and first chair of ASPA's National Campaign for Public Service, an effort to assert the dignity and worth of public service across the nation. He is also a member of the prestigious National Academy of Public Administration and a Fellow of the Canadian Centre for Management Development. Dr. Denhardt is the author of *In the Shadow of Organization, Theories of Public Organization, Public Administration: An Action Orientation*, as well as many other books and articles in the field of public administration. He has also been a consultant to various public and private organizations, including public universities, primarily in the areas of leadership and organizational change.

PREFACE

There is a revolution taking place in public management. Around the world, many highly regarded public managers are transforming hierarchical, rule-bound public bureaucracies into organizations driven by a commitment to common purpose, by a concern for serving the public promptly and well, by empowerment and shared leadership, by an approach called "pragmatic incrementalism," and, most of all, by a dedication to public service. *The Pursuit of Significance* portrays the approaches and philosophies that these managers employ in making dramatic improvements in the quality and productivity of their organizations. It tells of a variety of revolutionary public managers committed to an active and responsive public service and having enormous insight into how that might be done.

Most of the managers whose stories are told in these pages were "nominated" by their colleagues and by well-placed experts in the field of public administration through a somewhat informal but highly revealing process. The project began as I traveled across the United States as president-elect and president of the American Society for Public Administration, visiting with practitioners at all levels of government and in all policy areas. Later I represented ASPA at meetings in Australia, Canada, and Great Britain.

As I talked with people in different areas, I asked who they considered the very best public managers among their colleagues in government. Later I also asked a number of leaders in the field of public administration the same question. In turn, I contacted those "nominated" and asked about the approaches and philosophies of public management that characterized their work. In some cases, I was able to interview these individuals in person, in others we talked by phone, and in others we exchanged extensive correspondence.

What was surprising was that these managers sought organizational change in similar ways—and that their approaches were strikingly different from those that have traditionally characterized the management of public bureaucracies. Five approaches—a commitment to values, a concern for serving the public, empowerment and shared leadership, pragmatic incrementalism, and a dedication to public service—seem to capture the new style of management these highly regarded public managers employ. These approaches constitute the core of this book and provide a model for effective public management that I suspect is just the beginning of the "revolution."

Even beyond these alternatives, public managers today are constantly experimenting with new ways of coping with the terribly difficult circumstances under which they must operate. Over the past several years, government has been attacked, abused, and "hollowed out" to the point that public managers today are under constant pressure to do more with less. At the same time, public managers are committed to public service and to creating organizations that are efficient, effective, and responsible elements in the process of democratic governance. In all that they do, these managers are trying to make a difference in the world around them, trying quite simply to make the world a better place. They aren't necessarily motivated by the pursuit of profit, nor even by the pursuit of happiness. They are driven by the pursuit of significance.

In many ways, the work of these managers and this book itself were precursors of what is now being called the "New Public Service," a movement emphasizing change and innovation in government, extensive interaction between administrators and citizens, and a deep commitment to public service. Denhardt and Denhardt (*Public Administration Review*, forthcoming) describe the New Public Service as an approach emphasizing the role of values in public service, especially one that focuses attention on rebuilding trust between government and its citizens and establishing more humane and flexible public organizations. The New Public Service is built around the following principles.

1. *Serve rather than steer*—The primary role of the public servant is helping citizens articulate and meet their shared interests rather than attempting to control or steer society in new directions.

2. *The public interest is the aim, not the by-product*—Public administrators must make creating a collective, shared notion of the public interest paramount. The goal is not to find

quick solutions driven by individual choices; rather, it is the creation of shared interests and shared responsibility.

3. *Think strategically, act democratically*—Policies and programs meeting public needs can be most effectively and responsibly achieved through collective efforts and collaborative processes.

4. *Serve citizens, not customers*—The public interest is the result of a dialogue about shared values rather than the aggregation of individual self-interest. Therefore, public servants should not merely respond to the demands of "customers," but rather focus on building relationships of trust and collaboration with and among citizens.

5. *Accountability isn't simple*—Public servants must be attentive to more than the market; they must also attend to statutory and constitutional law, community values, political norms, professional standards, and citizen interests.

6. *Value people, not just productivity*—Public organizations and the networks in which they participate are more likely to be successful in the long run if they are operated through processes of collaboration and shared leadership based on respect for all people.

7. *Value citizenship and public service above entrepreneurship*—The public interest is better advanced by public servants and citizens committed to making meaningful contributions to society rather than by entrepreneurial managers acting as if public money were their own.

Described in this way, the New Public Service stands in some contrast to those ideas associated with "reinvention," the "new managerialism," and, most recently, the "New Public Management." That movement, which has dominated discussions of public administration and public management through the nineties, builds on the familiar refrain that government should be run like a business. Correspondingly, governments have come to rely on the use of market mechanisms and terminology, in which the relationship between public agencies and their "customers" is seen as involving transactions similar to those that occur in the marketplace. Public managers are urged to "steer, not row" their organizations and are challenged to find ways to privatize previously governmentally provided functions. As the New Public Management has evolved, its dependence on market mechanisms and business values has become more clear. For example, the New Public Management relies on market-like arrangements such as competition within units of government and across government boundaries; it involves privatization of previously public functions; and it employs a variety of incentives and measures of results to move employees toward given objectives. Most importantly, the New Public Management involves not merely applying private sector *techniques* in public agencies, but also transplanting private sector *values* into the public sector. Public managers are urged to think in terms of individual self-interest, to behave in an entrepreneurial fashion, to create conditions of competition wherever possible, and to rely on market mechanisms rather than public values.

The alternative, the New Public Service, exemplified by the work of those managers in this book, focuses much more clearly on values and the public interest rather than on markets and self-interest. The New Public Service suggests a sharing of leadership responsibilities throughout public agencies and in their interactions with citizens and external groups. In the past, public administration was often viewed as comparable to a vending machine—you put your money in and hoped that you got the product you wanted (and sometimes kicked the machine when you didn't!). Increasingly, administrators in the New Public Service will not merely respond to citizens by saying, "Yes, we can" or "No, we can't." Instead, administrators will share responsibilities both within their organizations and with citizens to identify important needs and interests and to develop ways of responding to them. Their role will not be one of "steering" but one of facilitating, negotiating, and brokering solutions to important public problems.

Over the past several decades, trust in government has decreased dramatically. The New Public Management suggested that trust would be rebuilt if only we created a government that works better and costs less. While these are important goals, advocates of the New Public Service suggest that trust in government will only occur where government is seen to be responsive and to act with integrity. As we demonstrate here, public administrators are, for the most part, people whose motivations and rewards are more than simply money or security. They are people who want to make a difference. They are people engaged in the pursuit of significance, and on that basis we can build a New Public Service.

ACKNOWLEDGMENTS

So many people have contributed to this book that any listing is bound to come up short. However, I want to give special thanks to those who guided me toward the managers whose work I examine here. In the United States, Enid Beaumont, Chet Newland, and Carl Stenberg, all recent presidents of the American Society for Public Administration, helped to identify the best public managers and were highly supportive of my work, as was Shirley Wester, former executive director of ASPA. Outstanding public managers were also suggested to me by Bill Hansell of the International City Management Association, Keon Chi of the Council of State Governments, Ray Kline of the National Academy of Public Administration, Mark Abramson of the Council for Excellence in Government, and Carolyn Burstein of the Federal Quality Institute. In addition, my work benefited greatly from extensive and very stimulating discussions with Bob Backoff, David Booker, Cheryle Broom, Linda Capra, Vera Coombs, Joe Coffee, Peter and Linda deLeon, Michael Diamond, Mary Faulk, Pat Florestano, Lou Fox, George Frederickson, Mary Guy, Sandy Hale, Barry Hammond, Larry Hesser, Marc Holzer, Jim Jarrett, Phil Jeffress, Ed Jennings, Katherine Jesch, Tom Kelly, Norm King, Gilda Lambert, Naomi Lynn, Astrid Merget, John Nalbandian, Lloyd Nigro, Elaine Orr, Mike Pacanowsky, John Parr, John Pelzer, Phil Penland, Jan Perkins, Ted Poister, Kevin Prelgovisk, Jim Pyle, Charles Sampson, Frank Sherwood, and John Thomas.

In Australia, Hal Colebatch was largely responsible for my first trip "down under" and has remained a source of great help and encouragement. Judy Johnston and Gordon Pratt were especially helpful in identifying outstanding public managers in Australia, while I was aided tremendously by conversations in Australia with Jenny Bedlington, Peter Brennan, Clare Burton, Chris Chaseling, Greg Clarke, Pieter Degeling, Alison Gaines, Michael Howard, Owen Hughes, Dick Humphrey, John Moller, Peter Murfett, Jean Sherrell, Chris Selby Smith, and Roger Whetenhall.

In Canada, Joe Galimberti of the Institute of Public Administration of Canada was enormously supportive of this project in a variety of ways; he could not have been more helpful. In addition, I received special help and often inspiration from Janet Austin, Otto Brodtrick, John D. W. Clarke, Jim David, Ken Kernaghan, John Langford, Brian Marson, H. J. Osborne, and Bruce Young.

In Great Britain, David Falcon, former Director General of the Royal Institute of Public Administration, was enormously helpful in setting up interviews with some outstanding public managers. I especially benefited from my conversations with Michael Clarke, Mike Fogdon, Pamela Gordon, Marianne Neville Rolfe, and Sandy Russell.

A final word of thanks to all those whose names appear here and the hundreds of others who shared their experiences and their insights with me over the course of several years. I count these people among the real heroes and heroines of public service today. If I have been able to capture, even in a partial way, the texture and brilliance of their work, I'll be terribly pleased. Many thanks to all!

Robert B. Denhardt

CONTENTS

CHAPTER ONE
A REVOLUTION IN PUBLIC MANAGEMENT
1

Studies of Management Excellence
3
The Roots of Rationalism and Managerialism
6
The Critique of Traditional Theory and Practice
11
An Alternative Approach
15

CHAPTER TWO
A COMMITMENT TO VALUES
21

Managing Cultural Change
23
Missions, Visions, and Getting the Work Done
33
Developing a Vision Through Strategic Planning
36
Developing a Management Philosophy 38
Planning for Water Resources 46

Organization Development Approaches
54
Organization Development in Palm Springs 55

Translating Vision into Action 60

Conclusion
67

Contents

CHAPTER FIVE
PRAGMATIC INCREMENTALISM
177

CHAPTER SIX
A DEDICATION TO PUBLIC SERVICE
225

Contents

CHAPTER SEVEN
THE PURSUIT OF SIGNIFICANCE
265

CHAPTER ONE

A Revolution in Public Management

Many people are now proclaiming a "revolution" in management thinking, a revolution that is making possible new gains in quality and productivity in both the public and private sectors. Rather than seeking uniformity and control, managers are talking about adaptability, creativity, and shared power. Rather than depending on traditional hierarchical forms of organization, managers are experimenting with flatter structures and more participatory ways of organizing. Rather than focusing on the internal workings of the organization, managers are becoming more sensitive to their clients or "customers" and more attentive to their relations with those in other organizations. And the results are impressive.

Public managers have been at the forefront of these developments. In Australia, Jenny Bedlington, Secretary of the Department of Community Services in the State of Tasmania, inspired people in her organization to reconsider their basic approaches to "business-as-usual" by paying special attention to emerging issues of social justice, by responding to the needs of citizens, and by establishing incentives for creative and effective management. In Canada, Brian Marson, Comptroller-General of British Columbia, embraced a new approach to managing a finance-based organization, emphasizing a strong service orientation and empowerment of employees throughout the organization to act effectively in pursuit of the department's mission. In Great Britain, Mike Fogdon of the Employment Service brought about a dramatic change in the culture of his organization, by emphasizing a strong client orientation and by decentralizing decision making. In the United States, Stephen Higgins of the federal Bureau of Alcohol, Tobacco, and Firearms worked hard to create a new organizational culture that redirected the mission of the organization and created a new spirit of commitment to its work. Similarly, Mary Faulk of the State of Washington transformed the Department of Licensing from a rigid control-oriented bureaucracy to a more flexible and responsive service-oriented agency. At the local level, Robert O'Neill, City Manager of Hampton, Virginia, remarkably restructured his local government management team to allow for increased employee participation and leadership.

The dramatic successes of these and other public managers have been driven both by broad social and cultural trends and by some specific and immediate challenges within their jurisdictions. Certainly, the world is moving at an ever-increasing pace, and change and complexity are commonplace. Under these circumstances, public managers are coming to recognize that maintaining control is far less important than encouraging creativity and change. For this reason, they are shifting their focus from "giving orders" to "promoting dialogue and innovation." Similarly, the interconnectedness of all aspects of society makes the relationships between and among organizations as crucial to their success or failure as their own internal ways of operating. Consequently, many public managers now view their work with other organizations as important or even more important than maintaining the internal system.

These changes have also been triggered by circumstances that are more immediate and, in some cases, peculiar to the public sector. Obviously, many public organizations have been forced to cut their budgets, while at the same time maintaining a high level of quality in their services; they have been asked to "do more with less." Agencies have been "hollowed out," drastically reduced in budgets and staffing levels. Consequently, many public managers feel that they are "too busy fighting the gators to drain the swamp." Yet, many of these managers have stepped up to the challenge and undertaken dramatic transformations of their organizations; they have begun comprehensive efforts to improve quality and productivity.

Some public managers have acted under the threat of cutbacks; but many others have acted simply in response to a weak public perception of the organization or a lackluster image of their agency's performance. This feature of recent change efforts in public organizations was pointed out by Sandford Borins of the University of Toronto, who studied a large number of innovative public organizations in Canada. He discovered that most comprehensive change efforts in those agencies were stimulated less by the kind of financial failure that often sparks massive changes in private organizations than by a public perception that the organization was failing to meet its mission or that the mission itself had somehow become irrelevant. For a variety of reasons, then, public managers have sought dramatic improvements in the work of their agencies. In many cases, they have cast aside older approaches to management, seeking new and different paths to achieve higher levels of performance.

STUDIES OF MANAGEMENT EXCELLENCE

The alternative approach that many managers in the private sector have chosen has been described in several publications, perhaps most notably in Thomas J. Peters and

Robert H. Waterman, Jr.'s *In Search of Excellence.* Peters and Waterman identified several private sector organizations in the United States with reputations for outstanding performance; then they tried to isolate the characteristics of management that made these organizations successful. Their list included such items as a bias for action, staying close to the customer, developing productivity through people, staying hands-on and value-driven, and permitting autonomy and entrepreneurship. (Incidentally, one of the special virtues of the Peters and Waterman study was its success in placing theoretical ideas in a practical context; theirs were ideas that managers could "feel" in their work.)

The factors that contribute to success in private organizations, however, are not necessarily those that advance success in the public sector. Public organizations are, for the most part, service-oriented and driven substantially by the needs, interests, and demands of their clients as well as the citizenry in general. At the same time, public organizations are constrained by a variety of rules and regulations, many of which (for example, due process requirements in employment issues) have developed in response to appropriate political concerns. By virtue of being part of the governmental system, public organizations are subject to important ethical demands associated with democratic governance, especially the demands for openness and participation. The work of those in public organizations is different from (some would even say harder than) the work of those in private organizations.

For this reason, there have been several efforts to identify characteristics of high performance *public* organizations. For example, prior to the Peters and Waterman study, Kenneth A. Gold of the U.S. Office of Personnel Management studied public as well as private organizations and concluded that management in successful organizations was most often based on such ideas as delegation of authority and responsibility, shared decision making, participation and involvement, and trust and integrity. Later, Barbour, Fletcher, and Sipel adapted the Peters and Waterman framework to their own search for excellence in local government, commenting on such attributes as an action orientation, closeness of citizens, autonomy and entrepreneurship, and an employee orientation.

Most recently, a study by Otto Brodtrick of the Office of the Auditor General in Canada focused on "well-performing organizations" in Canadian government, asking what aspects of management philosophy and management practice made them distinctive. The resulting list included an emphasis on people, participative leadership, innovative work styles, a strong client orientation, and, most important, a mindset that seeks optimum performance. In Brodtrick's view, those in well-performing organizations "hold values that drive them to always seek improvement in their organization's performance. When conditions change, they adjust their methods not their values. Because of this orientation toward performance and adaptability, the organization performs well even in a changing environment. This mindset may be the most important attribute of all."

Each of these studies has contributed in important ways to our understanding of what managerial approaches or philosophies underlie success in public organizations. Yet, there has been no comprehensive effort to draw together both the theoretical and the practical implications of these revolutionary efforts in a way that might help others improve their work in public organizations. That is the purpose of this book.

Over the past several years, both during my time as president of the American Society for Public Administration and since, I have had occasion to talk with public managers at all levels of government in Australia, Canada, Great Britain, and the United States. I asked them which of their colleagues are considered to have been the most successful —the people who have made the greatest strides in public sector management. I then contacted these individuals and asked about the strategies they found most effective. From these discussions, several themes emerged, ideas these highly regarded public managers feel hold great promise for improving the quality and productivity of their organizations. In the following pages, I will chronicle the approaches and philosophies that characterize the work of these revolutionary public managers.

THE ROOTS OF
RATIONALISM AND MANAGERIALISM

We should be clear up front about the changes that take place as public managers move in dramatic new directions. One way to do this is to examine some essentials of traditional management practice, as well as some of the problems associated with this conventional approach. Although we now recognize the drawbacks of rule-bound hierarchies, although we now resist the old concepts of authoritarian command and control, and although we now know of the ridiculous and self-serving things that happen in bureaucratic organizations (public and private), most of our organizations are still built along hierarchical lines and managed with the same attention to power and regulation as they were years ago. To understand the tenacity of these traditional approaches to organization and management, let's examine the ideas and practices that have historically provided the justification for centralized, hierarchical structures. Then, hopefully, we can begin to move beyond such patterns.

Administrators in public organizations around the world talk about the older approach to public management in various ways, but two terms that seem to characterize this approach are *rationalism* and *managerialism*. The idea of rationalism in the conduct of public affairs has a long history in thinking about public management. It was, of course, the German sociologist Max Weber who outlined the defining characteristics of the "ideal-type" bureaucracy—a hierarchy of impersonal offices to which people were appointed based on their technical qualifications, that is, their ability to perform those specialized tasks required by the division of labor within the organization, and through which they were subject to strict discipline and control. Weber felt that bureaucracy was important because "experience tends to universally show that the purely bureaucratic type of administration . . . is . . . capable of attaining the highest degree of efficiency and is in that sense formally the most rational known means of carrying out . . . control over human beings." In another passage, Weber stated, "For the needs of mass administration today, it is completely indispensable." For Weber, rationality in administration meant efficiency, and efficiency could only be attained through bureaucracy.

This same theme was at the core of other early approaches to management, particularly that of Frederick Taylor, whose "scientific management" was not only significant in its impact on the private sector but also, despite union (and legislative) protests, influential in the public sector. Taylor felt that through the rigid application of "scientific" principles based on rigorous and logical analysis the "one best way" of accomplishing any task could be found. A clever analyst, for example, could calculate (as Taylor did) the optimum weight of a shovelful of dirt lifted by an outstanding shoveler, then apply that lesson to improve the productivity of others. The same principles of "time and motion" could be adapted to most other tasks, just as today some organizations measure the number of keystrokes that data entry personnel make per hour or the number of rooms that hotel employees can clean in an hour. Interestingly, Taylor's philosophy not only changed various work processes, it also redefined the manager's role in public and private organizations, to include the calculation and design of the most efficient ways of getting things done.

In the field of public administration, the American "administrative management" theorists of the thirties and forties were also interested in efficiency and effectiveness, though their approach focused mainly on issues of organizational structure. Such a preoccupation with structure was understandable, for government organizations were growing rapidly, in both size and complexity. It only made sense, therefore, that Luther Gulick, the first chief administrator of New York City and one of the founders of the American Society for Public Administration, would write about ways a public manager should go about creating a new organization, dividing labor on the basis of purpose, process, persons, or place. Structural issues such as who reports to whom, how many people one manager could supervise, or how managers could best arrange the offices reporting to them were the paramount issues in public management theory and practice during this period and the next several decades.

In Weber and others, rationality is equated with efficiency; in Gulick and others, being attentive to organizational design is the first order of business for the manager. A final element of the rationalist paradigm is the idea that a science of organization can be built to support the quest for rational efficiency. Herbert Simon, whose book *Administrative Behavior* was first published in the late 1940s, argued persuasively for greater attention to the actual behavior of human beings in organizations and held that public organizations (like other organizations) could best be understood "scientifically" through a strict separation of fact and values. According to Simon, although facts could be said to be right or wrong, values were more elusive. Consequently, the theorist and, by implication, the manager would do well to stick to the facts, putting aside those troublesome issues of human values that sometimes arise in organizations. Understanding the factual basis for administrative behavior would allow the manager to explain, to predict, and eventually to control the behavior of individuals in the organization so that work could be accomplished with the utmost efficiency. In Simon's work, the rationalist view was given its classic formulation—a formulation still familiar today.

In these early writings, the idea of rationalism in the conduct of public organizations was complemented and, indeed, more recently has been extended by the notion of managerialism. Managerialism, which characterizes much management practice in the public sector today and is a topic of special debate in Australia, is essentially the application of market principles and business practices to the management of government. It is often associated with moves to implant private sector incentive systems in the public sphere. In some cases, both specific agencies and the public generally have benefited from this approach. For example, strategic planning activities (when properly carried out) and incentives for effective performance by managers or others have proven beneficial in a number of cases. Similarly, many public managers have found a more entrepreneurial style helpful. Unfortunately, managerialism can lead to excessive control and regulation. However, it is most vulnerable in its ethical content—or lack thereof. In its most extreme technical applications, managerialism embraces a variety of practices that are antithetical to those democratic principles that should guide work in the public sector (indeed, many are even antithetical to contemporary management practices in today's private sector). For these reasons, managerialism must be viewed with care and even some skepticism.

In the United States, the managerialist perspective received early and significant support in an essay by Woodrow Wilson—an essay many believe initiated the self-conscious study of public administration in America. Wilson argued, among other things, that government should be run like a business, with the principles and techniques of enlightened business management permeating its structure and its operations. For example, he contended that public organizations, like business organizations, should have a single source of executive authority, wielding power through a hierarchical system. For this to occur, however, the potentially corrupting influence of politics should be separated from the administrative sphere; that is, separate politics (or policy formation) from the management of government agencies. Political officials would set policies, and administrative personnel would carry them out. Only if this were to happen would the economic values of the market, especially the notion of efficiency, govern the conduct of public agencies.

These ideas sound surprisingly contemporary, especially as the permissiveness and rebelliousness of the late 1960s and the early 1970s yielded to the more conservative and market-oriented mood of the 1980s and the early 1990s. The result has been a more market-driven approach to the conduct and delivery of public services—an approach that seeks to transplant business-oriented concepts to the public sector. Some of these ideas have been quite positive: Public

9

managers have become more attentive to planning, more results-oriented, and more attuned to cost-effectiveness. But, as has always been the case, business concepts cannot be completely embraced in the public sector, because the circumstances and, more important, the core values are different.

A variety of politically driven efforts to bring business values to bear on the work of the public service crystallized in the 1980s. In Australia, for example, Neville Wran, former Premier of New South Wales, speaking about the new management practices being encouraged in Australia, stated, "In implementing these new management policies we have sought to impose upon our departments and authorities the same type of financial discipline and performance criteria as the private sector." In Canada, Brian Mulroney initiated a project called "Public Service 2000" and expressed his desire for Canadian government to become "leaner and meaner." In Great Britain, the Thatcher government launched the Financial Management Initiative "to promote in each department an organization and system in which managers at all levels have: a clear view of their objectives and means to assess, and, wherever possible, measure outputs or performances in relation to those objectives [and] well-defined responsibility for making the best use of their resources including a critical scrutiny of output and value for money." Finally, in the United States, the Grace Commission was appointed to ferret out waste and inefficiency at the federal level, while nearly all states and localities, under the pressure of limited resources, were forced to take action to "streamline" government.

There is no question that the values of rationalism and managerialism continue to dominate administrative practice in public organizations around the world. Not only are most contemporary public organizations governed by traditional values, especially those of hierarchy and control, but somewhat surprisingly there continues to be a significant academic justification for such measures. One American writer describes four preconditions for successful policy implementation: communications, resources, dispositions or attitudes, and bureaucratic structure. He suggests that orders must be clear and accurate, that resources must be sufficient, and that authority must be commensurate with responsibility. All of these admonitions were also part of administrative management theorizing in the thirties and forties. In a chapter on bureaucratic structure, for example, he describes the problem of fragmentation in public organizations, suggesting the importance of concentrated executive authority exercised through a hierarchical chain of command—recommendations straight from the earliest proverbs of public administration.

Other theorists continue to endorse the concept of hierarchy, another outgrowth of the rationalist/managerialist position. For instance, Aaron Wildavsky of the University of California, an internationally respected writer on the policy process, recently presented a defense of both hierarchy and bureaucracy, then asked pointedly, "What is left for public administration . . . if its hierarchical form of organization and its search for efficiency are rejected?" If we only slightly rephrase the question, the answer is that a public administration *preoccupied* with neither hierarchy nor efficiency has much to offer, including not only efficiency but effectiveness, reason, and responsibility.

THE CRITIQUE OF
TRADITIONAL THEORY AND PRACTICE

Against the mainstream of rationalism and managerialism in public administration, a consistent and important dissenting view has persisted, one that is now becoming prominent. Among the voices heard in support of an alternative more consistent with the norms and values of public service, none has been more important than that of Dwight Waldo, a leading American public administration scholar and longtime editor of the *Public Administration Review.* Quite early, Waldo challenged the scientific management of

Frederick Taylor as well as the implicit rationalism of the administrative management theorists and others, such as Herbert Simon, who continued the rationalist tradition. Waldo pointed out that the early theorists and practitioners in public administration, though highly pragmatic people concerned with immediate and practical problems, held implicit beliefs that constituted a normative theory of politics and governance. For example, Simon's supposedly value-free approach to understanding administrative behavior held one value paramount, the value of efficiency. In contrast, a variety of other criteria might be used to gauge the work of those in public organizations—liberty, justice, equity, equality, responsiveness, to name just a few.

Pursuing the same point, one that should be taken to heart by the managerialists of today as well as those of a half century ago, the American scholar and practitioner Marshall Dimock poignantly warned in the 1930s that although mechanical efficiency is "coldly calculating and inhuman," successful administration is "warm and vibrant." Public administration, he felt, "is more than a lifeless pawn. It plans, it contrives, it philosophizes, it educates, it builds for the community as a whole." The point is not that efficiency is unimportant; indeed, there is no question but that efficiency is extremely important in government. The point is that efficiency is not the single nor even necessarily the most important criterion for evaluating the work of public agencies.

More recently, there has been a sustained critique of bureaucracy and hierarchy as well as of their underlying motive, rationalism. Bureaucratic systems are often characterized as rigid and unresponsive, objectifying and depersonalizing both members and clients, and exerting unnecessary and psychologically demeaning control over their members. Perhaps most important, the values underlying bureaucracy have been found lacking; for example, the bureaucratic equation of rationality with efficiency means that other values, such as responsiveness to the public interest, are not only downplayed but are by definition considered "irrational."

The failures of traditional management practice in the public sector have been sounded frequently and by a diverse group of managers and public servants. Hugh Faulkner, Secretary General of the International Chamber of Commerce in Paris and a keen student of government, remarks that contemporary public institutions are

> far too process-driven, far too governed by rules, far too hierarchical and far too prone to built-in control mechanisms. In turn, these limit the freedom of action, limit the capacity to respond and limit initiative. Routine is a servant of control. The capacity for government to respond to change will in large measure depend on its ability to adapt institutionally, to build in more flexibility and responsiveness and to introduce what I describe as managerial adaptiveness.

Unfortunately, many of the negative features Faulkner discusses seem endemic to hierarchical bureaucratic systems, systems for making activities routine and predictable. Moreover, bureaucratic systems depend on tight controls to ensure that rules and regulations are complied with. But, as Otto Brodtrick points out, "the demands of customers frequently change, requiring the very flexibility and innovation that have been standardized out of the bureaucracy's operations." The rationality of bureaucracy may not be so rational after all.

Extreme applications of managerialism have also come under attack. While it is one thing to transpose business *practices* into the public sector, it is quite another to transpose business *standards* into the public sector. Two issues seem especially significant. First, there is the problem of technical overkill. In recent applications of managerialism, there is a tendency toward technical (rather than human) criteria for judging the work of those in the public service. The impulse is to concentrate on activities that can be quantified, not taking into account human values such as justice, equity, or compassion that should also be part of the evaluation of public employees and public programs. One student of the Australian public service explains: "The [new managerialist] approach to performance measurement . . . is concerned with unit cost and output, and has not developed indicators which address dynamic efficiency [responsiveness to change, innovation] or which focus on equality and effectiveness matters. It is distinguished by its fascination with targets and other forms of 'management by the numbers.'"

Second, managerialists tend to view the work of those in public organizations as detached from the political process. Just as Wilson believed that employing business techniques required a separation of politics and administration, a similar tendency exists in contemporary managerialism—the idea that elected political leaders can frame the agenda and an impartial civil service implements it. If that notion were ever true—and it likely was not—it is certainly no longer the case. Administrative officials at all levels are involved in developing policies, in exercising discretion in the execution of policies, and in making administrative policy decisions required of them by law. Indeed, the direction and complexity of modern society will probably extend rather than limit the policy role of the administrator.

Peter Wilenski, former Secretary of the Department of Transport and Communications and recently appointed Australian Ambassador to the United Nations, has commented, "In these terms, the danger in the new managerialism is that it is a return to 'instrumentalism' by the back door. The instrumental view—that the public service is a neutral machine that mechanically puts policy into effect—[is an] inaccurate and misleading description of what the public service is asked to do." Moreover, a narrow technical view of the conduct of public organizations may disregard important public values that lie beyond efficiency, notions such as equity, fairness, and compassion. Wilenski continues, "The problem, then, is that the new managerialism for all its virtues may become unduly mechanistic and, like the old instrumentalism, may have an unconscious bias which will make it difficult for disadvantaged groups to deal with the bureaucracy, to obtain their fair share of programs and to receive the high standards of courtesy and civility to which they are entitled."

AN ALTERNATIVE APPROACH

Beyond these somewhat abstract critiques, what may be even more important in changing our understanding of how public organizations might be managed with greatest success is the experience of a group of highly progressive managers who are willing to experiment with new organizational forms and behaviors and who are taking substantial risks in opposition to "business-as-usual," In short, managers willing to confront that most sacred of organizational maxims: That's the way we've always done it around here. Paul O'Neill, a former deputy director of the U.S. Office of Management and Budget, foresees a dramatic shift in the way public organizations are run: "I think we are on the verge of a major change in all organizations. There is an old culture which is slowly beginning to die . . . a culture which is very hierarchical and slow to change." In its place, managers in the public sector are being called upon to develop organizations that are adaptive, responsive, and well-focused; they are being required to place a premium on high performance but at the same time share power and take risks to achieve their goals. Public organizations today and in the future will require new ways of thinking and new ways of acting.

The shifts in public management that will be required to meet the demands of the 1990s and beyond are varied and complex. Yet there are several basic ideas that seem destined to replace the tenets of rationalism and managerialism that have so long dominated the field of public management. Together these ideas represent a dramatic change from the logical and detached, impersonal and control-oriented management of the past. They represent the future of public management and are already being worked out in many public organizations. The most progressive managers of today and tomorrow will emphasize creativity and innovation, empathy and understanding. They will move away from a focus on structure and toward a focus on values, away from the notions of control and domination and toward participation and involvement, away from rule-bound conformity and toward a sense of community, away from a preoccupation with the internal and toward a better understanding of those outside, away from rigidity and toward adaptability, and away from a pretension of value-neutrality and toward high standards of ethics and morality.

My discussion of these ideas will be organized around several themes or strategies for managerial success that practitioners in public management are finding useful in their work. As noted earlier, these themes developed through a long series of interviews and other conversations with public managers in Australia, Canada, Great Britain, and the United States. As I talked with these public managers, I asked about the people who were making a real difference in their organizations, people acknowledged to be among the leaders in public management. I followed up these conversations by talking more systematically with leaders of professional organizations in public administration in the four countries, again asking about the public managers they consider to have made substantial improvements in the ways they do business. These were persons recognized by their peers and by leaders in the field of public administration around the world for dramatically changing the organizations in which they worked; they represent (though they are hardly inclusive of) the "best and the brightest" in the field of public service today. Some of these managers work at the national level, while others work at the state and local level. Some are chief executives, while others are somewhere in the middle of their organizations. Some work in large agencies or jurisdictions, others work in organizations that are quite small. They come from a wide variety of policy areas, but all are recognized by their peers as outstanding public managers.

What was surprising was that when I contacted these highly regarded managers and asked about their approaches, a number of common themes emerged—themes that easily crossed national boundaries (at least these particular national boundaries). Certain strategies were mentioned again and again. And while these themes can hardly be said to have been "scientifically" demonstrated—they are impressionistic at best—they do represent the best and most contemporary ideas that public managers today are pursuing, and pursuing with apparent success. Some of these ideas are familiar, others more unusual; some are broad scale in their impact, others more focused. Few of these ideas would be described as mainstream, although all may serve as models for other managers to pursue. Generally, the following ideas seem to characterize the best in contemporary public management:

A Commitment to Values. The manager seeks organizational change less by attention to structure than by developing a pervasive commitment to the mission and values of the organization, especially the values of professionalism and integrity, service and quality. Values are clearly articulated by the chief executive and shared throughout the organization.

Serving the Public. The manager gives priority to service to both clients and citizens. That priority is supported by high standards of performance and accountability and by a constant emphasis on quality. Most important, the manager recognizes that technical efforts alone will fail unless equal or even greater attention is given to the human side, especially to building a sense of community within the organization and a sense of cooperation outside.

Empowerment and Shared Leadership. The manager encourages a high level of participation and involvement on the part of all members of the organization in efforts to improve the quality and productivity of the organization. Leadership from the top is complemented by empowering individuals throughout the organization to assume leadership within their own realms.

Pragmatic Incrementalism. Change occurs through a free-flowing process in which the manager pursues a wide variety of often unexpected opportunities to move the organization in the desired direction. The manager views change as a natural and appropriate feature of organizational life and employs a creative and humane approach to change, taking into account the personal concerns and interests of members, clients, and others.

A Dedication to Public Service. Individuals throughout the organization understand and appreciate the special character of public service, especially the role of public organizations in the process of democratic governance. The manager insists that members of the organization maintain high ethical standards and encourages them to make their organization a model of integrity for similarly situated groups.

These five characteristics, which many highly regarded managers consider essential to improved performance in public organizations, form the basis for our discussion. Each idea is treated in a separate chapter of the book. In each chapter, the basic ideas underlying these new managerial approaches are examined and illustrated through practical, "real-life" examples drawn from my conversations with successful public managers. At one level, then, this book is intended as a guide to improving performance in public organizations. For example, I will show how managers coming into poorly performing organizations have sought changes not through the traditional efforts at reorganization, but by focusing on the values of those in the organizations, often emphasizing new standards of service quality. I will also examine new approaches to empowerment and shared leadership in public organizations, as well as the ways these ideas are integrated into the work of public organizations.

Throughout, I will suggest that the approaches of these outstanding managers may serve as models for other managers to follow.

Beyond providing guidelines for effective practice, I will discuss some of the personal and interpersonal skills that public managers today and tomorrow will require to develop and maintain high levels of performance in their organizations. For example, since ambiguity is becoming a hallmark of organizational life (and will likely increase rather than diminish), the manager's ability to operate effectively and responsibly in vague and uncertain situations is becoming more important. Similarly, the interconnectedness of public policies in various spheres will require new skills in negotiating agreements across organizational boundaries, skills in sorting through the complex and often conflicting political pressures placed on the organization, and, perhaps most of all, the ability and self-confidence to know how and when to take risks. As we will see, changing a public organization requires a great deal of maturity and self-esteem on the part of the manager. Managers may benefit from careful attention to the psychological issues underlying change processes.

Finally, beyond the practices and skills associated with these emerging approaches to public management, I will point to some further and even more dramatic changes that may be expected in the future. In my view, the changes now being put into practice by the most progressive public managers around the world are merely precursors to far more significant changes likely to occur over the next decades. Interestingly enough, these changes, which will place questions of human meaning, personal and societal values, and individual responsibility at the core of our thinking about all organizations, must necessarily receive their first expression in public organizations. Despite the forward-looking practices of many private sector managers today, those who see their primary commitment as that of serving private interests may be limited in their expression of moral vision. Yet a sense of moral vision is exactly what will be required of all organizations in the future. Public organizations are and indeed must be permeated with a commitment to values, not merely values that reinforce self-serving behaviors but values that relate to the concepts of freedom, justice, and the public interest. In this way, they may provide a model of moral excellence for organizations elsewhere. In contrast to the often heard view that public organizations should be run like businesses, I will argue that the most substantial changes in organizational life in the coming decades will require that more and more organizations of all types be run like public organizations!

This book is a guide to improving public management and a forecast of changes yet to come, but it is also a celebration—a celebration of the achievements of public managers in many different policy fields and in many different parts of the world. One often hears about the bad things that happen in government. In these pages, however, I'll talk about some of the good things that happen. You'll hear of managers improving the quality of the services they deliver. You'll hear of managers saving the public thousands, even millions, of dollars. Most important, you'll hear of managers committed to the idea of public service, people concerned about the welfare of others and dedicated to improving the quality of life for all. In their work, these public servants are not merely engaged in instrumental actions designed to reach given goals and objectives, they are engaged in the pursuit of significance, and that idea permeates everything they do.

A Commitment to Values

The manager seeks organizational change less by attention to structure than by developing a pervasive commitment to the mission and values of the organization, especially the values of professionalism and integrity, service and quality. Values are clearly articulated by the chief executive and shared by those throughout the organization.

Imagine that you have just been appointed director of an agency known for doing exceptionally sloppy work . . . and doing it very slowly. Picture an organization that is "dead in the water," doing little to serve the needs of either its employees or its clients; an organization that is stereotypically "bureaucratic." Picture an organization torn by internal discontent to the point that quality suffers and productivity is severely curtailed. On the other hand, consider that the mission of the organization is a noble one directed toward an important public need or one that supports other agencies in their efforts to pursue the public interest. Maybe you have been appointed director of a finance department at the national level or head of the health department at the state or provincial level or city manager in a medium-sized community. You very much want to turn the organization around, transform it into a model of quality and service to which both members and clients will point with pride. Where do you start?

Traditionally, public managers faced with this situation began by establishing new organizational structures and new mechanisms for managerial control. Creating new lines of authority and responsibility was supposed to enable the manager to direct and supervise the work of those in the organization more closely. Presumably, the organization and its members would be made more accountable and service to the public would be improved. Countless organizations have been presented with reorganization plans by their top manager only to have those plans scrapped and replaced by a succeeding manager . . . and the next . . . and the next. Sometimes the reorganization worked, but frequently things just got worse.

Today, it is far less likely that an organizational "turn-around" will begin with a change in the structure of the organization or its patterns of authority and control. Progressive public managers are much more likely to focus on values. In doing so, these managers are seeking a basic transformation of their organizations, one far beyond what a change in structure could bring about. The Canadian Public Service 2000 report states the point quite well: "A fundamental change in corporate culture and management attitudes is . . . required if we wish to promote the kinds of behaviours which will achieve the desired results. For this reason, we encourage efforts to define a set of values and operating principles to guide the actions of public service managers. . . . These should encourage creativity and initiative, trust and teamwork, and excellence in the delivery of government services." These actions are not easy. Indeed, the report continues by noting that senior managers should be prepared to invest considerable time and effort in communicating and consulting with staff, preparing for the transition period, and overseeing implementation of the reforms.

An approach to organizational change based on a reassessment and a realignment of the values that guide the work of those in the organization has proven successful in a surprising variety of public organizations. Some of these efforts involved changing mission statements to reflect shifts in the way the organization does business. Others have resulted from broad-based strategic planning exercises. And some have come about through approaches based in organization development. All have involved the manager, often working in concert with many others in the organization, framing a new set of beliefs and values appropriate to the organization's future. The change has focused not on the organization's structure but on the organization's "culture."

MANAGING CULTURAL CHANGE

The idea of organizational culture has, of course, received much attention over the last several years, especially in relation to the capacity of leaders to bring about dramatic shifts in organizational cultures. One writer portrays the "transformational leader" as "a person who can literally transform an imbedded organizational culture by creating a new vision of and for the organization and successfully *selling that vision* by rallying commitment and loyalty to transform that vision into a reality." Such a characterization makes the leader sound almost superhuman, yet no one really doubts that changing the beliefs and values of an organization can make a profound difference in the focus and the performance of those in the organization.

Some managers feel that their organization needs a clearer statement of where it is going. In a recent quality enhancement effort in the college of agriculture at a major university in the United States, administrators and members of the faculty were asked the following question in a series of interviews by an outside consultant: "If you were to think of this college as a person, how would you describe that person? What would the person look like; what would he or she act like?" Although several different images were presented in response to this question, one image, a surprisingly specific one, was mentioned by the largest proportion of the group: "This is a man going through a mid-life crisis. He used to know where he was going, but now things are confused. He's lost his sense of direction and doesn't know exactly what the future will bring." Obviously, this organization needed to establish a clear direction for its future.

Other managers feel the need to clarify issues that have long confused those in the organization. When Sandra Hale became Minnesota's Commissioner of Administration, she wanted the department to shift to an "enterprise" model, one stressing the creation of value, flexibility, and customer service. This new vision of the organization was generally considered a departure from the long-accepted norms of control, consistency, and uniformity that had been dominant for years. The question was not one of completely replacing the old values but rather one of how the two sets of values might work together. Jeff Zlonis, Deputy Commissioner, explained, "We don't want to throw away . . . methods that promote efficiency and honesty. But we sensed people in the line agencies had come to see using our services as a burdensome necessity. We wanted to retain compliance with procedural norms but we wanted to provide mechanisms for making administrators accountable." The solution did not incorporate a completely new set of values, but it moved the organization toward a more positive, service-oriented outlook.

Other managers have discovered a need to emphasize long-held but recently neglected values. As Brisbane manager of COMCARE, the Australian Commonwealth agency dealing with safety, rehabilitation, and compensation of employees, Jean Sherrell wanted her employees to exhibit the highest standards of professionalism and integrity in their work. She told me how she talked about those values constantly, in staff meetings, in formal presentations, and in conversations in the hall. Apparently, the message was effective. One day, when she returned from a business trip, Sherrell's employees presented her with a statement they had written and individually signed. Titled "Our Commitment," the statement included (among others) commitments to "perform all our duties in a Professional manner demonstrating integrity, honesty and humanity . . . [and to] ensure that all our Customers and Clients are given fair and equitable treatment." Obviously, these values had long been a part of the agency's charge, yet Sherrell and, eventually, her staff felt that these values were worth restating and publicizing.

In cases such as these, public managers faced with the problem of operating in a complex world of competing values, a world typified by conflict and uncertainty, will likely find little guidance (or comfort) in the world of rationalism and managerialism. From the point of view of the real-world manager, organizations are not fully rational nor solely market driven. Rather they appear like somewhat amorphous swirling complexes of activity, sources of different and sometimes competing viewpoints, and arenas contested by those holding quite distinct values and philosophies. The problem for the manager is to intervene in such a way that this swirling mass will move in a new direction. That intervention may be small and seemingly inconsequential, but to the surprise of all concerned, it may make an enormous difference in the organization. On the other hand, the action taken may be dramatic and appear to address great issues, yet do little to affect the course of the organization's development. The chief skill of the manager, though one rarely addressed by theory, is that of intervening at just the right time, with just the right content, supported by just the right values.

Examples at the personal level are legion. The manager meets an employee in the parking lot and casually says, "How's it going?" The employee responds with one of those

"If you really want to know . . ." statements and proceeds with a litany of complaints about his or her inability to obtain needed information from people in another part of the organization, people who know the answer perfectly well but who are unwilling to share that information because they know their supervisor is at odds with the employee's supervisor. Though the manager's response is, of course, purely spontaneous, driven as much by emotion as rationality, that response may assume legendary proportions among those who hear about it. A quick dismissal of the complaint may signify to the employee, and to all who hear the story second hand, that the manager doesn't really care about resolving these difficulties and feels there are more important things to do. Conversely, an interested and responsive reply, a promise to look into the situation and do something to support more cooperative relationships—especially a response that is followed by action—may form the basis for one of those organizational "stories" that, when passed back and forth through the organization, can make a positive and significant difference in the way people act.

At a far different level, a major policy statement by the top manager may well be perceived by those in the organization as providing, or failing to provide, the answers to questions they have. The manager may be attempting to say something that will make a significant difference in the way people in the organization behave, but if he or she acts without consulting the employees and consequently fails to address issues members of the organization feel are most critical, if the manager fails to use the right language so that the policy statement makes sense to those in the organization, or if the manager fails to lead in a direction that seems both reasonable and appropriate, there will be little positive effect and often quite negative results. Typically, under these circumstances, employees will say, "She's out of touch," or "He simply doesn't know what's going on here." And they may be right.

The problem for the public manager, in either the informal situation or the more formal, is to affect the *values* of the organization in such a way that the organization, its members, and its clients benefit. That's very difficult, however, because in most situations there will be no clear answer (as you might expect when dealing with values). In contrast to the rationalist perspective, the proper path for the manager will not be easily determined by a logical analysis of the situation; in contrast to the managerialist perspective, there will be no apparent calculation of the costs and benefits of action. People may not act logically; they may not act solely in terms of their self-interest. Indeed there is a significant likelihood that they will not. Rather they will likely respond in terms of the full complexities of the human personality, swayed in part by logic, in part by their passions, in part by their ambitions, and in part by their apprehensions.

In the complex milieu that is life in public organizations, time and chance play an enormous part, one that can't be denied by the manager acting in the real world or by the scholar analyzing the results. The manager may try to act strategically, yet he or she must be prepared to suffer the consequences of irrational behavior or even random error. Linda Krefting of Texas Tech University and Peter Frost of the University of British Columbia express the role of the manager metaphorically as "rather like a surfer who must ride a wave to its conclusion, always facing the risks of un-expected swirls from the depths beneath the wave as well as the unpredictable air movements on and above the sur-face. In fact, it is likely that changes of high intensity will require the manager to ride out a succession of waves, fall-ing off some and striving to remain secure on others."

Certainly the public manager who interprets the orga-nizational universe as a complex of rational actions or market interests will often be disappointed. Contrary to theories of rationalism and managerialism, members of the organization will not easily nor consistently respond to orga-nizational decrees in a rational, maximizing, or even "satis-ficing" way. Rather they will be human in their responses—fallible, imperfect, irrational, and sometimes even immoral. On the other hand, their choices will sometimes be creative, outrageous, insightful, and virtuous. The public manager, acting in this complex world, will be ill-served by a "lens" for viewing the world that will only permit him or her to see the rational or technical in organizational life. Quite the contrary, the manager will be aided by a view of the world that takes into account the fact that human beings are indeed human, that they bring all the problems and complexities of life itself to the organization, that they respond to situations in novel and surprising ways, and that they act on the basis of their beliefs and their values as much or more than on their understanding of the facts.

Properly used, the concept of organizational culture can aid in understanding the remarkable flow of events in organizations, but care must be exercised. Edgar H. Schein of MIT, in his book *Organizational Culture and Leadership*, suggests that the concept of organizational culture has a number of different common meanings, among them the dominant values espoused by an organization, the philosophy that guides an organization's policy toward its employees and its customers, the feeling or climate that is conveyed in an organization, the rules of the game for getting along, the norms within working groups, and the behavioral regularities that are observed when people interact. Schein argues that these meanings reflect the organization's culture, but none is the essence of culture. Instead Schein holds that "the term 'culture' should be reserved for the deeper level of basic assumptions and beliefs that are shared by members of an organization, that operate unconsciously, and that define . . . an organization's view of itself and its environment."

These basic cultural assumptions are built in a number of ways and their formation is a key to effective leadership. Leadership in public organizations as elsewhere requires an ability to evoke a vision of the organization, a vision that gives content and character to the work of the organization's members. That vision, typically developed by many but articulated by the leader, not only describes a possible and desirable future for the organization but sets boundaries with respect to the types of behavior that will move the organization in that direction. It speaks directly to the issue of "how things operate around here" in language that those in the organization will read or hear and understand. Some scholars even argue that such a statement is absolutely basic to organizational change: "Vision is the goal that provides direction, aligns key players, and energizes people to achieve a common purpose. It is a statement of an organizational dream—it stretches the imagination and motivates people to rethink what is possible. It is the most critical element of a successful organization-wide transformation."

Typically, the vision of the organization is not stated in formal objectives alone; rather it is accompanied by statements of beliefs and values that touch the feelings, even the passions, of those in the organization. Judy Johnston of the Premier's Department in New South Wales is responsible for monitoring strategic management programs for that government. Her understanding of statements of vision emphasizes their nonrational side: "The vision is the creative, intuitive, sensitive, subjective, emotional, entrepreneurial thinking of the leader and the executives which provides direction for the organisation and keeps staff motivated and focused on excellence." Such statements of vision, though sometimes sounding naive, or trite, relate to the basic and sometimes even subconscious needs, desires, and interests of the members and, if successful, trigger responses that lead to actions in line with the statements. Organization development consultant Peter Block stresses the same point in his book *The Empowered Manager*:

> We know we create a great vision when it has three qualities:
>
> 1. *It comes from the heart.* A vision is in some ways unreason-able. The heart knows no reason. When our vision asks too much of us, we should begin to trust it.
> 2. *We, alone, can make this statement.* The statement needs to be recognizable as ours. It needs to be personal, and those who know us should be able to recognize who it came from.

3. *It is radical and compelling.* A vision dramatizes our wishes. This makes it radical and demanding. Radical in the best sense of service rather than rejection. Our willingness to take a unique stand is what empowers us.

Such statements of vision, however articulate and perceptive, require supportive and consistent behavior on the part of the leader or the leadership group. The chief executive must express commitment to the vision of the organization in every action. The leader must "Walk your talk," as many managers express it. Employees will not be convinced merely by seeing a statement of values; they will want to see and to evaluate the factors the leader considers when making decisions about hiring and promotions, the criteria for raises and promotions, and the leader's way of modeling new behaviors or training or coaching others. Shifts in culture will only occur when there is consistency between what is said and what is done.

Intuitively, then, the notion of organizational culture has great appeal. Certainly, the idea of shifting the norms, beliefs, and values of the organization to produce the desired results is quite attractive. Without a doubt, many contemporary public sector managers find it appropriate to focus on changing values in their organizations. But there are potential "land mines" in the terrain of organizational culture, and the most successful managers will be aware of the costs as well as the benefits of making cultural changes.

One obvious problem is that some organizational cultures can be quite destructive. Karl Weick of Columbia University writes, "Strong cultures are tenacious cultures. Because a tenacious culture can be a rigid culture that is slow to detect changes in opportunities and slow to change once opportunities are sensed, strong cultures can be backward, conservative instruments of adaptation." Any organization that adopts a particular set of values and beliefs without simultaneously creating systems for the review and alteration of those ideas is doomed from the outset. The manager must always ask, "What have I done to build in adaptability?"

Similarly, the particular values chosen as the bases for organizational change must be carefully considered. The manager must be particularly attentive to the ethical implications of value choices and be especially concerned with doing the right thing. To deal in the world of values means that the manager must recognize the consequences, especially the moral consequences, of the values selected. Working with values raises special questions of responsibility. As Robert H. Waterman, Jr. points out, "Management's efforts to gain commitment must stem from solid, worthwhile values. Leaders use the same means to gain commitment that others use to manipulate." And, as one manager told me, "Manipulation just isn't a good strategy in the long run."

Managers can also be tempted to devise internal "propaganda" campaigns extolling particular values or virtues designed to secure compliance with the wishes of top management. A more honest and more effective approach to value change involves the participation of many people in the organization. The values of the organization must be subject to debate and deliberation by those throughout the organization so that there is little question that the choice of direction has been thoughtfully crafted in a cooperative framework. Values selected in a less public process are simply not as likely to endure.

Most important, the beliefs and values that help define an organization's culture must capture and express deep-seated meanings that reside in the hearts and souls of the organization's members (and often citizens generally). Unfortunately, much of the corporate literature on organizational culture is fully rationalist in content and is concerned with an instrumental manipulation of organizational culture to achieve the results desired by top management. For example, two writers on business management approvingly note that organizational culture serves as an "organizational control mechanism, informally approving or prohibiting some patterns of behavior." Using culture as a "control mechanism" is completely inappropriate in public organizations, and probably elsewhere as well.

That doesn't mean that discussions of culture are unimportant. As Linda Smircich of the University of Massachusetts has correctly pointed out, the "instrumental" interpretation is only one interpretation of "culture" in organizations. An alternative view sees culture as consisting of the shared meanings that members of an organization bring to their work. Smircich describes the differences between these two approaches to organizational culture in terms of "culture as a variable" and "culture as metaphor." As a variable, culture is used for instrumental purposes in the service of management interests. As a metaphor, culture is used to indicate the expressive nature of organizational life, that it is life filled with meanings.

Since I will argue later that public organizations of the future need to be especially attentive to the meaningfulness of organizational life, it is important to understand this point clearly. The anthropologist Clifford Geertz describes human beings as creatures "suspended in webs of significance," webs of their own making. An analysis of culture can add to understanding those webs and enhance the search for meaning that human beings inevitably bring to their actions. To emphasize the importance of interpreting not just the behaviors but the meanings that people bring to social situations, Geertz distinguishes between "thin" and "thick" descriptions of human behavior. A thin description describes what has occurred, the actual behavior; a thick description provides a sense of the meaning or significance of the act. For example, a person may be thinly described as running through the woods, but more thickly described as trying to elude the sheriff's bloodhounds. The failure of the rational model of administration is in providing only thin descriptions of organizational behavior; what is missing is the thickness provided by understanding the meaning and significance of those actions.

What do the ideas of thinness and thickness mean in the real world of management? Consider an employee who constantly complains about the type of work he or she is doing. A thin analysis of the situation might lead the manager to conclude that the employee is a complainer or a malcontent in need of discipline and constraint. A thicker understanding of the situation might, however, reveal that the employee has discovered a much better way to do the job and is complaining about the restrictions that limit the implementation of that improvement. Now, any modern manager would obviously respond by saying that a thick analysis of this situation would be clearly advisable; however, in practice, the distinction between thin and thick responses to organizational situations is much harder to make. It's simply too easy to respond to what's on the surface, especially if your approach to organizational life emphasizes the facts of human behavior or the design of organizational structures and disregards the meanings and values that people in the organization hold.

MISSIONS, VISIONS, AND GETTING THE WORK DONE

The manager seeking to change an organization must understand the organization in a contradictory way, seeing clearly and with great depth and insight the meaning and significance that members attach to the organization, yet seeing beyond ingrained patterns or webs. The trick for the manager interested in cultural change is to be at once "in" the organization but not "of" the organization, to be close enough to the existing culture to understand the way people in the organization think, yet to be attuned to the environment as well as the needs, interests, and desires of the organization's members so that some sort of vision can emerge. While understanding the culture of the organization is essential, that understanding must not provide blinders that prevent the manager from seeing the possibilities, the subtle openings in the web that permit future growth.

For this reason, managers anticipating changes in their organizations spend considerable amounts of time getting a sense of the existing culture. Some managers do so in formal ways, for example by developing questionnaire surveys or interviews of organizational members and clients, trying to determine their beliefs and attitudes, their understanding of the strengths and weaknesses of the organization, and their sense of the organization's future, especially the opportunities and constraints it faces. Others seek this information more informally, though nonetheless systematically, by spending hours talking with organizational members and those outside about their views of the organization. Some managers hold these conversations not only to obtain an understanding of the uniqueness of their organization but to begin to shift the dialogue among individuals and groups in a more positive and creative direction.

Pamela Gordon, Chief Executive of the Sheffield city council, persuaded me that, "It's important to analyze the organization you are in. There's not a magic formula that you can apply in any organization. If you're going to make progress, you have to find the right way of evolving from what is there. I've always seen it as my function to ask questions, to challenge the basic assumptions, to ask the sort of basic, stupid questions that other people don't ask. And sometimes to astonish everybody by taking a much more rash approach than the others; that sometimes lifts the conversation onto a different level of debate."

Gordon's comments underscore the importance of language in the process of change. Language shapes our perceptions of reality, and our perceptions of reality shape our behavior. For this reason, changing language may be a prerequisite to changing behavior and changing attitudes. Jenny Bedlington of the State of Tasmania spoke about the importance of changing language as a prelude to changing behavior. "Some people try to change the employees' attitudes. I want to focus on their language. I don't care if they're fascist if they use the right language and treat clients well. Change will then occur. If their language changes, then their behavior will change—and that's what I'm ultimately interested in."

One way public sector managers seek to change the language used in their organizations is through revamping statements of mission or developing new statements of vision or philosophy. Many public managers have found that a new articulation of the mission of their organization can make a surprising difference in the way people do their work. The key seems to be simply that the mission statement effectively communicates a vision or direction for the organization. John L. Manion, a former high-ranking Canadian federal executive now associated with the Canadian Centre for Management Development, places development of a concise mission statement at the center of his discussion of communications in public organizations. Manion advises, "A short, clear and concrete mission statement for the department is essential. This statement combines statutory obligations, goals, policies and priorities of the political leaders, and the goals and policies of the department's leaders. Such a statement must be strategic and future oriented. It must establish a framework and motivate staff to meet current objectives and carry the department into the future." The mission statement then becomes the initial device in the manager's efforts to communicate his or her view of the organization.

Such statements need not be lengthy or detailed to have an impact. For example, the City of Portland Police Bureau staff recently developed a community policing program. As part of the transition, a new mission statement was developed. The old statement, reflecting a more traditional view of police work, read as follows: "The Bureau of Police is responsible for the preservation of the public peace, protection of the rights of persons and property, the prevention of crime, and the enforcement of all federal laws, Oregon State statutes, and City ordinances within the boundaries of the City of Portland." The new mission statement was considerably shorter, but the changing emphasis was clear: "The mission of the Portland Police Bureau is to work with all citizens to preserve life, maintain human rights, protect property, and promote individual responsibility and community commitment." Obviously, this new mission statement said to police officers and others that a new orientation toward the role of the community in law enforcement was to guide their work.

Changing the mission statement of an organization may focus attention more clearly on what needs to be done, but typically says little about the *way* in which the work should be done. Also, the mission statement may not reveal the aspirations of those in the organization or what they would like to accomplish. For these reasons, many public managers encourage people in their organizations to state the *values* of the organization more explicitly, including both guidelines or standards of behavior expected in the organization and statements intended to inspire and to animate those in the organization. Such statements present a variety of images and may be developed in a number of ways. Some are statements of management philosophy, some are stated as commitments of the organization, and some are stated as principles. Some are developed through strategic planning processes, some through organization development efforts, and some through extended dialogue within the management team. All these statements provide an opportunity for the manager to help articulate a vision and a way for the manager to begin to change the organization's culture.

DEVELOPING A VISION
THROUGH STRATEGIC PLANNING

Strategic planning is surely one of the most frequently used, and most frequently abused, tools of modern management. Many organizations undertake strategic planning programs these days, yet many of these programs fail miserably. Those in the organizations or communities involved in the programs feel let down; they feel they have wasted their time. One state level administrator responded to my suggestion that the organization develop an improved planning capacity by saying, "I have a list of 127 things to do in my top drawer. I don't want this planning effort merely to be number 128." Another administrator said, "If we are going to get into a planning process, I want planning to be a tool not a task."

The task of planning was painfully experienced by faculty at a major American university who recently engaged in a long series of exercises projecting goals for the future. Each unit presented plans and objectives to the next higher level, where in turn plans and objectives were prepared for the next higher level. There were targets for enrollments, targets for graduates, and targets for research dollars. But when it all was over, no one felt satisfied with the result, and nothing about the university seemed to change.

To make planning a tool and not a task, many contemporary public managers distinguish between traditional long-range planning and more contemporary strategic planning. Most who do so find the ideas underlying strategic planning far more satisfying than those implicit in long-term planning. The most important difference is that traditional long-range planning is concerned primarily with establishing goals or objectives for performance over a period of time. Strategic planning, on the other hand, implies developing a vision of the organization's future, then moving to a series of action steps that will guide activities in the immediate future.

A group of job training specialists recently gathered at a retreat to think about the future of their program. At the beginning of their work, those in the organization wanted to talk about performance targets or objectives for the future. Someone asked, for instance, how many people the organization should have placed in permanent jobs by 1995? After considerable discussion, however, the focus shifted. The group began to talk about what they expected in terms of economic growth in the community, then realized that local economic conditions played a critical role in opening jobs for program applicants. As a result, they started focusing on what they could do immediately that would help the economic situation in the community and, in turn, the possibility that new jobs might be created and filled by their applicants.

Notice the difference. In the first case, the group set abstract goals but failed to develop specific actions to give them guidance as to what to do. In the second case, the group looked to their vision of the future to develop specific action steps they could undertake today. Their planning made it possible for them not only to set a desired end state but to determine how to get there. The difference seems to be one of objectives versus vision.

William Ouchi, author of *Theory Z*, illustrates the implications of this distinction in describing a series of conversations about a couple of American vice presidents working in a Japanese bank. Both the Americans and their Japanese president complained that their counterparts "didn't understand objectives," by which the Americans meant specific and measurable performance objectives. When Ouchi interviewed the Japanese president, however, the banker said, "If only I could get these Americans to understand our philosophy of banking. To understand what our business means to us—how we feel we should deal with our customers and our employees. What our relationship should be to the local communities we serve. If they could get that under their skin, then they could figure out for themselves what an appropriate objective would be for any situation, no matter how unusual or new, and I would never have to tell them, never have to give them a target." Again, a strategic approach implies a consideration of values and aspirations as well as an analysis of what immediate steps are needed to position the organization to confront the future. That's what strategy is all about—positioning.

DEVELOPING A MANAGEMENT PHILOSOPHY

A good example of a more strategic approach in the public sector comes from the State of Missouri. When John

Pelzer became Commissioner of Administration in the early 1980s, he inherited an organization known not only for its heavy-handed top-down management but also for its tactless control of other state agencies. Quite simply, the Office of Administration was seen by people throughout state government as a roadblock to effective management. The Office of Administration housed a number of central management agencies: the Division of Budget and Planning, the Division of Personnel, the Division of Purchasing, the Division of Design and Construction, the Division of Data Processing, and the Division of General Services. From the point of view of those in other areas of state government, the various divisions within the Office of Administration bombarded them with a constant stream of "thou shalt nots." The Personnel Division interfered with the agencies' efforts to hire or move personnel; the Division of Purchasing interfered with their efforts to buy new equipment or contract for services. Worst of all, the Budget Office tried to exert control over nearly every aspect of their work. In addition, those in other departments believed that people in the various divisions within the Office of Administration never talked with one another. Guidance given by those in one division would often be contradicted in another. (Many suspected that this lack of cooperation had been fostered by Pelzer's predecessor who often bragged that he never held staff meetings.)

Internally, things weren't much better. The Office of Administration was seen as being rigid, uncaring, and under the strict control of top management—in essence, as being a department where creativity and innovation were discouraged. Operations went "by the book," and many activities were performed the way they were only because it had been done that way for years. Throughout the department there was little sense of accomplishment associated with the work being done and scarcely any pride in the involvement of members of the department in the public service.

Although Pelzer immediately confronted a number of important policy issues, he also spent time trying to change the management of the department. Several key personnel changes were made, resulting in a highly competent and professional group of top managers. The next step, however, was ensuring that those people operated as a team and had a clear vision of where the department, not just the various divisions, was going. To address these issues, Pelzer hired a consultant to work with the top management team (the commissioner, the deputy commissioner, and the division directors) on a series of team-building activities. These sessions focused on developing the individual skills of managers in the department and, more important, on developing effective patterns of interaction among various division directors. The team-building activities, held outside the state capital, allowed various top managers to come to know one another personally, and a sense of camaraderie began to develop. At the end of one team-building session, for example, the director of the Division of Data Processing commented that what he found most important about the sessions was not their specific content but the opportunity they provided for him to get acquainted with the other division directors on a more personal level.

As the top management team began to coalesce and to talk about ways the department could become more focused on its activities, someone suggested that an integrated planning process be developed. Again, a consultant was employed to analyze the existing planning activities within the Office of Administration and to work with members of the top management team in designing an integrated strategic planning effort. The results of the initial survey were not surprising; little planning was being done, and none seemed to have much impact on the organization. Consequently, Pelzer and his management team made a commitment to develop an improved strategic planning process.

The model chosen was one that focused first on developing clear statements of the mission and the management philosophy of the department, then on formulating specific action steps to pursue those values. The mission statement was fairly easy to derive from statutes and other formal statements, all of which spoke of the role of the Office of Administration as the central agency responsible for the management and operations of state government. Developing a statement of management philosophy, however, was much more difficult—though in the long run much more dramatic. (The statement of management philosophy that was eventually proposed is reproduced in Box 2.1.)

As you will see, the statement the management team hammered out focuses on several key issues. First, there is a concern for balancing the role of the Office of Administration in "serving the line agencies of state government and in assuring the accountability of governmental operations." Commissioner Pelzer and his top management team were trying to rid the department of its old image of "controlling" the other agencies of government and seeking to establish the role of the Office of Administration as one of providing "the highest quality of *service* to other agencies." A key statement of the new philosophy is: "We recognize that our own effectiveness is directly related to the services we provide others."

Second, the framers sought to assert a more open and participatory form of internal management, while acknowledging the importance of communication and coordination throughout the organization. Pelzer and his colleagues also sought a philosophy of caring about employees, communicating with employees, involving them in the work of the department, and utilizing their talents to the fullest.

Third, several items specifically dealt with the role of the Office of Administration in providing quality public services to the citizens of Missouri. While the managers recognized that most of their work served "customers" who were internal to state government rather than serving citizens directly, they were careful to be sensitive to the public nature of their activities and their "ultimate responsibility" to the citizens of Missouri. The statement concludes: "Though we come from many professional backgrounds we are brought together in the public service. We take seriously the special responsibility that the concept of public service implies and we value our participation in the process of government."

As members of the team talked about the final wording of the statement, they recognized that making such a statement public would "put the pressure on them." Publicly committing themselves to the ideas contained in

BOX 2.1
State of Missouri
Office of Administration:
Statement of Management Philosophy

We are PROUD of our role in providing EFFECTIVE and RESPONSIBLE government to the citizens of the State of Missouri.

As the chief agency responsible for the management and operations of state government, the Office of Administration plays an important role in serving the line agencies of state government and in assuring the accountability of governmental operations. Despite the fact that the Office of Administration provides less direct services to the public than some agencies, we are constantly reminded of the public nature of our activities and our ultimate responsibility to the citizens of Missouri.

We RESPECT the elected officials of the State and will perform our responsibilities in a way consistent with their direction.

As the management arm of state government, we provide leadership in various policy areas and, more generally, we seek to improve the managerial effectiveness of state government. In these areas, we will seek to be responsive to the state political leadership and to build professional competence on which our leaders and the state's citizens can depend.

In our relationships with other agencies, we will seek to be SENSITIVE to and SUPPORTIVE of the special needs of those agencies.

We will provide the highest quality of service to other agencies. In our dealings with them, we will be helpful, courteous, and respectful; in our decisions and recommendations, we will be open and flexible, fair and consistent. We recognize that our own effectiveness is directly related to the services we provide others.

We CARE about our employees and we RESPECT and VALUE their work.

In our internal operations, we will place the highest regard for the worth and dignity of each individual member of our organization. Through programs enhancing the quality of work life, we will seek to develop a more humane and caring organization. We care about those who work in the Office of Administration and we wish that caring to show. We also appreciate the excellent professional work being done by those in the Office of Administration and we will remember to say "thank you" more frequently.

We will seek to improve COMMUNICATIONS and COORDINATION throughout the organization.

We recognize that in an agency as diverse as ours, communications and coordination are of special importance and we will give priority to ways of improving our capabilities in these areas. As managers, we will seek to establish a clear direction for the development of the organization, and within that framework we will seek mechanisms for the involvement of all employees in building a more effective department. We will listen carefully to their ideas and, where possible, we will act promptly on their suggestions.

We recognize the importance of personal GROWTH and organizational DEVELOPMENT and will seek ways of constantly extending our capabilities.

We recognize that as individuals we must always be attentive to our growth needs. We recognize that improvements can always be made in the quality of service and in the productivity of all organizations, including our own. For these reasons, we will be attentive to the developmental needs of our members and to the building of programs for improving the skills of the organization.

We value our participation in the PUBLIC SERVICE and will strive for HIGH QUALITY in all our activities.

Though we come from many different professional backgrounds, we are brought together in the public service. We
continued

Box 2.1 continued
> take seriously the special responsibility that the concept
> of public service implies and we value our participation
> in the process of government. We want our agency to be
> one of the recognized leaders in Missouri state government,
> one to which others will look for professional, technical,
> and ethical guidance. With the full cooperation and in-
> volvement of all members of a caring and concerned
> organization, we are confident this goal will be attained.

the statement would provide a standard against which
employees as well as citizens or legislators could evaluate
their work as top managers. The managers were willing to
make such a strong commitment and worked hard to
publicize their commitment. Framed copies of the statement
were placed in offices throughout the department, newsletter articles were written clarifying various sections, and
paycheck envelopes periodically contained items from the
statement.

Managers also undertook a number of specific steps to
support the values contained in their statement. For example, Commissioner Pelzer began periodic "walk throughs"
of various divisions and held a variety of public meetings
to discuss his philosophy of service and accountability and
to listen to ideas and suggestions from people throughout
the organization. Similarly, he set up a series of Quality of
Work Life Committees to elicit suggestions and recommendations of employees throughout the organization. (Unfortunately, before Pelzer was able to convert this work into
specific behavioral objectives for the organization, he was
the victim of a political controversy in the legislature and
resigned.)

The extent to which the statement of management
philosophy made a difference in the organization can be
judged in several ways. Perhaps most telling is the comment
of Pelzer's successor, James Moody. A number of years after
he had taken charge, I asked him about the most significant
aspects of the work of the Office of Administration. Moody
commented:

Having worked in another department of state government for fourteen years before coming to OA, I had the ability to view it from afar and form some opinions. Based on that view, I had seen an evolving of management philosophy in the Office of Administration, and a maturing of the agency. Much of the credit for this actually belongs to John Pelzer, my predecessor in this department. John and the present management team, all of whom I inherited from John and who still work for me, had as a group developed a management philosophy. This management philosophy stressed work they were trying to accomplish and how they were trying to accomplish it. I believe this statement provides a baseline from which we determine how we will operate on a day-to-day basis.

The importance of the OA philosophy and the maturation of the organization is our development from an agency that was especially interested in the control of other agencies' actions to one who serves agencies, while having to keep in mind the control functions which statutorily we must administer.

Moody's comments address one question that is often asked about changes in organizational culture—whether such changes can survive a shift in top leadership. In this case, the cultural change initiated by Pelzer did survive and indeed thrive under new leadership.

The Office of Administration in the State of Missouri was an organization in need of a sense of vision, direction, and unity. The statement of philosophy that was developed clearly communicated to those throughout the organization that a new orientation toward service to other agencies had been initiated and that top managers were going to be much more open, more caring, and more conscientious. In retrospect, the statement was more important than it was recognized to be at the time. By stating their commitments in such a public manner, the management team began to change the language used in the organization and in turn the behaviors and the attitudes of those in the organization. Questions remain about the degree to which the statement was converted into specific measurable objectives to guide individual behavior; however, as you will see later, this is a frequent question when managers seek changes in their organization's culture.

PLANNING FOR WATER RESOURCES

A similar case, one in which the need for converting a vision into more specific objectives has been clearly recognized, comes from Australia. The Department of Water Resources of New South Wales was created in 1986 out of the earlier Water Resources Commission and its predecessor the Water Conservation and Irrigation Commission. The Water Resources Commission had been concerned primarily with water development activities but had not adapted well to its new responsibilities in water resource management. Additionally, the commission had developed a poor reputation among its increasingly demanding users or "customers." The newly created department now has responsibility for building dams and supplying water, as well as for environmentally sound water resource management.

By most accounts, creation of the new department occurred with considerable "bloodshed and pain." For example, a totally new executive group was employed. Since none of this group had any experience in water resources, their credibility was low in the eyes of both the staff and the water customers. Consequently, when Peter Millington became director—following the relatively quick departure of the previous executive group—he faced an organization with serious problems, among them "a reorganised entity that was battered and bruised, an old and conservative culture, a lack of appreciation of our new role, no strategic outlook, poor resource policies, and a monolithic structure driven by self interest with no cross fertilisation."

Millington felt that changing a public sector organization presented special difficulties because of unclear objectives, peculiar problems in industrial relations, and the number of controls exercised by central agencies. For these reasons, he was especially sensitive to issues of communication in bringing about organizational change: "The purpose and the nature of the change must be communicated to all relevant stakeholders, both inside and outside the organisation." Consequently there was a lot of up-front communication, by both Millington and his deputy, about the changes under way: restoring morale, creating a new organizational culture, building the confidence of the department's customers, changing to a participative style of management, focusing significant attention on management development, and designing a new staff reward system. Nothing was more central to communicating this new vision of the organization than the products of the department's newly instituted planning process.

In Millington's view, "Managers in the public sector must devote large amounts of energy towards ensuring that there is a clear understanding about *why* the organisation exists, *what* it is trying to achieve, [and] *how* it gets things done . . . if they are to manage pressures for change successfully." Millington and his executive group set about to answer these questions through an extended strategic planning exercise. Their planning activity culminated in three sets of statements: first, a corporate planning document addressing questions of product and service mix as well as issues of public accountability (issues of extensive staff involvement in the planning process were included here); second, a set of corporate strategies designed to achieve value for money and organizational success (included here were items such as regionalization, commercialization, environmental accountability, and human resource management); and third, a statement of corporate philosophy designed to encourage a common vision of how the organization should operate. The corporate philosophy statement, which was eventually circulated widely in booklet form as "The D. W. R. Way—How We Manage to Get Things Done," provides an excellent model for such a statement.

In "The D. W. R. Way," Millington expresses his own philosophy of management and commits the executive group to that philosophy. According to Millington:

> Simply put, there are three principles that should dominate our attitude: Respect for our staff and their abilities, and encouragement of their development, giving the best possible customer service, [and] seeking excellence in all we do.
>
> Perhaps these principles have always been there; perhaps not. Irrespective, they are the crux of my outlook on how the Department should operate.
>
> They are principles which are not always simple to follow or adhere to in the public sector when often we don't have direct control over budgets and staff numbers.
>
> Nevertheless, they are the symbols of the organisation and the platform upon which the "culture" of the organisation will grow.
>
> That, then, is what staff can expect of the Executive—an adherence to those three basic principles in whatever we do.

In turn, managers and staff members were asked to follow the eight guidelines or commitments: a commitment to teamwork, a commitment to a businesslike attitude, a commitment to achievement, a commitment to innovation, a commitment to strategic thinking, a commitment to customer service, a commitment to excellence, and a commitment to accountability. (These ideas are presented in Box 2.2.)

As in the earlier Missouri case, the statement alone was helpful in clarifying the direction the organization was moving toward and the values that should guide that movement, but Millington and the executive group also recognized that a number of actions must follow upon declaring these principles or aspects of organizational culture. Certainly, the vision of the organization must be communicated to all those in the organization—through publications, management

BOX 2.2
The D. W. R. Way:
How We Manage to Get Things Done

COMMITMENT TO TEAMWORK

Teamwork is vital to the D. W. R. simply because it improves our performance in two crucial ways. First, teamwork helps us to raise our individual standards by sharing talent and by improving each other's creative performance.

Second, no individual can look after every aspect of a major task unaided. We have to work closely with others to harness all the skills the job requires.

Even when formal team structures are absent, we have to get into the way of talking to each other and working together whenever it would improve individual performance. Through leadership, managers must stimulate teamwork as a means of obtaining better results. Teamwork is achieved by developing individual talents, building on the ideas and know-how of the team, and gaining commitment by way of listening, involving and communicating.

Leading by example, being seen, being involved, providing common understanding and direction: these are essential elements of a manager's role in developing the cooperative teamwork attitudes which are imperative for obtaining the best results.

COMMITMENT TO A BUSINESS-LIKE ATTITUDE

Private companies need to plan for the future and to provide the very best and most cost-effective service for their customers.

If they don't they will not survive.

The facts are the same for the Department; if we don't perform, the Government will re-arrange the organisation and its people. Being business-like is a combination of many things. It involves the attitude of our people. It certainly means that we must have efficient financial and management information systems to guide us, we must recover a fair share of our costs, be committed to excellence and research our markets.

Box 2.2 continued

We must explore every opportunity to promote ourselves to our customers and be openly accountable for our performance. Joint venturing of projects must be explored.

We must strive to keep our costs down and at the same time introduce new technology. In the end, the organisation must be "smaller," and we must work "harder and smarter."

Being business-like is a way of life that must become part of the normal every-day thinking of a manager. It is absolutely vital for survival that all our activities are continually viewed from the perspective "Is it good business practice?"

COMMITMENT TO ACHIEVEMENT

Achievement in the Department is about output, that is, performance, not necessarily input or effort. More specifically it means high value output . . . output that creates a demonstrable impact on our visible performance.

Managers must ensure that the work tasks and actions of their staff reflect this basic principle.

Managers are obliged to identify and eliminate substandard performance and ineffective work situations. High performance of a low-value job provides a poor return for the individual and the organisation. This is where priority setting is so important. It allows our resources to be directed to areas of greatest need or benefit.

High performance objectives will be realised only if accompanied by an equally strong commitment to self-assessment. Managers must continually challenge and appraise their own management actions and the way they as individuals, and their work units, contribute to the organisation results.

Managers must measure their own effectiveness as people managers, for their ability to provide leadership is vital. They must balance the attitudes of staff with the targets sought, to produce the organisational effectiveness necessary in our operations.

The achievements of managers are dependent on the achievements of their staff.

The Executive is committed to developing its employees to the full extent of their potential; to giving everyone a fair go. Managers must first ensure that optimum use is being made of current skills and that individuals are given tasks which "stretch" them in their existing jobs. They must ensure that equal opportunity is implemented throughout.

They must encourage staff to contribute. There is a staff suggestion/reward system operating so use it; both the staff and the Department will benefit.

One of the most important elements in developing the right culture in an organisation is the feedback given to staff. To develop the right culture we must "reward" the right sort of actions/work/initiatives. In most cases this "reward" will only be in the form of a compliment or public recognition of a job well done. Even though it may seem only a small "reward," it is essential that we make conscious efforts to recognise jobs well done by personally complimenting those responsible.

COMMITMENT TO INNOVATION

Innovation is the key to managing change and to meeting our commitment to excellence. Managers must consciously strive for improvements in their personal and work unit performance.

They must exploit modern management techniques and information technology as ways of increasing output of all activities. It is the manager's obligation to set the framework for creativity . . . a very clear understanding of the need; freedom to challenge the traditional and try out new ideas; and encouragement provided by a supportive teamwork environment. Encourage risk taking, do not repress initiative and do not punish mistakes that could come from being innovative.

Managers are required to set the pace and lead by example. Their "can-do" attitude to tackling tasks must be infectious, influencing others to adopt the same willingness and positive approach. We have much expertise in this Department; encourage people to use it.

The successful manager thinks in terms of opportunities rather than problems, uses initiative to pick up the "loose ball" and willingly volunteers relevant skills to help others achieve their objectives. When a commitment is made it is invariably carried through, and carried through quickly.

All successful managers take a degree of risk. Without such a philosophy we will only "plod" toward our target.

COMMITMENT TO STRATEGIC THINKING—
THE BIG PICTURE

The greatest challenge facing managers arises from their responsibility for identifying changing long-term needs and

Box 2.2 continued

for planning effectively to meet them. Predicting, managing and exploiting change are key demands calling for foresight, judgement and leadership of the highest order.

Managers are expected continually to identify future trends in the water resources field, to monitor present performance and to take corrective action to avoid poor performance.

By analysing the critical long-term issues which confront the organisation, managers can establish for their teams a clear vision of the future. They can also develop the strategies upon which that future will be secured.

COMMITMENT TO CUSTOMER SERVICE

The Department has many customers; each has a different need and the Department's aim must be to satisfy these needs (as constraints permit) with high quality service.

We cannot begin to achieve this aim unless our thinking is directed towards the evolving needs of our customers.

Managers are expected to identify and understand customer needs. Managers need to be sensitive to the customer's environment as well as the Department's and to the issues concerning them. Programs are expected to be developed to meet the varying needs with innovative solutions and high quality service.

All work units within the organisation also have to adopt the same attitude toward their in-house customers.

Managers must adopt an attitude of high quality, efficient service in the dealings with other units of the Department.

The customers must always feature strongly in our work programs and we must never allow our own problems to distract us from understanding and when possible, solving theirs.

COMMITMENT TO EXCELLENCE

Excellence . . . it is one of our basic beliefs. Without it, customers will simply see us as "just another outfit." Excellence will be achieved only by adopting a "can-do" attitude and the highest levels of co-operation and teamwork right throughout the Department.

We CAN deliver a service to our customers that is seen to be the best.

We CAN undertake and produce technical work of the absolute highest order.

We CAN develop new techniques and procedures that are at the forefront of the water industry.

We CAN develop a culture and commitment for the organisation and its staff that is second to none in the Public Service.

Excellence is an attitude which never overlooks a need, never allows an opportunity to slip. It is also an attitude that recognises the need for teamwork. "Can help" is as important as "can do."

Every new project or task demands that we look for standards of excellence, define ways in which those standards are to be met and then go on to achieve them.

Only by doing this, day in and day out, can we expect to make real progress and be seen as "an excellent public sector organisation."

COMMITMENT TO ACCOUNTABILITY

The community now expects greater levels of scrutiny and accountability in the public sector, and we must respond by openly presenting our performance for assessment.

Managers must have detailed knowledge of the organisation's objectives and strategies. It is a Senior Management responsibility to ensure that all managers fully understand what the organisation is doing and where it is going.

It is every manager's responsibility to provide the basis for determining sub-unit objectives and work priorities. Managers must ensure that all employees clearly understand their individual roles and responsibilities, and the standards required for the successful completion of tasks. It is equally important that there is a clear standard of measurement not only for the Department's performance, but also for that of all staff.

Managers are accountable for the achievement of the Department's objectives through the achievement of sub-unit objectives. Also they are accountable for the performance and development of their staff.

Managers will be given sufficient delegation and encouragement to get the job done on their own initiative. However, in accepting greater levels of responsibility and independence, they must also accept a greater level of accountability.

development sessions, and employee orientation materials, just to name a few used in D. W. R. Beyond this, as Judy Johnston told me, developing action plans often proves most difficult; it is this stage that continues to occupy Millington and his colleagues. "Plans alone will not guarantee results. Successful implementation will only be achieved when staff, as the most valued resource, have the commitment, skills, and knowledge to carry out the plans and turn words into actions." Broad strategies must be translated into specific and measurable objectives against which performance can be monitored. Initially, the report is positive. Millington writes, "As Director of the Department of Water Resources, my experience has been that if the vision, strategies, and philosophy of an organisation are clear and are well communicated to all relevant parties, then managing change becomes an intrinsic organisation capability." Such an intrinsic capability to manage change is something all organizations would value.

ORGANIZATION DEVELOPMENT APPROACHES

Many agencies and communities have approached the task of establishing a vision in the context of larger organization development programs. Organization development (OD) is a process-oriented approach to planned change, that typically involves a third-party interventionist who helps members of the organization analyze, confront, and solve work-related behavioral issues. Organization development programs may have multiple purposes, among them the following:

- To create an open, problem-solving climate throughout the organization so members can confront problems rather than fight about them or flee from them
- To increase the sense of ownership of organization objectives throughout the work force

- To build trust among individuals and groups throughout the organization
- To maximize collaboration between individuals and units whose work is interdependent
- To increase self-control and self-direction for people within the organization
- To create conditions where conflict is brought out and managed
- To increase awareness of the group process and its consequences for performance

One important feature of work in organization development is that it is based in the needs and interests of those in the organization. Although a third-party interventionist may serve as a facilitator or even a catalyst, the interventionist does not impose or prescribe solutions to organizational problems. Rather, the interventionist works with members of the organization to enable them to do this (presumably at the same time building a greater organizational capacity for dealing with future issues as well). Chris Argyris of Harvard University, one of the foremost practitioners of organization development, describes the classic role of the interventionist as follows:

- To help generate valid and useful information
- To create conditions in which clients can make informed choices
- To help clients develop an internal commitment to their choices

Again, the emphasis of organization development programs is on building the capacities of those in the organization to confront and to resolve behavioral issues that inhibit successful performance.

ORGANIZATION DEVELOPMENT IN PALM SPRINGS

When Norm King became city manager in Palm Springs, California, in late 1979, he discovered a municipal organization battered and frustrated by Proposition 13, the California tax limitation requirement, struggling to find a sense of direction. Based on his familiarity with the values and approaches of organization development theorists and practitioners such as Neely Gardner of the University of Southern California, King felt strongly that most employees want to do a better job and that managers should be responsible for creating a work environment in which they can do so. Early on, King initiated an organization development program that continued in various phases throughout his decade-long tenure in Palm Springs and became one of the leading examples of local government organization development efforts in the United States. The program began with exercises in group problem solving, then proceeded to address other areas such as training of trainers, developing internal consultants, holding team-building events, ensuring public participation, and developing commitment to the goals and values of the organization (though not necessarily in this order). Although the process of developing commitment to the values of the organization is of great interest here, I will briefly review each of the other components of the effort to provide a better context for the "commitment" exercise.

Initially King brought together, for a day, about a hundred management and professional staff to identify and prioritize issues facing the organization. The group identified seven issues—topics such as communications, computers, personnel rules—to be dealt with by task forces comprised of volunteers from throughout the organization. A consultant worked with the task forces to build their members' capabilities in communications, group dynamics, and problem solving. The task force concept soon became an accepted way of doing business in Palm Springs and was helpful in building trust and communications throughout the organization. Its matrix format also allowed subordinate employees to play more of a leadership role, thus breaking down some of the traditional limits imposed by the organization's previous structure.

A second element of the city's organization development effort, a training of trainers program (TOT), sought to prepare a number of city employees to train other city employees in areas as diverse as communications skills, personal health, engine repair, and stress management. The internal trainers were trained in workshop design, group facilitation, and experiential learning, then allowed to conduct workshops for their fellow employees. The city manager participated in the program and occasionally conducted workshops himself, modeling the program and allowing for what King described to me as "quality time" with his employees.

In a similar effort, hoping to improve the organization's capacity for work units to solve problems and to build teamwork, King encouraged training a group of employees as internal consultants. The external consultant trained the new consultants, who were then made available to departments or divisions (other than their own) to serve in a consultant role. Typically, the internal consultants worked with a unit for at least three sessions. They were often able to develop a climate in which supervisors and employees felt free to talk more openly and creatively about problems they faced in their work.

At the same time, King wanted to develop a diverse set of activities to increase trust, openness, and teamwork. Staff retreats, city council retreats, mid-management meetings, a wellness program, and a number of social events were conducted. About three times a year, the management and professional employees came together for a management meeting, typically planned by representatives of the various departments. Some meetings were quite serious, but others were simply fun. For example, departments competed for a "bragger award," which went to the department that presented the best skit bragging about its accomplishments. Similarly, King conducted a series of department visits to learn about the work of each area. King commented that without such visits, he never would have climbed the ladder on the fire department's snorkel truck with hose in hand or joined a street crew squirting hot asphalt on the street with a crack-filling gun.

One of the city's most interesting exercises in public participation, known as the "Palm Springs Project," was initiated at the suggestion of Mayor John Doyle, who wanted to see the city council, staff, business people, and residents working together to identify important issues and to co-operate in coming up with solutions. This turned the legislative process upside down:

> Instead of problems being identified by the council, they are identified by the public. Instead of issues being probed only by the staff, they are researched, with the help of staff, by residents and business owners who are interested enough to devote volunteer time to addressing them. Instead of the city council trying to "sell" ideas to the community, the public suggests programs and ideas to the council or the governing body for program implementation.

Initially, most observers were skeptical, but even the skeptics eventually concluded that the process was a success. A steering committee was organized, initial broad issue areas were identified, a town hall meeting was held to identify specific concerns, and six task forces of local citizens were established. The Palm Springs Project placed city employees in a new role in which they would develop skills in group facilitation and conflict resolution. At the same time, they became even more sensitive to their role as "public servants."

A final element of the city's organization development effort tied the various pieces together. This was development of a statement of philosophy for the City of Palm Springs and a City of Palm Springs management philosophy. The city council worked for more than a year developing the philosophy statement. In the process of doing so, they engaged in a series of stimulating discussions about the values and purposes of city government. The resulting document featured a new mission statement including language such as the following:

> Our primary objective is to be the best in our job of providing municipal services, at the same time re-

taining Palm Springs' position as America's foremost desert resort and retaining an ideal environment for living. Our rewards for achieving these objectives are social harmony, respect from the public, satisfied constituents, pleasing environment and a healthy local economy.

In addition, many city employees were involved in producing an internally oriented statement of management philosophy, crafted during a long series of meetings. The statement (see Box 2.3) focuses on values represented in the city's organization development program as well as on King's own approach to management. For example, the first item closely parallels King's belief, noted earlier, that the role of management is to provide a work environment in which employees can do a better job. Additionally, there are statements dealing with interdepartmental cooperation and exchange, flexibility, self-awareness, two-way communications, responsibility, and accountability. Working together toward creative and innovative solutions to the city's problems is emphasized.

The City of Palm Springs' organization development effort through the 1980s produced a number of important successes, and certainly Norm King's personal involvement in the program and his modeling of the values and attitudes he sought in the organization contributed to that success. Most important, however, King's effort was solidly based in a consistent set of values communicated and reinforced throughout the organization over a sustained period of time. In the concluding paragraph of a letter accepting an award for innovation in local government, King reflected on this perspective. After listing a series of two dozen or more innovative efforts on the part of the city, King wrote:

It is not a single program or even several that contribute to our recognition for innovation and productivity; it is a conscientious effort to continue evolving toward excellence by constant attention to improving our values and our organization, both of which are centered on communication, trust, participation, risk taking and fair play. And that, we freely admit, is harder to do than to say.

TRANSLATING VISION INTO ACTION

In my earlier discussion of strategic planning, I made the point that planning is best considered by looking at the future to establish specific action steps for today. In the same way, statements of vision are most helpful when accompa-

---

BOX 2.3
The City of Palm Springs
Management Philosophy

The management philosophy sets the tone for operations throughout the organization and establishes a model which management strives to achieve. The management philosophy is embodied in the following principles:

- We believe the organization's most important resources are the employees and we strive to provide a creative work environment where employees feel comfortable in participating in the decision-making process.
- We work together to develop a consensus of purpose.
- We help in organizing assignments so that work is meaningful and provides a sense of accomplishment and personal satisfaction.
- We believe employees should enjoy freedom to experiment and we support them in their risks to benefit the organization; we try to catch and recognize employee successes.
- We provide a safe, pleasant working environment, necessary equipment and needed resources so that each employee is able to reach his or her ideal level of productivity.
- We realize that in order to respond to changing conditions, we must be flexible, self-critical, aware of where we need to improve and open enough to accept suggestions.
- We share responsibility and accountability at all levels of

---

nied by specific steps that translate that vision into reality. As we have already seen, however, that is a difficult process. The more progressive public managers recognize that although developing a statement may itself be important, it is important as well to translate a vision into specific guidelines or behavioral objectives that make sense to those in the organization. Public managers often argue that policies should take into account the difficulties of implementation; similarly, translating a vision into reality needs to be done with great care. How then can a statement of vision be translated into reality?

the organization so that the commitment to teamwork is felt by all employees.

- We recognize that employee talents can be useful in interdepartmental problem solving and we encourage employees to apply their creativity and skills where they are most valuable, both inside and outside their own departments.
- We work toward the development of a system which recognizes employees not only for their required work but also for their individual efforts that go beyond the scope of the regular duties.
- We encourage the development of mutual trust by being open and honest with the public and with employees.
- We foster two-way communication and the flow of information to employees and citizens so that they are knowledgeable about programs and issues affecting them and the organization. We strive to notify everyone who has a stake in information.
- We practice the management philosophy by transmitting City Council goals and policies, as well as a sense of mission, to employees throughout the organization and to citizens.
- We learn from the public and employees by listening to and considering their ideas and by being aware of their feelings.
- We attempt to anticipate future challenges and plan for their resolution, while at the same time addressing current problems.
- We serve all members of the community and wherever possible help them identify issues and reach solutions that are understood and supported by the public.

One way to approach this question is through training and development. Following an extensive survey of opinion, top executives of British Rail felt a need to communicate their vision of the organization more clearly. At a conference involving the top thirty executives, key values that should guide the work of British Rail were listed: "To place renewed emphasis on the customer, to value our people and to give them scope to commit to excellence and to quality, and to encourage enterprise, initiative, and innovation." To implement these values throughout the organization, the executives of British Rail sought to bring about a major cultural change through a series of management development efforts.

Their first step was directed at their top 500 managers, all of whom were involved in a program that sought to combine a new awareness of the values of the organization with the leadership skills needed to implement those values. The objectives of this program—called "Leadership 500"—were to create the conditions and momentum necessary to bring about a change in the culture of the organization and to develop a critical mass of trained and committed leaders. After a week of training, these managers followed individual action plans designed to introduce concepts of quality improvement throughout the organization. These plans focused on key management qualities:

Urgency—Persisting in making the future happen.
Responsibility—Being in charge of your own behaviour.
Empowerment—Giving the mandate to yourself and to others to create and achieve.
Trust—Giving confidence to the individual and inspiration to the group.
Vision—Having the image of the cathedral as we mix the mortar.

As the quality improvement process was extended throughout the organization, all managers leading work groups became involved in a new phase of training emphasizing the new values of the organization and the skills needed to achieve those values—Leadership 500. To ensure that the training and development activities didn't simply train people and send them out into a vacuum, a new performance review system was instituted and extended to the top 900 executives of British Rail and to some 10,000 managers throughout the organization. The review system emphasized the new values of the organization, stressing communications and feedback rather than confidential reports and judgments.

Another approach to extending the values contained in a statement of philosophy is by developing specific guidelines for performance in keeping with the mission and philosophy of the organization. For example, on becoming Secretary of Community Services in Tasmania, an appointment based largely on her ability to turn other public organizations around, Jenny Bedlington sought significant changes in her new organization. She described these changes to me in great detail. Like the other managers whose work we have already examined, Bedlington began with a statement of mission and philosophy, a statement she termed "Business Rules." In the statement, she noted the commitment of the Tasmanian government to balancing economic development and social justice. Specifically related to the work of the Department of Community Services were the objectives of the Social Justice Strategy:

- To reduce disadvantage caused by unequal access to economic resources and power
- To protect, extend, and ensure the effective exercise of equal legal, industrial, and political rights
- To increase access to essential goods and services according to need
- To expand opportunities for participation by all Tasmanians in decisions which affect their lives

Beyond these general goals, Bedlington's Business Rules described the operation of an agency that would pay special attention to affordable, accessible, and appropriate services meeting the needs of clients. The Business Rules told those in the organization that "clients have a right to sensitive, responsive and quality service. Clients are the reason the department exists, and the reason the taxpayer pays our salaries. So the balance between providing the best service possible while getting maximum value from taxpayers' funds is our responsibility." Finally, the Business Rules expressed Bedlington's deep commitment to an open and caring working environment: "As managers, our aim is to create a client-focused organisation which is innovative and vital, productive and efficient, open and supportive and an enjoyable and satisfying place to work." In these ways, Bedlington sought to articulate a vision for the Department of Community Services.

But, as we have said, more specific mechanisms to actualize the vision are necessary as well. In Bedlington's case, the connecting point between vision and reality was the program management plan, a statement Bedlington asked all managers in the department to prepare showing how they intended to implement the values expressed in the Business Rules. Having articulated values such as client rights and consultation, Bedlington asked for strategies that would enable the organization to achieve its goals in a way that was consistent with these values. The key question Bedlington asked her managers—the main question that needed to be addressed in the program management plan—was, "What are we trying to achieve for whom?" That is, how do our actions translate into measurable outcomes that demonstrate a benefit to our clients? How much can we do, in what time frame, and at what level?

Managers were then asked to isolate more detailed strategies and to accompany these with performance and work load indicators. In keeping with Bedlington's philosophy as stated in the Business Rules, these activities were to be accomplished with substantial participation by all members of the organization. Indeed, Bedlington argues convincingly that having a strong statement of mission and philosophy makes it possible to localize decision making and focus on client needs. And, happily, such devolution of responsibility doesn't mean that standards are lowered.

Indeed, Bedlington reports that the staff consistently set their own standards higher than those her managers or she would set.

After requesting the program plan, Bedlington asked each manager to report back in three months and to indicate how they were doing with respect to the goals and strategies contained in their program management plan. This report provided an opportunity for managers to review their plans, note progress toward their objectives, but also to change their plans to meet new conditions. Initial reports were often confused and contained data irrelevant to the central question of "What are we trying to achieve for whom?" But in time the answers became more precise, and the indicators of successful outcomes became more positive. Bedlington acknowledges that the transition was not without pain, especially for those who missed the point the first time around: "When people stand out, they hate it—in fact, they hate me. It's very stress-inducing. Typically they have a lot of data that I'm not interested in; it's just not what I need. And this tells us something. That lasts about six to nine months. Then they discover it works!" And quality and productivity increase dramatically.

Halfway around the world, Lamona Lucas of the Alabama Division of Rehabilitation and Crippled Children Service pursued a similar strategy. Lucas assumed leadership in an organization known for its classic approach to the rehabilitation of children and adults. Her organization had been characterized by tight control and close oversight on the part of top managers. The division was a male-dominated agency that closely regulated its front-line workers (mostly rehabilitation counselors) through demands for compliance with agency policies and extensive reporting activities.

Lucas wanted to institute a structure for decision making in the agency that clearly defined the mission and associated values for the organization and provided a set of goals and objectives consistent with the organization's values. She wanted people to achieve congruence between what the agency said and what it did. Over a twelve-month period, all personnel in the division and many clients of the agency participated in developing "Blueprint for the Future," a statement that would focus not on immediate problems (or symptoms of problems) but rather on the desired end states of the organization. The statement set out four primary values of the Rehabilitation Agency:

- We value the worth, dignity, and rights of persons with disabilities.
- We value the contributions of all staff in achieving our mission.
- We value an agency management style that provides opportunities for staff participation.
- We value maximum acquisition and the efficient and effective management of resources.
- We value public support.

Following development of these guideposts, goal statements for each value were derived by asking questions such as, "If we value the worth, dignity, and rights of persons with disabilities, then what will we do?" Evidence of goal accomplishment was also ascertained by asking, "How will we know if the goal is accomplished (what are we willing to accept as evidence)?" For example, valuing the worth, dignity, and rights of persons with disabilities led the organization to posit advocacy for the rights of such persons as a goal. Following development of these statements, members of the organization considered questions about whether the agency was organized in a way that reflected its newly stated values, and whether supervisors were behaving in a way that would reflect those values. (Interestingly, in developing these sets of goals and criteria for evaluation, the agency tried to follow a model consistent with its interest in staff participation in decision making. Staff were involved in all phases of the effort, thus communicating the agency management's interest in building a new structure for decision making in the organization.)

Finally, a system for "quality assurance" was developed to guarantee that the values and goals of the organization were in fact being followed. This approach sought consistency with the stated values of the agency. A first effort involved extensive training for both managers and service delivery personnel that focused on outcomes of the work of individuals in the agency. Additionally, instead of continuing the more traditional and punitive approach in which the primary roles were played by central staff, performance review was decentralized, with immediate supervisors being responsible for improvements in individual and unit performance. In this way, the values of the Rehabilitation Agency and its goals and objectives were translated into specific behavioral guidelines that would orient the work of those in the organization.

CONCLUSION

Establishing a vision for the future is an important act of leadership and a step that the more progressive public managers deem essential to improving the quality and productivity of their organizations. To state clearly and publicly the desired direction of the organization and the values that should guide the organization as it moves into the future is something members of the organization not only need but actually appreciate. Although such a statement may seem remote from the day-to-day activities of those in the organization, it is surprising how relevant and applicable such a statement can be. Simply saying to those in the Missouri Office of Administration that the organization was not merely concerned with controlling the actions of other agencies but was interested in serving those agencies, in helping them to achieve their objectives, made a substantial and immediate difference in the way people throughout the organization interacted with their "clients" in other agencies. Indeed, in the interviews preceding the statement, it was surprising to hear how many people very much wanted a resolution of this issue—because it made a difference in the work they did.

Manager after manager reports that while a statement of vision is important, it is often less important than the activity involved in producing the statement. Jim Bragg, City Manager of Abilene, Texas, helped his city through a four-month-long exercise aimed at developing a joint planning process involving the city, the county, the school district, and the Chamber of Commerce. The resulting plan was helpful, but Bragg later commented that the process was even more important than the plan itself. By working on the plan, members of a somewhat politically fragmented community pulled together, and the community was soon named an "All-America City" by the National Civic League. Bragg's comments are reminiscent of Robert H. Waterman, Jr.'s characterization of planning activities in organizations seeking major transformations: "Renewing organizations . . . think strategic planning is great—as long as no one takes the plans too seriously. They often see more value in the process of planning than in the plan itself."

For a planning or visioning process to be effective, the manager must be extraordinarily sensitive to communications with those involved in the proposed changes. Robert Gray of the Australian Post put it nicely when he told me, "One cannot underestimate, in my experience, the amount of 'knitting together' that can, with advantage, be carried out in a large organisation." Inevitably, there is a tendency in large organizations for things to fly apart, as Gray says, "Something like centrifugal force!" People from all parts of the organization need to talk with one another. "There's nothing more destructive of a participative planning process than to send proposals out into a void. Yet how often do we see this happen!"

Finally, at a personal level, managers engaging in major organizational renewal efforts report that the creative process of analyzing the needs of a particular organization, envisioning a desired future state of the organization (and the values that might support that vision), and articulating that vision in language that is clear, meaningful, and relevant to members of the organization is just the beginning. The manager must then seek opportunities to reinforce the main ideas, sometimes formally but often informally, sometimes in speeches and agency publications, sometimes in conversations in the parking lot or during a golf tournament. In always being aware of such opportunities and taking advantage of them, the manager must exhibit a certain tenacity of purpose, having "the desire, commitment, and simple doggedness to keep walking into that wall until it finally collapses." The manager, the leader, the visionary must ultimately be well connected to reality by demonstrating his or her personal commitment to the vision and the organization.

Serving the Public

The manager gives priority to service to both clients and citizens. That priority is supported by high standards of performance and accountability and by a constant emphasis on quality. Most important, the manager recognizes that technical efforts alone will fail unless equal or even greater attention is given to the human side, especially to building a sense of community within the organization and a sense of cooperation outside.

The concept of public service has always been central to the work of those in public organizations. Unfortunately, today many public agencies are too inward looking, concentrating on organizational and professional standards for evaluating their work rather than asking how the public can be better served. Certainly, government cutbacks and restrictions in recent years have forced some public managers to focus more narrowly to conserve resources. But a dilemma for many is that if service to the public is performed well, demand may increase, even though resources for the operation probably will not. Despite these difficulties, the most progressive public managers today are boldly emphasizing improved service and improved quality, both supported by a caring and concerned organization.

In restoring a sense of priority to public service, managers have some very special qualities to build on, not least among them is the intrinsic appeal of public service itself. People are attracted to public organizations for many reasons, but primary among them is a desire to serve—to contribute something meaningful and significant to the world. This deeply personal element of commitment distinguishes public organizations from others and cannot be ignored by managers wishing to improve the performance of their organizations. The most progressive public managers recognize that fact, and the special sense of responsibility that the desire to serve confers on their organizations. These managers know that their organizations and their people are special and that they must take that specialness into account in all they do.

Because public organizations are imbued with such an ethic and such a responsibility, ideas and practices found useful elsewhere cannot easily be transferred to government. This is especially true of the values examined in this chapter—a concern for service, a concern for quality, and what I will call community within/cooperation without. Some of these ideas, especially service to the customer, have received considerable attention in recent literature on private sector management in such books as *In Search of Excellence*. The public sector managers with whom I talked found these notions appealing; indeed, many had already developed highly advanced programs in areas such as service quality, quality management, job satisfaction, and the quality of work life. They cautioned, however, that transferring ideas more often associated with the private sector into their public organizations was not as easy as one might imagine.

More important, many of the people I talked with pointed out that public sector organizations themselves have a significant history and tradition of service, quality, and caring. Indeed, it could be argued that those in public organizations historically have been much more committed to these ideas than those in business and industry. Public servants deserve credit for that history, but they also are shaped by that history. Ideas such as serving the public have a significant heritage in the public sector; that heritage cannot be dismissed in an effort to copy techniques that seem to have worked elsewhere. If ideas appropriate to the private sector are used in the public sector, a simple transfer of techniques from one arena to the other is not what is required. What is needed is to build upon the tradition of public service by incorporating new ideas *in the right way.*

Certainly, that admonition applies to the new interest in customer service. The relationship between a public organization and its clients or the citizenry generally is just not the same as between a business and its customers. The idea of public service is absolutely central to public organizations, but to speak of a "customer" orientation is to speak in terms more closely associated with private business. At the most basic level, the user of government services rarely pays directly for those services in an open marketplace as do customers of private businesses. As you will see, this is just one of a set of differences that can be subtle but very significant. (Despite these problems, I will bend to the popular usage and occasionally use the word "customer" in relation to the recipients of government agencies.)

Many public managers advise caution in the casual adoption of ideas such as Total Quality Management (TQM), the basics of which are clearly associated with production-based industries. Although this approach to organizational change has much to offer, its recommendations need to be adapted to the peculiar setting within which public organizations operate. Most notably, programs to enhance quality need to acknowledge the public purposes sought by the agencies of government and the fact that those purposes demand attention not only to doing things right (the goal of

TQM) but to doing the right things. The ethical context of government permeates all that public agencies do, even their adoption of management techniques that, on the surface, appear neutral in their application. These new ideas must be fully consistent with the ethics and traditions of the public service.

As you saw in the previous chapter, many forward-looking public managers seek to transform their organizations through attention to the norms, beliefs, and values held by members, clients, and others. In this chapter, I will focus on particular values typically found in such statements that help orient the work of these organizations. In each case, whether looking at a concern for service, a concern for quality, or community within/cooperation without, I will review the ideas that have caused such attention and explore some of the ways they have been used to guide the work of those in public organizations. I will also consider how the public setting of these organizations is likely to shape the application of these ideas, now and in the future.

A CONCERN FOR SERVICE

The importance of staying close to the customer was an important theme in Peters and Waterman's *In Search of Excellence* and, indeed, a theme voiced frequently in the literature on corporate management ever since. Peters and Waterman opened their discussion on a note of irony. They remarked that it should go without saying that a business ought to be close to its customers, yet, not all do so. What seems to distinguish excellent companies from the rest is that "the excellent companies *really are* close to their customers. That's it: Other companies talk about it; the excellent companies do it." These firms seem obsessed with notions of quality, reliability, and service. That obsession permeates the organization, affecting every aspect of the business.

Interestingly, the same comment probably could have been applied to the best public agencies in the eighties and early nineties (and earlier). Those perceived to be the best public organizations—and there were plenty of good ones—were those most attentive to the interests of clients or users *and* the citizenry generally. There is no doubt that those public managers held by their peers as examples of the best in the public sector place a strong emphasis on serving the public, both clients and citizens. Not surprisingly, the importance of a service orientation in public agencies is a recurring theme in major reports issued in all four countries. A quick review of these reports will provide a context within which to examine the actions of individual managers and individual organizations; in addition, such a review will give some understanding of the way the service issue is being approached in each country.

A first reason for increased attention to serving the public is to help improve the image of the public service. This reason is clearly reflected in the report of the National Commission on the Public Service (the Volcker Commission), an independent body primarily concerned with improving the recently diminished public image of the United States public service, a body that was especially battered during the Reagan years. In keeping with its mission, the commission spoke of a service orientation in the context of changing the public's *perception* of government services. The report argued that government must shed its image of being isolated, complex, and impenetrable and move away from a public impression of government as involving endless lines, second-rate facilities, and quarrelsome officials bound by a set of outdated rules and regulations. In other words, government must become more "user-friendly." The commission held, "If government is to be for the people, it must go where the people are. Government must go to the shopping malls and the branch libraries, even if that means occasionally contracting out to 'franchisees' who deliver services. Instead of making the people fit government schedules and government locales, government must fit the people's schedule and needs."

In Australia, the authors of the APS 2000 report more substantively and perceptively placed their discussion of serving the public in the context of a general cultural change affecting private business, public organizations, and the customers and employees of both. The report pointed out that providing good service is no longer a discretionary activity for business; today if good service is not provided, customers will look elsewhere. The report held that the same criterion also is being applied to government today. "The public service cannot stand aside and apart from this new service culture. Those same consumer expectations which if not met can result in a company losing customers will also cause those same customers to react negatively if they do not receive a comparable level of service from a public service department or agency." Interestingly, and somewhat paradoxically, the report contends that since public employees want to give good service, emphasizing high quality service helps motivate employees; on the other hand, "organisations that are not oriented toward their own employees find it difficult to develop a strong service culture." As you will see, the interconnectedness of various strategies clustering around the service theme has important implications for the renewed interest in developing a service orientation.

The Report of the Canadian Auditor General, mentioned earlier, also reflects a strong client orientation as one attribute of such organizations but, in addition, emphasizes the connection between such an orientation and other features of the organization's activities. "People in the well-performing organization focus on client needs and preferences. People in the organization derive their satisfaction from serving the client, rather than serving the bureaucracy. Interaction is strong within the organization, but it is perhaps even stronger between the organization and its clients." What is especially interesting about the Canadian report is the way client service is embedded in a series of other strategies for achieving excellence in the public sector. The report's discussion of a client orientation, for instance, is contrasted with traditional patterns of hierarchical authority in public organizations as well as approaches to change that depend on structure and control. The implication is that a serious commitment to a strong client orientation requires substantial changes in many aspects of traditional management practice.

Finally, an Occasional Paper produced by the Office of the Minister for the Civil Service in the United Kingdom addressed the distinctive service orientation appropriate to the public sector. In its opening statement, the report held that "all civil servants serve the public through their service to Ministers. The majority deal with the public directly. . . . They regard the efficient and helpful performance of their duties as a matter of personal and professional pride." Public service, therefore, involves not only the immediate customer but the citizen as well; it also involves accountability to elected political leaders—both points of great significance. The private sector relationship between customer satisfaction and commercial success is a direct one, but in the public sector "the reasons for providing a service in the first place, the nature of that service and the manner in which it is delivered, are not dictated by markets. In these circumstances the balance between public expectations and the level of service to be provided is decided on the basis of political judgments about economic and social priorities." The report concludes that public servants have a professional responsibility to adhere to the highest standards of service possible within a given level of resources.

These broadly stated commitments are reflected in specific programs undertaken in a wide variety of public agencies in the various countries. Although some programs are fairly easy adaptations of private sector marketing practices to public sector problems, others have involved the difficult and challenging task of figuring out what is distinctive about serving the public and how those differences affect efforts to improve service. Before looking at some exemplary programs developed by public managers, a review of the special characteristics of public services should be helpful. As you will see, a clear understanding of these distinctions grows out of a combination of practical experience and thoughtful reflection.

One of the most interesting state or provincial efforts in improving the quality of service occurred in British Columbia in 1990 when the government approved a proposal by the Deputy Ministers' Council to undertake a government-wide initiative called "Service Quality B. C." The new program was designed to create more affordable, innovative, and customer-focused government agencies across the board. A secretariat, consisting of line managers on loan from their "home" agencies, developed a business plan recommending changes in central control and service functions, a delegation of authority to the front line, improved training, mechanisms to coordinate service delivery across departments, and individual ministry efforts to enhance service quality and customer satisfaction. The project has just "lifted off" across the provincial government, with some departments obviously taking the lead and others still working on the basics; but the program is in place.

The British Columbia plan is outstanding not only for its scope but for its careful conceptualization of many important issues in the design and implementation of programs to improve the quality of government services. Joan Barton and Brian Marson of the Service Quality Secretariat present their overall goal, service quality, as a combination of two movements: the *service movement*, which means knowing what the customer wants and satisfying that need; and the *quality movement*, which means doing it right the first time and continually improving the product and the service. Barton and Marson recognize that government services are diverse and that not all such services easily fit the market model of customer behavior or the manufacturing or product model of improving quality. The public service, they point out, has at least three related and overlapping functions:

> The Service/"Operations" component, which sometimes resembles the private sector. It provides benefits to customers by transferring resources or information directly to the public, through various facilities such

as schools, hospitals, parks, ferries, recreation and cultural centers, public health care and welfare services.

Regulatory and enforcement responsibilities, which protect the public interest by imposing constraints, duties and obligations on citizens and institutions. These include collection of taxes and fines, detention and imprisonment, surveillance and supervision of citizens.

Development of policy proposals and legislation to support ministers, and help achieve the objectives of the government. This includes the advice given to decision-makers and the drafting and re-drafting of legislation to facilitate policy decisions.

Obviously, the varied functions of government do not represent uniform products or even a unified "product line." Rather, they are extraordinarily diverse in the ways they are created; the ways they are communicated, performed, or transmitted; and the ways they are received and valued. Some, like issuing traffic citations, are services that the immediate recipient doesn't even want. For these reasons, the relationship between those in public organizations and their customers is certainly more complicated than the relationship between those behind the hamburger stand and their customers.

Similarly, the diversity of government activities means that even the first step in a service improvement effort, identification of an agency's customers, can be quite difficult. Private sector customer service efforts often distinguish between internal and external customers, but the problem for government goes far beyond that distinction. Included among the categories of customers dealt with by government might be those who immediately present themselves for the service, those who may be waiting for service, those who may need the service even though they are not actively seeking it, future generations of possible service recipients, relatives and friends of the immediate recipient, and on and on. For example, who is the customer of a program that was designed to respond to the AIDS epidemic? Should the government's response to AIDS be oriented toward those victims who seek medical treatment, toward those who might potentially be affected by the virus, or toward the population as a whole? Obviously, choosing one answer to this question over another determines how the agency targets its analysis of customers, designs a strategy to meet customer needs, and opens possibilities for feedback and participation.

The problem of identifying the customer is even more complicated. Obviously, some customers of government have greater resources and greater skill in bringing their demands forward. Does that fact justify their being treated any differently? Moreover, many public services, such as environmental quality or police protection or schooling, are designed to have a collective benefit. For example, we generally assume that having a more literate society is an important general goal that goes beyond the effect schooling has on particular individuals. How should collective services such as this be assessed in terms of customers' needs or wants? Finally, the consumer of business products or services is rarely the producer of those goods or services; yet in the public sector the customer of any government service is almost always at the same time a citizen—in a sense, the boss. As a citizen, the individual has a stake in all services that are delivered, not just those that he or she consumes directly. Citizens, of course, are involved in transactions denoting more than a market relationship; they are participants in a political process.

Public sector discussions of service quality are further complicated by the relative lack of choice involved in public sector activities. The consumer of business products presumably wields some power because of business competition; the individual may be able to make the same or a similar purchase somewhere else (although there are obvious practical limitations to this). The same simply doesn't apply in the public sector. For exactly this reason, Police Chief James O'Dell of Kettering, Ohio, is highly concerned about obtaining effective feedback about his agency's performance. "If the citizen is not satisfied with (the service he or she receives), the result is perpetual dislike for [an] agency each time he or she must deal with it. When that agency is the police department, the citizen cannot take their business elsewhere. The end result is that the police agency's image and credibility suffers and the agency is held in low esteem. Thus, we in Kettering are concerned with our citizens' satisfaction and how we measure up." (Incidentally, the same lack of choice is maintained even when certain public services are privatized. Individuals cannot switch their water company or fire department, even if privatized. Instead, in all these cases, the appeal—the effort to change things—is not market appeal but political appeal.)

Michael Clarke, Chief Executive of the Local Government Management Board, and John Stewart, of the University of Birmingham, have written extensively on what they term the "public service orientation" in local government (though their work also extends to other levels of government). Their writing appropriately captures the special character of public services:

- The service must meet a public purpose.
- Public purpose in turn can mean that the service is of concern to more than its immediate user.
- Political processes, subject to public accountability, are central to the determination of public purpose.

Public purposes are distinct because they are directed toward "the collective needs of society and give expression to community values." They can override individual choice; indeed, individuals may be compelled to accept certain services (even services they see as limitations on their freedom). Similarly, customers may be statutorily restricted from receiving certain services. On the other hand, they may have statutory or even constitutional rights to certain services. (One ongoing complaint about the consumer programs of the British National Health Service focuses on whether those programs are solely about customer relations or are about patient rights.) Finally, public services may be directed at a need that has not been requested or demanded by the recipient or by potential recipients of the service . . . and appropriately so. Because of these characteristics, the character of public services is not determined in the marketplace nor according to the laws of supply and demand; it is determined through the political process. Judgments concerning the provision and distribution of public services ultimately can be legitimized only through appeal to recognized political actors.

Despite the difficulties of applying a service perspective to the operations of public organizations, that perspective is essential to the nature of public organizations, and not surprisingly, more progressive public managers seek such an orientation, in most cases with great care and thoughtfulness. Karl Albrecht and Ron Zemke, authors of *Service America*, suggest that the outstanding service organizations have (1) a well-conceived strategy for service, (2) customer-oriented front-line people, and (3) customer-friendly systems. Better customer service programs in public agencies seem to follow these guidelines, while taking into account the special circumstances within which they operate. In the more developed service improvement programs, public managers started with efforts to identify the products or services of the organization, as well as its customers, both members of the public and others within government who serve those who serve the public. (These are sometimes called internal and external customers.) Then, in most cases, those in the agencies have sought to assess their own performance *in the eyes of their customers* through surveys or other assessments. Of course, as several managers cautioned, "If you ask someone what they think, you'd better be ready to listen to what they say."

Developing a response means not only communicating to those throughout the organization the importance of delivering services properly and well but also creating specific customer-oriented strategies for service delivery, strategies that will improve the speed of the service, the choices available to clients, the quality of the service, the extent of coverage, the openness of the organization to feedback, and other features. These strategies, given the nature of the public service, must be measured not only against the potential demand but also against the resources available for any one particular activity as opposed to the many others that may present themselves. Obviously, public services are constrained by limited public resources. Following implementation of these strategies, managers typically try to measure the results of their efforts by instituting some sort of internal performance review that ensures that those in the organization are doing all they can to enhance service quality. Finally, though it sounds obvious, the most progressive managers actually take time to recognize and reward individual and group successes in improving service quality.

In a number of public sector efforts, agencies have used marketing techniques quite similar to those employed in the private sector to meet their customers' needs and expectations. For example, the Minnesota Department of Natural Resources conducted a survey to determine the reasons attendance at state parks decreased significantly. One thing that stood out in the survey results was that potential users of the parks wanted to pay for services with credit cards, something the state's finance department had long opposed. The Department of Natural Resources prevailed, however, and made this change along with several others suggested by their customers. As a result, attendance increased 10 percent over a one-year period!

In another case, Michael E. Horsey, President of the British Columbia Pavilion Corporation, wanted the 1.4 million annual visitors to his various exhibition and convention facilities to have, as it was expressed in the corporation's mission statement, "The Best Event Experience in North America." He wanted to emphasize service excellence; he wanted to tune his systems to what the guests wanted. Feeling that the attitude of employees is critical to service excellence, Horsey tried to make sure that new employees were hired based primarily on their attitude toward service. Their hiring was followed by eight hours of training, which

Horsey designed after consulting with those doing staff training at Disney World in Orlando. These training and orientation programs were based on a highly visible "Yes We
Can" slogan, a slogan reinforced by a set of award programs
(with buttons, badges, hats, certificates, and all the rest).
Horsey also empowered his employees to make service-
oriented decisions on their own. For example, employees
were told:

- Admit when you are wrong and correct the problem now.
- If a customer complains that the hot dog is cold,
  give him another one immediately.
- If he gets ketchup on his shirt and it's our fault,
  clean his shirt; or buy him a new one!

Horsey's service excellence program has been so successful
that he now offers a course on service excellence to businesses and other public agencies.

For many in the service and operations areas, this type
of marketing approach has worked quite well; but in other
areas a more complicated, politically based analysis has
been required. For example, given the multiplicity of interests represented in the political process, the interests of
different customers may conflict with one another. Mary
Faulk of the Department of Licensing in the State of
Washington worked hard to develop an attitude of courteous
and responsive service to the public, including those who
applied for drivers' licenses, only to have the Washington
Commission on Efficiency and Accountability point out the
difficulty of reconciling such an orientation with the older
paradigm of driver safety. For the individual seeking a
license, excessive testing is often considered a nuisance; but
from the standpoint of the public, such procedures may
mean the highways are safer for everyone. You can please
some of the people, some of the time . . .

Another difficulty is the limited resources in most
government agencies. William D. Mitchell, Director of the
Government Agents Branch in British Columbia, someone

who has successfully developed a strong service orientation in his organization, recognizes these barriers. Mitchell commented, "If you provide superior service, it's going to lead to increased workloads, but if you get increased workloads without increased resources, the very service you provided in the first instance will deteriorate." And, of course, in the public sector, increased demands have often been countered not by increases but by diminished resources. Obviously, this situation raises difficult questions for staff; why should they work hard to improve a level of service, so they will have to work even harder to sustain it? (Fortunately, many managers have found that staff are so interested in providing quality service that they find ways to resolve this dilemma. It's another manifestation of a deep-seated commitment to public service.)

Another barrier Mitchell pointed out was that "improved service leads to rising expectations. If they see you as an organization that provides a superior product and you provide anything less, you're in trouble." This raises a question about what the proper expectation should be and, of course, that can only be answered politically. What should be done and at what level of expenditures is a political choice. In any case, as these examples illustrate, the easy application of "supermarket" principles simply doesn't fit the reality of work in public organizations; an approach much more sensitive to political circumstances is required. Let's look at a few examples.

• Ron Christie is Director-General of the Public Works Department of New South Wales, an agency charged not only with construction and maintenance of the governmental infrastructure of New South Wales but also with providing architectural and engineering design and project management services on a commercially competitive basis. The commercial work has intensified in recent years, especially after a NSW task force on business development pointed out that there is a "vast reservoir" of technical and engineering talent "embedded" in the public sector that might be exploited in export markets, particularly those in

ticularly those in Southeast Asia. Christie responded by placing service to both public and commercial clients at the top of his list of organizational values: "Client service is our top priority. We believe in providing the Government and our other clients with a highly professional, responsive, and timely service, value for money, sound commercial dealings, a choice of options, and what they need." Interestingly, this concern for service underlies a statement of values that the department produced, one structured in terms of the needs of various stakeholder groups. Typical statements are: "Government wants value for money, accountability, proper financial management, etc." "The community wants safe and useful infrastructure, sensitive treatment of the environment, etc." "Our state and local government clients want their needs satisfied, effective design solutions, a choice of options, etc." As one indicator of the success of this approach, the department is currently providing consulting services on overseas projects worth over $500 million.

• Pierre Niedlispacher, Assistant Director of Client Services in the City of Montreal, has been deeply involved in development of Acces Montreal, a storefront, neighborhood-based network of public information offices built on a human scale. Today Acces Montreal offices are located in thirteen key districts of the city, providing a direct link between these districts and the city administration. (This approach was especially well suited to Montreal, a city known for its strong sense of neighborhood identity.) The neighborhood offices serve as consultation centers, information points, and outlets for direct transactions with the city. Staff handle everything from zoning requirements, to cultural activities, reports of defective light posts, voter registration, payment of parking tickets, obtaining renovation permits, registering new babies, and much more. Businesses are major clients, with one-third of the clients representing businesses and one-half of all contacts being business related. As one measure of the success of the program, demand for Acces Montreal has increased dramatically since its beginning, growing by 300 percent from the first to the second year of operations.

During the first months of operation, managers of the project recognized the considerable amount of time spent by staff in district offices responding to telephone inquiries. A representative would sit down at a desk across from a client and begin to work on a problem. Then the phone would ring. The representative would take several minutes handling the telephone inquiry, then return to the client across the desk. Then the phone would ring . . .

In response, the city developed Acces Montreal "First Line," a telephone-only information intake service staffed with specially trained personnel who are available from 7:00 A.M. to 11:00 P.M. five days a week. It is anticipated that "First Line" will receive a million calls during its first year alone. With the addition of enhanced computer equipment, it will soon be possible to access municipal data banks or even to reserve tennis courts from a television set or home computer. Quite a step forward from long lines in many scattered locations.

- In the United States, interest in improved service to the public has been especially strong at the local level. Leland Nelson, City Manager of University Park, Texas, told me that "successful managers in the future will be strong advocates of customer service. The quality of service delivery, especially in one-on-one situations, and the perception of that service among the citizen customers is more important than ever." Toward that end, Nelson and his staff developed a computer-aided tracking system to monitor how various departments respond to citizen complaints. Nelson stresses viewing citizens as customers with needs rather than enemies with demands (though, just in case, they also developed training in how to deal with difficult people). They have also purchased uniforms for field employees to give them more pride and more visibility.

"Just down the road," as they say in Texas, Camille Cates Barnett, City Manager of Austin, started a program called "BASICS—Building Austin's Standard in Customer Service." This program focuses on managing moments of truth (those contact points between a citizen and a city employee), knowing and understanding the customer's needs (through surveys and so forth), developing systems and procedures that are user-friendly, and recognizing and treating both employees and customers with dignity and respect.

- At the state level, the State of Minnesota has been a leader in developing a strong service orientation in many of its key agencies. In 1988, the state began offering two courses: "Creating Satisfied Citizens and Customers," a two-day foundation course; and "Coaching Extraordinary Customer Relations," a one-day program for supervisors. Vera Vogelsang Coombs, Manager of Training and Development for the state, told me that the courses, which help employees identify customers and ensure that all citizens— "even the most irate, defiant, confused, or upset"—receive high quality service, have now been offered to over 10,000 employees or nearly a third of the state's work force. Meanwhile, the state's Department of Employee Relations is setting up an evaluation system to gather public opinion data on citizens' reactions to the improvements.

- Just a few years ago the U.S. Internal Revenue Service was known as one of the least customer-oriented public organizations anywhere, but changes are even occurring in the IRS—changes centered on serving the public. Fred T. Goldberg, the Commissioner, puts it this way: "Our responsibility is to foster voluntary compliance. We have a tax system that is reaching every individual, every business, everyone. Somehow we need to get back in touch with the notion that our primary responsibility is to make it as easy as possible for all those groups, all those diverse constituencies, to live with the tax law." Rather than succumbing to the natural impulse to ask for more people to do more enforcement, Goldberg thinks that the IRS should work with individuals and businesses "so that they do it right the first time, rather than waiting till they fall in a ditch and then trying to drag them back out."

Charles Gilbert, a veteran of many years with the IRS, recognizes the changes from his position as Assistant Director of the San Francisco office. He told me that in the old days the IRS would hide away and seldom talk with anyone. Now, each time even a minor change in a form is proposed, someone from the IRS is out there trying to see what the users would think about the change. Each time a customer contacts the IRS—and in the San Francisco office alone that is 10,000 times a day—the IRS is trying, often under great pressure, to make that experience a positive one. Gilbert believes these changes are best expressed in a new IRS mission statement that says: "The purpose of the IRS is to collect the proper amount of tax revenue with the least cost; serve the public by continually improving the quality of our products and services; and perform in a manner warranting the highest degree of public confidence." The new language represents quite a change in tone from the old IRS.

• In Great Britain, questions about customer service are a significant part of the privatization debate, a debate John Beishon, a former public manager who is now Chief Executive of the Consumers' Association, watches with great interest. Beishon saw the Thatcher moves to privatize services as an effort in part to improve services by creating a more competitive attitude. "What Thatcher said was, if we stand the thing on its head, if we introduce a much harsher, more exploitative, business competitive mentality . . . the service will become more responsive to the consumer. And in a certain sense she's been proven absolutely right. You now have rough tough managers—not the kind of people we would like to know, certainly not the people we would like to have dinner with, not like our daughters to marry. But, by God, we like going on their trains!"

Beishon feels that the performance of many government agencies, especially local authorities, had reached the point where delivery was unacceptably bad and that shaking things up so that greater attention would be given to consumer interests was positive—and, indeed, there are numerous customer service success stories throughout the U.K. But Beishon points out the dangers of the pendulum swinging too far in the direction of a strict market orientation toward customer service. The problem, he says, is that a point may be reached "where people start saying, we could be even more efficient and effective if we bent this rule a little bit more or if we weren't quite as fair to this person as to that. I worry that the values of the marketplace start to corrupt." For this reason, Beishon sees a role for the Consumers' Association (as well as those in the agencies themselves) in monitoring the quality of service delivery in the public sector, in promoting avenues for proper feedback and the redress of grievances, and in assuring that proper ethical standards are maintained.

LOOKING TO THE FUTURE

As we look to the future, at least three possible developments with respect to an expanded public service orientation may be quite fascinating to watch. First, many public managers pursuing a service orientation have been struck by the way in which a serious commitment to service affects and is affected by everything else that happens in the organization. Consequently, the public manager espousing a service orientation should be prepared to follow through with organizational changes needed to support a service orientation. That kind of follow-through can mean establishing new channels of communication in the organization, channels in which first-line employees have greater access to data previously denied them; it can mean decentralizing decision making or empowering first-line employees to make decisions within a significantly expanded range of discretion; or it can mean establishing a more caring and concerned attitude toward service delivery personnel, one that recognizes that the way employees are treated will affect the way they treat customers. Some managers portray these changes as an inverted pyramid with the customer at the top and all in the organization supporting those who deal directly with the customer (see Box 3.1),

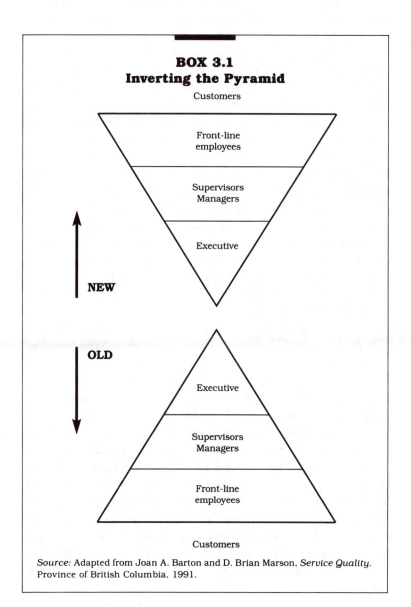

**BOX 3.1
Inverting the Pyramid**

Customers

Front-line
employees

Supervisors
Managers

Executive

NEW

OLD

Executive

Supervisors
Managers

Front-line
employees

Customers

Source: Adapted from Joan A. Barton and D. Brian Marson, *Service Quality.* Province of British Columbia, 1991.

though admittedly such drawings represent more of a shift in attitude than a shift in power or pay.

Second, although many efforts to improve public service remain somewhat cosmetic, what one writer called the "charm school and better wallpaper" approach, a serious commitment to a public service orientation opens the door to more radical, though certainly not inappropriate demands by citizens. As an example, information sharing as currently conceived in most service improvement plans means providing better signposts, better schedules, or more complete lists of services. Alternatively, it could mean providing performance data so that a customer could decide whether to use a bus or a train or whether a health care facility in one neighborhood is better than one in another. In turn, questions such as these could lead to establishing specific expectations for performance—for example, that the trains run on time—and could open the possibility not only for complaint but even redress when those standards are not met. (In responding to issues such as these, the public manager cannot stand alone; eventually, questions about levels of performance and resources to support those levels must be placed in their inevitable political context and handled by elected leaders as well.)

Third, responding to customer demands is only a short step from efforts to create more avenues for citizen involvement in both the policy process and the process of structuring service delivery systems. Robin Hambleton of the University of Bristol writes, "Thus, getting closer to the consumer might well involve decentralizing services to neighbourhood offices and the localization of services might well provide a starting point for attempts to widen public involvement and extend local democracy." And, indeed, in all four countries, moves toward decentralization, such as parental involvement in the governing of local school systems, tenant self-management schemes in public housing, or user control of sports facilities, are evident. As we noted earlier, the public sector interest in being responsive to clients and citizens carries with it more than a market interest in efficiency; it involves as well a political interest in the expression of the public will, one aspect of which may turn out to be a strengthened sense of participation in public decision making and a devolution of power to the grass roots. In the long run, this may be the most significant implication of the movement toward improved service quality in the public sector.

A CONCERN FOR QUALITY

Without question, among the most progressive public managers, a reinvigoration of the concept of public service is a high priority. As you have seen, these managers emphasize the importance of being sensitive and responsive to customer and citizen interests and of building programs that reflect a public service orientation. But doing so requires more than simply encouraging an improved attitude or developing a greater understanding of customer needs and desires among front-line personnel. Indeed, developing a strong service orientation in a public organization has implications for nearly everything that happens in the organization. It may even have political implications going far beyond the bounds of the immediate agency.

How organizations can improve the quality of their work has, of course, been the subject of considerable debate and experimentation over the past several years. Answers range from broad scale, systemic, and even government-wide approaches to efforts focusing more on the personal dimension of life in public organizations. Although we will examine the human element in the next section, here we will look at two systemic approaches that have received considerable currency among public managers in very recent years: developing high standards of performance and accountability, and creating a constant emphasis on quality.

Chapter Three

PERFORMANCE AND ACCOUNTABILITY

One would hope that high standards of performance and accountability would come naturally to the agencies of government, but that's not always the case. Sometimes public managers simply haven't been as insistent on high levels of performance as they should be. Sometimes the service objectives of agencies are not defined with precision in legislation and, consequently, performance standards are difficult to establish. Sometimes measurement issues interfere with effective monitoring of objectives. Whatever the reason, the more progressive public managers today are highly attentive to performance standards and accountability. They are concerned with setting high standards and seeing that those standards are met. (The phrase "managing for results" could be used in this connection, but that phrase has come to symbolize the managerialist movement in some places, and thus carries with it some special connotations.)

Recent political/managerial debates in the United Kingdom reflect the concern for high performance, although similar examples could be drawn from other countries as well. The Thatcher administration, of course, placed considerable emphasis on privatization of public services and tendering or contracting for services not completely amenable to privatization, but there still remained considerable activity in the civil service. The creation of the Prime Minister's Efficiency Unit, designed to develop "scrutiny exercises" to assess the efficiency and effectiveness of various agencies of government, and the subsequent Financial Management Initiative (1982) had, as their primary concerns, setting objectives and performance indicators as well as development of more effective information systems so managers would be able to assess how they were doing against established standards. While the Financial Management Initiative increased the sophistication of information systems, it also raised fundamental questions about personnel management practices in the civil service. One problem that concerned the Efficiency Unit early on was that those who rose to high positions in the government often did so based on their policy expertise and their capacity to provide expert advice to ministers, rather than on their competence as managers. Consequently, the efficient and effective management of government agencies was impaired.

In 1983, Sir Robin Ibbs, subsequently Deputy Chairman of Lloyds Bank, became head of the Efficiency Unit. Under his leadership, a study was conducted, resulting in a report in the late 1980s indicating "Next Steps" that should be taken in the reform of the civil service. Most of the concerns addressed in the report related to performance standards and accountability:

- a lack of clear and accountable management responsibility, and the self confidence that goes with it. . . .
- the need for greater precision about the results expected of people and of organisations;
- the need to focus attention on outputs as well as inputs;
- the handicap of imposing a uniform system in an organisation of the size and diversity of the present Civil Service;
- the need for sustained pressure for improvement.

The main recommendation of the Ibbs report was to create "executive agencies" to carry out the management work of government within policy and financial guidelines established by ministers. The idea was to provide executive agencies with a set of general policy and resources guidelines, contained in a "framework document," as well as yearly performance standards. The chief executive of the agency would then be held responsible for meeting that set of guidelines. It was basically a trade-off: Executive agencies and their chief executives would be given considerable latitude in terms of strategies for implementation as well as budget and personnel policy but would be required to meet stringent standards of accountability. Following endorsement of the Ibbs report by the prime minister in February

1988, the concept of creating executive agencies was adopted, and certain agencies began moving toward that status. As agencies did so, Peter Kemp, director of the project team overseeing the creation of the Next Steps agencies, expressed the hope that "individual managers should be given the maximum possible power to manage their business, at the lowest possible levels. It is not enough to create new flexibilities; they must be capable of being used widely." Again, the rationale for creating these so-called Next Steps agencies was to provide high standards of performance and accountability while allowing managers maximum flexibility to meet those standards.

Many of the same issues are being discussed in local authorities in the United Kingdom. One local government manager highly regarded for establishing a greater sense of managerial accountability is Paul Sabin, Chief Executive of the Kent County Council. Sabin has transformed the Kent County Council with ideas such as getting close to the customer, devolving responsibility, and implementing strategic management. Sabin believes that managers in his organization must be given clear responsibilities for performing specific tasks, they must control the resources that are needed to do so, they must be given the freedom to manage, and they must be held accountable for the results. Although these proposals sound reasonable enough, they were not in place in Kent before Sabin arrived, and unfortunately they are rarely found in other public organizations even today.

Sabin uses social services as an example of how previous budgeting practices failed to take performance into account: "In the past a home help organiser had been given a budget at the beginning of the year—if they were lucky—and willy nilly through the year pushed green buttons and sent home helps out to home help. They weren't aware that they were consuming money, that home helps had offices and used vehicles and materials." The same pattern held at the upper levels of the organization as well. "Previously strategic plans were largely budget-led, for example, 'we'll spend £30 or £60 million a year on social services,' with no output definition, no statement of what we were trying to put forward. It was merely a case, at the end of the year, of adding up how much you'd spent and seeing how near it came to £60 million."

Sabin pressed his elected council members for more specific statements of what outcomes they wanted for the money they were spending on infrastructure, on education, and other areas; then he translated these objectives into appropriate goals for the various departments. Sabin notes that in the private sector performance is balanced against profit, while in the public sector performance is measured against political values and priorities. Under these circumstances, "We are working to a simple concept of strategic management, balancing the 'performance requirement' against 'operational capability.'" Sabin views his job and that of his management team as maintaining this balance or, better yet, a dynamic equilibrium.

Again, however, the key is to establish clear performance objectives and then hire managers who can move their departments in the needed directions. Most of those managers were hired on fixed-term contracts ranging from three to seven years, and Sabin has implemented a performance-related pay scheme. (Sabin himself received one of the first fixed-term contracts in British local government.) In these ways, managers know exactly what is expected of them, and they have an incentive to produce. Sabin speaks bluntly of the change in performance and accountability: "The aim of the change was to clarify accountability—that was the driving force. To identify who stands up to be counted, patted on the back, kicked in the backside or kicked out. If you can't answer that question we've fudged it somewhere."

One obvious problem with working in a system that pays particular attention to high standards of performance is the difficulty of measuring success or failure in meeting the agency's objectives. Indeed, Sandy Russell of HM Customs and Excise is adamant in arguing that the single most difficult task in government is defining objectives and systems of accountability clearly so that "people who are ultimately accountable for policy and to Ministers know whether this is working or not." Russell argues, "People say that policy is among the most intellectually demanding jobs in government. Phooey. Policy formulation is dead easy. Policy analysis is dead easy. The most difficult task in the public sector . . . is how do you define objectives and how do you define accountability in terms of whether you're moving forward, sideways, or backwards. Are we doing better in relation to the drug problem, or are we doing worse, or are we doing about the same? That's the battleground. It's hugely more difficult in the public than the private sector; and it continues to be grossly underestimated as an intellectual exercise."

Although it's hard enough just to tell whether you are going "forward, sideways, or backwards," many managers have sought much more precise measurements of service delivery. There is potential danger in doing so, as even the most fervent managerialists admit. Michael Keating, Secretary of the Australian Commonwealth Department of Finance, acknowledges "that performance measures and assessment could concentrate too much on outputs that can be quantified and that this would lead to distortions. For example, measuring the number of clients dealt with each day by Social Security counter staff could reduce the incentive to provide comprehensive advice, which may lead to a beneficiary being worse off." Unfortunately, despite this concern, some public managers, probably spurred by the drive for rationalism and managerialism, have become preoccupied with measurement to the detriment of the organization's performance. However, public managers who are careful in both choosing and using reasonable indicators often develop a clearer picture of the organization's performance. When used with care, performance indicators can be an aid to managerial and political judgment.

Obviously, some indicators make more sense than others. But, in general, organizations that have direct contact with the public have focused on such areas as punctuality, reliability, customer queuing, product quality, and customer complaints. For example, British Rail measures train punctuality in terms of the percentage of trains arriving on time, and measures train loading by the ratio of passengers to seats and the time that customers spend standing. Airport authorities in the United Kingdom analyze their baggage claim service in terms of the time that elapses from the first passenger out of immigration to the last bag onto the belt or carousel. Water supply authorities measure the quality of water in terms of compliance with bacteriological standards and color standards. Despite these examples, developing performance measures is often quite difficult. For example, would the number of complaints to an aviation board be an adequate indicator of "Community Satisfaction with the Environmental and Economic Impact of Air Services"? Probably not.

Again, note the various uses to which performance data can be put. In this section, I am concentrating on the use of such data for internal management purposes, establishing whether or not the organization is moving in the desired direction. But, as you saw earlier, such information may also be of great interest to the public. Interestingly, public organizations are already much more open to sharing such information with the public than are their private sector counterparts; in the future even more public presentations of performance data will be available upon which citizens can make decisions about the quality of government services.

One variation of the movement toward specifying standards and holding managers accountable is the effort to "commercialize" certain public services or to create conditions so that managers can take a more entrepreneurial posture. There are various approaches to this issue that require political action, including transferring certain governmental functions to the private sector, creating separate authorities with semiautonomous status, or requiring contracting out or competitive tendering. My focus here, however, is on *managerial* approaches, and indeed there are several examples of public managers seeking to create a more entrepreneurial spirit within the regular departments of government.

Sandra Hale, Commissioner of the Department of Administration in the State of Minnesota, is known for her development of the STEP program—Strive Toward Excellence in Performance—a program designed to encourage more entrepreneurial and risk-taking behavior in state government through a particular strategy for change. The change process involves project teams from the target agencies, supported by trained management analysts, often working with persons from the business community or from universities to improve the quality and productivity of the target agency. Six STEP hypotheses guide each change effort:

- Close contact with the customer will provide a better understanding of the customer's needs.
- Increased employee participation taps the knowledge, skills and commitment of all state workers.
- Increased discretionary authority gives managers and employees greater control over and accountability for a bottom line.
- Partnerships allow the sharing of knowledge, expertise and other resources.
- State-of-the-art productivity improvement techniques will enhance productivity.
- Improved work measurement provides a base for planning and implementing service improvements and giving workers information about their performance.

Working within these guidelines, those involved in the change effort follow a specific set of steps: determine and create an awareness of the need for change, assess the work environment before designing the change, design the program, assess the impact, organize for change, maintain the momentum, celebrate the change, evaluate the change process, and fine-tune the process.

One spin-off from the STEP program was an effort by Hale and others to instill more of a market-driven attitude within the Department of Administration itself. Under the concept of "enterprise management," each service within the department is viewed as a separate enterprise, with most operating from a revolving fund supported by revenue received from other agencies using the products or services of the agency. Other state agencies and departments using the services become the customers. Some of the functions of the department are described as "marketplace acitivites" and operate much like private groups, competing for their revenues with other firms. The state bookstore, the motor pool, and consulting with state and local government are of this type. (Some services have not survived the competition; after it was discovered that private vendors could produce software programming as well as those in the department and with less cost, that function was moved outside the department.)

Other areas are called "utilities," services where economies of scale make a central operation appropriate. For example, installing one telephone system for the entire state government makes more sense than installing a separate system for each agency. Rates charged agencies for such services are set by rate panels, made up of customer (agency) representatives, and service level agreements are reached with each customer. Like marketplace activities, these activities are also financed through a revolving fund based on revenue from the agency's customers. Obviously, managers of the various services have considerable incentive to serve the other agencies of government well.

A close parallel is found in the Australian Commonwealth Department of Administrative Services (DAS), which handles transport and storage, design, construction, repairs and maintenance, mapping and surveying, publishing and printing, meteorology, and so forth. In the late 1980s, the department moved toward a system in which the various DAS "businesses" began operating under a trust fund arrangement through which they could spend only what they could raise. Funds previously held by the department are now held by the other agencies of government who can use DAS or a private supplier. Charges levied for services must obviously be commercially competitive and be sufficient to cover all operating costs. The changes appear beneficial to all concerned, saving the government considerable sums of money, providing other agencies with flexibility in the use of their funds, as well as improved client-oriented service from DAS, and forcing strong discipline on the various "businesses" of DAS.

Graham Bashford, General Manager of Finance and Corporate Affairs with the department, makes an important point: that commercialization of public services doesn't mean that profit or immediate gain is the only concern of the agency. Bashford illustrates the point this way: "I used to say that these commercialisers were hell bent on 'Reform At any Toll to Society'—or 'RATS' for short. They wanted us to pay our own way, make a profit whatever the consequence, *forget social objectives, public interest, service to the government.* Then there were the people who were a little more conservative. . . . I called them 'Men/Women Implementing a Changed Environment'—or 'MICE' for short. The MICE believed that DAS should deliver its services in the most efficient and effective manner with due regard to the full range of economic and social objectives to be achieved." Happily, the MICE won the day, and just such a provision recognizing the broad objectives of government was written into the principles that guided the commercialization effort. Again, here is a situation in which the transfer of business practices to the public sector may be acceptable, but the transfer of business values is not.

A CONSTANT EMPHASIS ON QUALITY

Although the best public managers recognize the importance of high standards, they also recognize that merely setting standards and devising sets of rewards and punishments to enforce those standards won't work. It's important as well to build a cultural commitment to high levels of performance and to devise management practices that help support those who must try to meet those objectives. These are the goals of the "quality management" movement, the most visible aspect of which is Total Quality Management (TGM). TQM has been defined as a "total, integrated organizational approach for meeting customer needs and expectations that involves all managers and employees, and uses quantitative methods and employee involvement to improve continuously the organization's processes, products, and services." As you will see, although TQM has attracted great attention in both government and the private sector, especially in the United States, the faddish TQM label may promise more than it can deliver, especially in its public sector applications.

Although TQM is often associated with the rise of Japanese industrial prowess, it actually has its roots deep in American industrial history. In the 1920s, Walter Shewhart developed a system of statistical quality control as a method for improving quality in mass production manufacturing. This notion was taken seriously by the U.S. military in World War II, and Shewhart's student Edward Deming was hired to teach statistical quality control to the War Department. After the war, most U.S. companies stopped using the techniques, but the Japanese, having been exposed to quality control by the occupation forces, took the idea quite seriously and hired Deming and Joseph Juran, among others, to teach them the techniques. Juran is particularly credited with extending quality control techniques beyond the production and inspection functions to all parts of the organization. He also changed the definition of "quality" from simply meeting technical standards to looking at the entire product cycle in terms of customer expectations. Kaoru Ishikawa expanded the idea to include all employees and added the team concept, the basis for quality circles.

The new techniques of quality control required an important shift in management thinking. The recommendation of Deming and others was to de-emphasize mass inspections of products to meet quality standards; the logic was not to correct mistakes "downstream" but to build in quality "upstream." The key argument is that quality can't be "inspected into" the product; instead, everything must be done to assure that quality is built in from the beginning. This means that persons throughout the organization, from top to bottom, must be committed to meeting customer expectations and that all employees should participate in the process of improving product quality. Eventually, Deming's thinking evolved to the point that a change in organizational culture became central. If quality were emphasized throughout the organization, everything else would fall into place.

Obviously, that recommendation fits quite well in businesses where "quality sells," but the fit in most public agencies is imperfect at best. First, there are the difficulties of identifying customers, noted earlier in this chapter, to say nothing of the possible conflicts between immediate customers and the citizenry at large. In many areas, the citizenry simply isn't willing to pay for the quality of service an individual client might desire. Second, the basic recommendation of TQM management is to do things right the first time; but when TQM has been applied to public organizations, the ethical basis of those organizations requires a restatement. Thus, the U.S. federal government's definition of TQM speaks of meeting customer expectations, achieving ever higher standards of quality, timeliness, and efficiency, and *doing the right things* right the first time. The difference is significant. Third, some theorists and practitioners argue that TQM is really "rational systems theory dressed in behavioral clothing," that the roots of TQM are deeply imbedded in the need for control and that although contemporary expressions of TQM use more humanistic language, the manipulative intent is still the same.

In a certain sense, these criticisms of TQM don't really matter, for TQM has lost much of its original meaning and is now regarded by many as a somewhat faddish label for good management practice, broadly defined. In 1990, the U.S. Office of Management and Budget drafted a circular that would have required TQM in all agencies. One part of the circular is an appendix describing TQM, including topics such as top management leadership and support, strategic planning, focus on the customer, commitment to training and recognition, employee empowerment and teamwork, measurement and analysis of processes and outputs, and, only lastly, quality assurance (to be achieved through control, optimization, and standardization). Most of the public managers I have talked with were already doing at least some of these things; they didn't need the TQM label to justify their efforts, and some just found it confusing.

Others, however, consider the widespread interest in and support for TQM a stimulus to agency reform and, in those agencies, TQM applications have occasionally been quite successful. Fred Williams has had a long and distinguished career, working in many different areas and at many levels of the Internal Revenue Service. In 1987, he realized a long-held ambition as he became Director of the Cincinnati Service Center (CSC) of the IRS. Immediately upon his arrival the center experienced a large increase in workload with the addition of the State of Indiana to its area of operations; thus, the CSC became the largest of the IRS's ten service centers, receiving and processing approximately 15 million individual tax returns and 8 million business returns each year. In addition, the CSC staff issues tax refunds, helps solve tax account problems, answers taxpayer correspondence, and engages in taxpayer education and compliance efforts. Moreover, the CSC is forced to use a largely seasonal work force that must be completely retrained each year to meet changes in the tax code. To develop quality within this context was obviously a challenge for Williams.

Many of the changes he brought about had their roots in 1985, when the Internal Revenue Service nationally experienced a "crisis" of service brought about when computer upgrades and new software simply didn't work very well. Battered by negative publicity, the IRS took a close look at its operations and determined to change things for the better. A strong new emphasis on quality, especially as measured through meeting customer needs, was key. Specifically, the organization shifted its focus from "quantity with minimum cost" to "quality is first among equals with schedule and time." Following the national lead, Williams and his staff developed a CSC goal statement: "The goal of the Cincinnati Service Center is to do a superior job of meeting customer needs and expectations with products and services of the highest quality and value."

Total Quality Management in the CSC was launched with a strong commitment from Williams and his chief deputies. Not only did they "preach" quality at every opportunity—at one point Williams placed a slogan above the entrances to CSC's seven sites, saying "Through these doors come quality people who do quality work"—they also made quality objectives an integral part of their own performance plans as well as those of managers throughout the organization. A Joint Quality Council, involving CSC management and representatives of the National Treasury Employees Union, oversees the operation of a variety of quality improvement efforts and encourages the development of "quality improvement teams" (very much like quality circles) throughout the organization. A new and more systematic approach has been devised to determine errors and, more important, the root causes of those errors.

Williams takes great pride in these accomplishments, but emphasizes the human element. In a recent letter, he told me, "I think if you worked at our center you would see that it isn't just brick and mortar, that we are empowering the people to do the job in the way that it can be done best. If you provide people with the type of work environment that makes them feel that they can do the job in an effective way, then indeed they will." And there is some evidence that Williams is right. In 1989, employees at the CSC initiated a quality improvement effort to reduce the amount of interest paid to taxpayers requesting extension returns. At the end of the year, the CSC announced that interest paid had dropped from $1.6 million in 1988 to $195,000 in 1989. Similarly, the CSC pioneered the use of electronic filing in 1986, when 25,000 returns were electronically filed. By 1990, over 1.75 million returns were filed electronically, saving on direct labor costs and cutting the error rate dramatically. In 1990, the Cincinnati Service Center won one of three Quality Improvement Prototype Awards presented by the Office of Management and Budget.

While Total Quality Management has been urged by the U.S. federal government, many states and localities have also undertaken TQM programs, some within particular agencies, others more across the board. One such community is Madison, Wisconsin, where Mayor Joseph Sensenbrenner became acquainted with the Deming approach in the mid-1980s and set in motion a quality enhancement effort in his city. His first target was the city garage, where an earlier audit had indicated long delays in repair of vehicles and where there was a scarcity of major pieces of equipment to repair the city's cars, dump trucks, refuse pickers, and other vehicles. Sensenbrenner secured the cooperation of the union president, and a small team set out to discover the problem.

The team first discovered that many delays resulted from not having the right part on hand, a situation the parts manager explained by noting the incredibly wide variety of vehicles the city had bought, a variety increased by the fact that the city had a policy of buying the vehicle with the lowest sticker price on the day of purchase. "It doesn't make any sense," a mechanic said. "When you look at all the downtime, the warranty work that weak suppliers don't cover, the unreliability of the cheaper machines, and the lower resale value, buying what's cheapest doesn't save us anything." In turn, the parts purchaser agreed with the analysis of the problem but said central purchasing wouldn't allow anything else; central purchasing agreed but said the comptroller wouldn't let them do it differently; the comptroller agreed, but said the city attorney wouldn't approve. But the city attorney did approve, pointing out how contracts could be written to accommodate the concerns of those up and down the line—and saying that he had assumed the policy had always been that way.

The problem was interesting to Sensenbrenner because it suggested that with increased teamwork, a breakdown of departmental barriers, and involvement of front-line employees in problem solving such system failures as that involving the city garage could be effectively corrected. The next question was how to implement the quality improvement process throughout the organization. Essentially, the city administration identified a few "champions," and a second wave of projects began in the streets division, the health department, day care, and data processing. The quality improvement projects undertaken here were impressive enough that momentum surged. By the end of 1988, two dozen projects were under way and all city department ments were invited to apply for "transformation status," a long-term department-wide commitment to continuous quality improvement and to training all employees in quality improvement techniques. From this point, the city's quality improvement effort was an integral part of its operations.

These two cases demonstrate the important successes that result from a conscious and organization-wide effort to improve the quality of customer service. In retrospect, it appears that in both cases a general "cultural" emphasis on quality enhancement was far more compelling than the introduction of more specific quality control techniques; however, don't underestimate the power of such a cultural commitment. Both cases also demonstrate the importance of strong leadership at the top of the organization, complemented by a willingness to permit employees throughout the organization to become involved in making improvements. As the perceptive chair of a state-wide effort to improve quality and productivity put it, "The people who do the work know the work best and know best how to improve the work."

Although the TQM label is probably being overused today and extreme advocates of TQM run the risk of overselling what TQM can do, its endorsement of management practices such as high levels of employee involvement, demonstrated to be successful in various organizations, is undoubtedly helpful. However, outside a few production-oriented public agencies, recent applications of TQM have paid only limited attention to the original elements of quality techniques such as statistical quality control, preferring to emphasize leadership, teamwork, and group problem solving, ideas that don't really require the TQM label. (The real winners may be the new TQM consultants who stand to benefit greatly from continued use of the TQM designation.) Certainly everyone is in favor of higher quality products and services, but whether customers of organizations formally committed to TQM receive better service than those in other organizations that emphasize quality service without the TQM label is open to question. In any case, there is little reason to believe that the customers of TQM organizations have any greater power over those organizations. Whatever one's view of TQM, public managers, like their counterparts in business, must experiment with radical departures from traditional management efforts. Formally calling new efforts TQM may not be necessary, but actions that depart from the failed practices of yesterday are essential.

COMMUNITY WITHIN/ COOPERATION WITHOUT

Serving the public and providing consistently high quality in all that you do are lofty goals, but the best public managers recognize that these goals are simply unattainable without proper attention to the human side of organizational life. The most progressive public managers as a group seem to be unusually caring and concerned individuals, people who recognize the needs, interests, and desires of others in the organization and attempt to respond to those concerns, not in a manipulative way but with authenticity. In a balanced way, these managers acknowledge the limits of what they or anyone else can do for another person. On the whole, however, they don't see their organizations and their employees as mechanical systems or aggregations of individual self-interest, or even as resources to be used (or used up) in fulfilling the goals of the organizations. Rather they see their organizations as collections of individual human beings, with skills and talents, with hopes and potential, with feelings and passions, and, most of all, with great dignity and worth.

This is not simply to say that these managers recognize the value of human relations in organizations, for the human

relations movement has only rarely evidenced a real concern for members of the organization as individuals. The
human relations approach, perhaps better considered as an
enlightened form of rationalism, has largely viewed organization members as resources (now politely called "human
resources") to be drawn upon, or more accurately, to be used
in the pursuit of the organization's goals. Far too much of
what continues to pass for effective human relations—and
this applies in the private sector as much if not more than
in the public sector—amounts to sophisticated boss-ism, an
ideology that says that the manager is more knowledgeable,
more focused, and more adept than anyone else in the
organization. Consequently, the job of the manager is to
achieve compliance with his or her wishes through threat,
bribery, trickery, or whatever else might work.

The alternative, expressed by many of the best public
managers, views individuals as being of value in themselves
(not merely for what they might contribute to the organization). The organization is not simply a device for meeting
certain goals (though it surely is that) but is a community
of human beings who may in the long run not only be better off but may be better people by virtue of their participation in the organization. The organization itself is not seen
as a competitive, purely self-interested entity fighting off
others who intrude on its territory; it is a cooperative and
contributing member of the broader social and political
system. The differences between this view and the traditional view are substantial and worthy of some exploration.

A SENSE OF COMMUNITY

As I talked with the public managers in many different
locations, I was struck by how often the term *community*
came up. "We're trying to build a sense of community in
this organization." "Community builds pride, and pride can
absolutely transform an organization." "Community is
much more important than control." At the same time, the
people I talked with seemed to experience a certain discom-

fort when talking about community. It was a little too nebulous. It sounded too soft, maybe even unprofessional. It was difficult to explain how it worked. There was a feeling that a greater sense of community fit with the ideas of improving service and quality, but no one could really demonstrate that. Yet community came up again and again. There was something so intuitively appealing about the notion of community in the eyes (in the hearts?) of these managers that they wouldn't let it go away. Otto Brodtrick of Canada clarifies the importance of community when he says, "The values, attitudes and policies of the [well-performing] organization are based on an overall sense of caring. . . . In the long run, high organizational performance is a product of *people who care rather than systems that control*" (italics added).

Certainly, there are many reasons *not* to expect the term *community* to be associated with the term *organization*, the inherent impersonality and depersonalization of members and clients by traditional bureaucracies being foremost. It might be asked whether community is possible in any group where the common bonds uniting the group seem limited, where members appear to have little in common other than their interest in holding a job, and where status and pay differentials seem designed to separate people rather than to bring them together. Indeed, many commentators on contemporary life have specifically blamed the rise of large and complex organizations for the lack of a sense of community in modern life. Theorists embracing a long philosophical tradition argue that community can be found only in face-to-face relationships, not in the impersonalized world of bureaucracy.

On the other hand, many people have experienced a sense of community within their organizations and have felt the strength, excitement, and exhilaration that comes from being part of a group engaged in a task of significance. Certainly, those who worked in the National Aeronautics and Space Administration during the period in which America first sought to put a man on the moon felt such a sense. However, such broad-scale projects of national and international significance are not necessary to stimulate feelings of community within an organization. Pamela Gordon of Sheffield commented that any intense project in which people share a dedication to a goal and a dedication to working together toward that goal can produce the euphoria of community. She described a redundancy exercise in which her personnel department had to design and implement a massive early retirement and voluntary severance program within a month and a half. Their success not only brought the group much closer together but also raised the credit of the personnel function throughout Sheffield local government.

A sense of community can arise even in the absence of an intense goal-oriented activity. Most often, it seems to accompany a pervasive attitude of caring and sharing within an organization. Katherine Jesch of the U.S. Forest Service told me about a particular work group that had been struggling to accommodate a more diverse work force involving more women in nontraditional roles. The pressures and difficulties associated with those new roles were made clear to all, including the men in the organization, when one of the women had a baby and started to deal with problems of child care. Soon, the entire work group took up the cause and "adopted" the baby as its own, even sharing in child care duties from time to time right in the workplace. Many of the workers later reflected that this event was the one that "really brought us together." From diversity, with understanding, came community.

What does establishing a sense of community within a public agency mean, and how might the building of community be brought about? Community involves feelings of identity, belongingness, and a commonness of purpose, and includes a belief in a common set of values, a sense of interdependence, mutuality and trust, and an understanding of common obligations and responsibilities. Beyond these features of community, the relationship between an individual and a community is marked by a set of shared commitments that touch the individual's very heart and soul. Rosabeth Moss Kanter of the Harvard Business School began her career writing about community (specifically utopian communes) rather than writing about corporations. Early on, she argued that "the search for community is also a quest for direction and purpose in the collective anchoring of the individual life. Investment of self in a community, acceptance of its authority and willingness to support its values, is dependent in part on the extent to which group life can offer identity, personal meaning, and the opportunity to grow in terms of standards and guiding principles that the member feels are expressive of his own inner being." Belonging to a community allows the individual a way of expressing deeply personal meanings in a setting that confirms and applauds those meanings. As you will see in a later chapter, the notion of a community of meanings built around the notion of public service may be essential to the operation of public organizations, and perhaps even all organizations, in the future.

Caring, Sharing, and Working Together   The managers I talked with mentioned many different aspects of community, though few were precise. One aspect is a sense of caring, sharing, and working together, qualities John Gardner, former Secretary of Health, Education and Welfare and a frequent writer on leadership and now community, comments on as essential to the idea of community. "The members of a good community deal with each other humanely, respect individual differences and value the integrity of each person. A good community fosters an atmosphere of cooperation and connectedness. There is recognition by the members that they need one another. There is a sense of belonging and identity, a spirit of mutual responsibility."

This spirit was evident in my conversations with public managers at all levels. City Manager Leland Nelson talked about the importance of the city manager being seen as a "humane, caring and involved" person; John Pelzer of Missouri, a state executive, was forceful in including a sentence in his statement of management philosophy that said: "We CARE about our employees . . . and we wish that caring to show"; Jack Manion of the Canadian Centre for Management Development hoped that staff would be convinced that their leaders are "competent and care about their welfare." Most striking, however, was the comment of a wing commander in Desert Storm who expressed the hope that the "chain of command" could be turned into a "chain of concern."

Some organizations, such as the State of Iowa, have developed institutionalized forms of caring and concern. Several years ago the state developed a mentoring program for new employees coming into the state system, especially for those working for the first time or who are coming off welfare. The volunteer mentors, also state employees, meet with the new employees as often as twice a week during work breaks to hear their concerns, either those on the job or personal concerns that might affect the job, and to offer advice and help. The volunteers are trained in personnel policies and departmental procedures, but, according to Jan Shockemoehl, director of the program, it is even more important for the mentors to have "a caring attitude, have good listening skills, and be resourceful."

Community involves not only caring but sharing, and the managers I talked with clearly valued openness and interaction. Indeed, one of the most frequent comments among these managers, somewhat to my surprise, was that they wanted people in their organizations to have fun. They valued a sense of "looseness," a relaxed atmosphere in which people felt free to be themselves. Gaylen Duncan, Senior Vice President of the Canadian Mortgage and Housing Corporation, was somewhat typical in this regard: "We must introduce the concept of having fun on the job. Perhaps as I age I take more importance from Mark Twain's quote, 'Enjoy life, you are not going to get out of it alive anyway!'" Duncan went on to lament the fact that in times of budget constraints "visible efforts to improve life in the public sector are the first to go—yet they should be the last."

A final aspect of the caring, sharing style of the best public managers is a certain humility and a willingness to take on any task in the organization themselves, no matter how messy or how unseemly. Linda Bowman, President of Parks Junior College in Denver, learned the lesson well and shared it with me in this way: "The power of leadership is weighty. However, I recall the day that water began seeping under the wall of the college lobby because the urinal in the men's room was overflowing and no janitorial staff members were available. I made a real management decision. My assistant and I removed our high heels and waded in, sloshing around until we found the water shut-off. Thus, I was reminded of the awesome power of the administrator, the requirement for creative problem solving, the essential decision-making ability, and that power should not ever cause one to believe his or her own press!" In my mind, this attitude is one that is likely to promote a sense of community.

Wholeness Incorporating Diversity   The concept of community clearly implies a spirit of mutuality and understanding, even a broadly defined consensus on important, guiding values, but community does not mean blind obedience to organizational rules or policies. Indeed, if anything, it implies the opposite—that members of the organization have an obligation to dissent from the prevailing view if they feel that view is not in the best interests of the community and, moreover, that members are always obligated to express their differences and to be respectful of others who do so. John Gardner captures the inevitable (and productive) tension associated with community in this way:

> To prevent the wholeness from smothering diversity, there must be a philosophy of pluralism, an open climate for dissent, and an opportunity for subcommunities to retain their identity and share in the setting of larger group goals.
>
> To prevent the diversity from destroying the wholeness, there must be institutional arrangements for diminishing polarization, for coalition-building, dispute resolution, negotiation and mediation.

Certainly the best public managers recognize the importance of dissent and diversity in meeting the challenges they
face. The older bureaucratic notions of limiting discussion
and controlling the thought patterns of members of the
organization are fast fading away. In their place, managers
are seeking to increase opportunities for those throughout
the organization to communicate effectively with one
another, regardless of organizational status or position. If,
for example, managers are serious about front-line service
delivery people being the most important people in the
organization, then they must devise ways for those voices
to be heard. If managers believe that creativity and innovation are among the most important attributes of high
performance public organizations, then they will promote
imaginative discourse, even if that involves dissent. If managers truly believe that both change and responsiveness to
the public are enhanced by differences rather than similarities (or conformity), then they will especially value diversity in their organizations.

No manager, however progressive or traditional, denies
the importance of effective communications in an organization. Indeed, the manager's role can almost be encompassed
by the activity of communicating with others. Rosslyn
Kleeman of the U.S. General Accounting Office told me
about the time her five-year-old granddaughter spent a day
with her. Later the youngster's mother asked what her
grandmother did at work. "Her answer was that I didn't
work—I just walked around talking to people!" All managers
spend an inordinate amount of time communicating. Yet the
most progressive public managers recognize that communications is not just a matter of information exchange
but a vehicle through which power and leadership are
widely distributed throughout the organization, again a
subtle but important distinction.

The traditional bureaucratic model envisions communications as moving through hierarchical levels and only
rarely across organizational divisions, but in practice the
best public managers are now encouraging rather than

limiting such communications. The benefits are obvious: being able to talk with anyone at any time to solve a problem enables information to flow much more quickly and permits more people (and consequently more views) to be part of the decision process. And, of course, modern information technology supports widespread communication. The results speak for themselves. Staff in the Canadian Spectrum Management Sector (dealing with the allocation and management of radio frequencies) are particularly proud of the free and open communications that exist within their organization. "When somebody has a problem that's unique," a staff member reports, "they can turn around and talk to anybody in the organization easily. The organizational climate supports that communication and the technology facilitates it."

Communications is one part of the puzzle, but valuing diversity is another. Differences in the composition of the staff can broaden the range of information and viewpoints brought to the discussion of important issues and can stimulate the kind of direct and revealing conversation that is often essential to building an effective community. Seeking diversity in such areas as race and gender (among others) is desirable for many different reasons, but especially as it brings new experiences and new perspectives to the organization. Diversity in the workplace can enable members of an organization to understand diversity in the population with which it works much better. For diversity provides a peculiar kind of mirror on one's personal life story, a mirror that is simultaneously distorting and clarifying, one that enables people to understand themselves and their experiences better.

The U.S. Forest Service has been working on the issue of diversity for some time. Like other organizations, the Forest Service passed through a time when diversity was important because it was the law and through a time when diversity was important because it was thought to be right. Now members of the Forest Service recognize that diversity is a very important value in improving all aspects of organizational life. Their reasons are worth detailing:

1. The character of our nation's work force is changing rapidly. Already women, members of minority groups, and people with disabilities collectively outnumber able-bodied white males. What is the future of an organization that excludes a majority of the talent pool in recruiting its employees?

2. Americans are coming to realize how difficult it is to understand one another. For the Forest Service to serve the diverse publics, all cultures must be present at all levels of the organization. A man cannot fully appreciate what it is to be a woman. A white American can never truly understand what it is to be an African American. Taping your eyes closed for a day or a week cannot tell you what it feels like to be effective without sight.

3. To be competitive in a business sense, the Forest Service must have a multicultural work force that is representative of our multicultural society. Such a work force will increase the productivity and quality of the organization.

   [The need for representation] requires more than a change in the makeup of the Forest Service work force. It requires a change in decision-making and supervisory behavior in the Agency. It is no longer enough to be sensitive to the needs of people of many kinds. Human diversity must be present throughout the Forest Service. All natural resource decisions have human impacts. We must adopt a decisionmaking process in which many views are heard, valued, and incorporated.

This statement and similar statements from those in other public organizations are compelling testimony to the increasing recognition of the value of diversity in our societies and our organizations, but they also provide support once again for the idea that many of the approaches being pursued by the very best public managers are dependent upon one another. Earlier, you saw evidence that a strong public service orientation requires changes in the entire management approach of traditional organizations. Now, as I comment on the importance of diversity, you'll see the same recommendation—that valuing diversity is important but incomplete without full attention to the kinds of organizational changes that permit the full expression of diversity within an organization. That means increased openness, improved communications, and the encouragement of involvement, even leadership, at all levels of the organization.

Enhancing the Quality of Life   Finally, as John Gardner puts it, for a sense of community to develop and to be sustained there must be a variety of "bonding experiences" for members of the organization—shared social activities, celebrations of excellence in the organization, chances for people in the organization not to work together but simply to be together and, perhaps most of all, opportunities for people to share pride in the organization and community of which they are a part. Pride was definitely the watchword in an organizational transformation that occurred in Santa Clara County, California, a few years ago. The county had withstood a series of devastating budget reductions that hurt in many ways but, according to Chief Executive Officer Sally Reed, "The most troublesome aspect of the cutbacks . . . may have been the message public servants felt the voters were giving them: 'We don't value the work you do.' This message struck a blow at their life's work."

Reed and her executive staff felt quite the contrary— that the employees of the county were the county's most important asset. As a group, the employees were highly skilled and dedicated to their work. They believed in the notion of public service and took seriously the obligations and commitments that notion involved, but they were bitter and disappointed. Where once they felt important and needed, they now felt cast aside. Where once there was a feeling of "family" in the organization, that sense had now been shattered.

Reed set about to change the culture of the organization, primarily through rekindling pride in the workplace. The first step was simply to assert publicly and forthrightly the strengths and capacities of the organization. Consequently, the county adopted a four-point "affirmation":

- Santa Clara County has the highest caliber employees.
- Santa Clara County is a well-managed organization.
- Santa Clara County provides quality services.
- Santa Clara County provides community leadership.

Although recognizing that exceptions exist—that all employees weren't of the "highest caliber," for example—the affirmation not only sent a message of support and encouragement to those in the organization but set a standard for the future work of the organization.

County employees responded at first with cautious appreciation, but Reed followed up with a series of concrete actions that reinforced the statements of affirmation. Efforts were made to recognize outstanding contributions by employees through public statements, formal recognition programs, or just informal notes. A conscious effort was made to make employees aware of the good things others in the organization were doing so they wouldn't feel isolated but rather feel they were an important part of an excellent organization. The county sought to significantly improve the work environment: painting offices, remodeling work spaces, buying better furniture—whatever it took to say to county employees, "We value what you do." Finally, and perhaps most critically, the county invested in a series of training and development activities for its employees, ranging from improving skills in public contacts (to reinforce the service orientation) to instituting a Leadership Academy for the county's 1200 managers. The approach chosen sought not to create a new organization but was designed to bring out the very best in an existing organization. In brief, Reed worked to build a sense of community and to allow that community to blossom.

Community and Technology   There is a certain irony in including a discussion of introducing new technology in a section on community, for the two are usually thought of as being absolutely at odds. However, their connectedness is just the message I received from many managers. Technology, especially information technology, is extremely important in the work of pubic organizations today. But technology is absolutely ineffective unless introduced in a humane and caring way. To do so requires sensitivity to the fears and concerns associated with introducing new technology and often requires significant investment on the human side of the equation.

Public Technology, Inc. (PTI) has been helping local governments apply new technologies. (PTI actually began in 1969 when a group of local government managers joined together to explore ways to employ technologies developed by NASA; for example, through conversations with NASA experts involved in designing life-support systems, the managers learned about new equipment, such as lightweight air tanks and devices that help firefighters see through smoke.) In addition to its work with new technologies, PTI has also been concerned with what it calls "orgware," the combination of human skills needed to cope with the frustrations and fears often associated with the introduction of technology. Costis Toregas, President of PTI, describes a formula for applications of technology—for every $5 spent on hardware, $15 must be spent on software, and $80 must be spent on orgware.

Managing the human side of technological applications may be the most difficult part, but it can be done. David Garson of North Carolina State University makes this recommendation: "Participatory (management) and other organization development approaches, typically facilitated by nontechnical generalists, need to be mobilized to foster a support, team-based information culture with the enterprise of agency if MIS (Management Information Systems) implementation is to achieve its greatest potential." Notice once again the themes of employee involvement and cultural change, themes that recur time and again.

COOPERATION WITHOUT

I have spoken of community in terms of its impact on the organization internally, but it is also important to point out that the caring and concern of the manager extends not only to those in the organization but to individuals and groups outside. No community, as it is encouraged in public organizations, should ever be exclusive or patronizing; rather, members of the community should value a significant measure of interaction, even reciprocity, with those outside. The Australian philosopher Stanley Benn makes exactly this point, distinguishing those organizations having some transcendent and even noble purpose but still treating clients impersonally from those we would call true "communities." Communities are defined by the common experiences of their members, but a degree of openness is also essential. "Community Within" is incomplete unless relations with those outside are based on similar standards of mutuality and concern, something we might call "Cooperation Without."

Jenny Bedlington of Tasmania spoke eloquently about involving clients in the work of her community services agency. In her view, social services agencies (and we would guess many other public agencies) are driven by a stated commitment to client-based values, but in practice they are often paternalistic with respect to client rights and client service. As an example, she noted that efforts at public participation in social services delivery often break down, and that staff members frequently "blame" the clients in a rather patronizing way. "They weren't all that interested" or "They just hadn't done their homework" or "If they were really concerned about this, you'd think they'd at least show up for the meeting." Bedlington rejects such a position out of hand: "If our efforts to involve the community break down, then we have to assume that it's our fault and that it is our responsibility to do something about it. Any other posture would continue to distance our organization from the community and would be evidence of the fact that we aren't really living up to our commitments."

As Bedlington implies, much if not all of what we have said about community within the organization applies to the relationships public managers and their employees develop with those outside the organization, and of course, those relationships are of increasing importance today. No longer can a public manager focus only on the internal workings of his or her organization. Today, what occurs in the environment and in other organizations is every bit as important as what happens inside. For this reason, any public manager must pay attention to what happens outside the organization and establish effective and (hopefully) cooperative relationships with other groups and organizations. Public managers today realize that the effective performance of their duties depends not only on what happens in their own organization but on the effectiveness of the interorganizational networks in which they participate. In such efforts, the old values of organizational self-interest and competition no longer apply. Cooperation is the watchword.

The current term, of course, is "networking." Gerry Meier, Deputy Minister for Human Resources, Labour and Employment in Saskatchewan, told me that "networking is more important than ever, both within government as well as with interest groups, clients, etc. What I have tried to do is 'reach out' to external audiences, even though such overtures may be politely rebuffed because of how those groups related to our current government. As long as the effort is sincere, people are inclined to accept it at face value—even if nothing will come of it." Marianne Neville-Rolfe of the British Civil Service College spoke of the difficulty in establishing good relations with other organizations; after all, it's a time-consuming job. On the other hand, when I asked her advice with respect to external relations she put it very directly: "Grab any network you can!"

CONCLUSION

The values of service and quality are constantly on the minds of the best contemporary public managers. A reinvigorated notion of public service, what some have called a "public service orientation," embraces the contemporary concern for more effectively serving the customers of the organization while at the same time remaining sensitive to the broad citizenry to which public organizations are ultimately responsible in a democratic society. Similarly, many public managers are urging their organizations to strive for greater quality, whether under the banner of Total Quality Management or under less pretentious guises. Meanwhile, though the notions of "community within/cooperation without" fly directly in the face of traditional organizational ideals of control within and competition without, my discussions with leading public managers suggest that a major shift is now under way with these issues at its core.

Many of these concerns have been explored by those interested in private sector management, yet, as you have seen, they take on new and important qualities as they are employed in the public sector. Public organizations are not guided solely by market behavior. Thus, for concepts such as service or quality to be appropriate to the public sector requires that they be placed firmly in a democratic political context. Instead of being an addendum to the manager's repertoire of techniques, they must express the highest values of a democratic society. This means, among other things, that the manager's consideration of service and quality issues must ultimately confront the question of whether responsiveness to the customer or an emphasis on quality in the work of the organization really involves a shift in power relations. Christopher Pollitt of The Open University is correct when he writes, "The aim is not merely to *please* the recipients of public services (difficult and worthy though that may be) but to *empower* them." Unlike the private sector, in the public sector, the logical path from an emphasis on service and quality to more political questions of citizen involvement, even greater empowerment, is quite clear.

In a related vein, the notions of service and quality, as well as that of community within/cooperation without, have interesting implications for the internal management of public organizations. Many public managers suggested to me that the new strategies being pursued require shifts in the way employees are treated. For example, several persons commented that if you expect front-line employees to treat customers with dignity and respect, then, as one manager told me, "you'd bloody well better treat your own people that way." Others pointed out the importance of recognizing that service and quality build on one central value—a dedication to public service. For a commitment to public service to be expressed, the organization must orient itself toward building community within and cooperation without. That, in turn, suggests extending lines of communication, improving the quality of work life, and empowering people to assume leadership, whatever their level in the organization. It is the latter topic to which we turn in the next chapter.

Empowerment
and
Shared Leadership

The manager encourages a high level of participation and involvement on the part of all members of the organization in efforts to improve the quality and productivity of the organization. Leadership from the top is complemented by empowering individuals throughout the organization to assume leadership within their own realms.

Although highly regarded for their leadership skills, the top public managers speak modestly about their own abilities. But when they talk about leadership in the abstract, or when they describe the leadership of others, they do so with great clarity and insight. Sometimes they describe leadership in a conceptual way, typically and somewhat surprisingly neglecting the hard side of leadership ("the leadership of the sword") and emphasizing leadership's more ethereal side. Sometimes they describe the *skills* of leadership, skills

less associated with the effective use of power and authority and more with vision, articulation, and empathetic
understanding. And sometimes they describe the deeply
personal qualities—of character, maturity, and judgment—
required of successful leaders.

In the comments of these managers, there are hints of
a dramatic change in the way they approach leadership
responsibilities. Leadership is no longer conceived in terms
of control but is instead associated with the development
of effective cooperation. Leadership is no longer conceived
as a position someone holds but as an activity engaged in
by different people at different times. Leadership is no longer
the prerogative of those at the top but rather something to
be encouraged at all levels of the organization. Perhaps most
distinctive, leadership is viewed as sharing power and, even
more dramatically, stimulating in others the capacity for
leadership and their willingness to assume leadership in
critical situations. In these ways and others, contemporary
public managers are demonstrating new attributes of leadership in their day-to-day work that remain obscure in management theory.

Because the emerging ideas and images of leadership in
public organizations are so ambiguous and seemingly contradictory, that obscurity is understandable. Camille Cates
Barnett speaks eloquently of the peculiar paradoxes of
leadership today: "The old concepts of leadership by command, the old notions of authority, are declining. No longer
can we rely on the infallibility of management, [the] cer-
tainty of management tasks, [the] distinction between management and workers, and the unquestioned authority of
management. The organizational and political environ-
ments are more complex and less predictable. There is more
uncertainty, interdependency, and persuasion." Today's
understanding of leadership bears little resemblance to the
old and excessively simple political-military model; indeed,
what is so striking about leadership today, in addition to its
being far more widely shared, is its complex and almost
dialectical character.

In this chapter, we will examine some of the principles
and approaches to leadership that seem embedded, if not

always fully articulated, in the work of many outstanding public managers. We will examine the concept of leadership that is emerging in administrative practice, consider the new skills of leadership in public organizations, and point out some of the inner qualities that characterize managers considered to be successful leaders. Following this discussion, we will explore applications of this new public leadership that range from involving others in decision making to fully empowering those throughout the organization to assume real leadership—and the sense of responsibility that must accompany such leadership.

THINKING ABOUT LEADERSHIP IN NEW WAYS

Among the most progressive public managers, as well as many of their counterparts in the private sector, the word "boss" is an anachronism, a reminder of earlier times, even those in which we also spoke of "masters" and "slaves." Today's managers are much more sensitive to the complex and subtle ways organizations are led; they recognize the paradoxes and contradictions endemic to leadership in the contemporary world. City Manager Barnett describes the public manager's approach to leadership under these difficult circumstances:

- We must use power to empower others;
- We must change behaviors while staying in tune with existing values;
- We must act as though we are in charge and be aware that we are not;
- Our logic must be guided by our intuition;
- We are judged by the success of the existing operation, yet that very success may blind us to the changes needed in the future;
- We must create a vision of the future that already exists in the minds of others.

Again, the idea of moving beyond traditional concepts of leadership and recognizing the complexity of contemporary leadership was reflected everywhere I visited. For example, the Australian APS 2000 report notes that in the public sector today "more emphasis within management is being placed on leadership, on communicating a vision and a sense of direction and purpose to people within the organisation. The leadership in question is not the military style of leadership, nor that found in sports teams, but rather a model of leadership which is as much earned as taken, in which the relationship with subordinates involves low levels of overt control and direction. Such leadership is not the preserve of the head of the organisation alone. It operates, and is vital, at many levels in the organisation."

The new leadership takes many forms, although the key issue in all cases is sharing power. Today's leaders must find ways to tap the skills and energies of those throughout the organization, and that requires a significant shift in the distribution of power and responsibility. This shift occurs at several levels. At one level, the shift simply suggests greater participation and involvement by members and clients in the major decision processes of the organization. At another level, the shift involves a clear devolution of power, authority, and responsibility to those closest to the action, something that is often called empowerment. And, finally, at its most progressive, the shift involves encouraging persons throughout an organization to assume leadership in making improvements in the quality and productivity of the organization.

INVOLVEMENT

The most significant changes in public organizations in the last decade are those that have reshaped the relationship between what we used to call "superiors" and "subordinates." Involvement of individuals throughout the organization is now considered essential to organizational survival. As a result of social and political events over the past couple of decades, people today simply expect greater participation in choosing directions for their lives in general and their lives at work more specifically. (We might even speculate that the wave of democracy that has so dramatically changed the former Soviet republics and eastern European countries is a part of a worldwide trend that has already affected the major Western countries by raising expectations about an eventual democratization of all kinds of public and private organizations.)

In any case, today people are more concerned with expressing their views—being heard and being listened to. Though stated in a somewhat academic tone, Warren Bennis is correct when he writes that "leadership . . . will become an increasingly intricate process of multilateral brokerage, including constituencies both within and without the organization. More and more decisions will be public decisions; that is, *the people they affect will insist on being heard.*" More practically (and cleverly), Gerry Meier, Deputy Minister of Human Resources, Labour, and Employment in Saskatchewan, put it this way: "Greater employee involvement is something I've believed in since I was an employee—when my fellow employees and I grumbled about not having any."

In addition to the cultural shift toward participation and involvement, more practical reasons explain why these values have moved to the fore. Modern society has been correctly described as (1) highly turbulent, subject to sudden and dramatic shifts; (2) highly interdependent, requiring cooperation across many sectors; and (3) very much in need of creative and integrative solutions to the problems that face us. Under such conditions, we are more in need of creativity than control. The problems of the past were often problems requiring uniform and repetitive actions. Exercising precise control over the actions of those in organizations seemed necessary.

Today's problems are different—more than anything else they require creativity. Although uniformity can be achieved through control, creativity is limited and constrained by control. Creativity is enhanced by autonomy, flexibility, and adaptiveness. As a practical matter, rigid and unchanging organizations are more likely to fail while those promoting change and innovation succeed. Involvement can broaden the creativity of an organization by calling upon many minds rather than a few; it can also prepare the way for change as people throughout the organization "buy in" to proposed changes they helped design.

Increasing the involvement of individuals throughout the organization in its decision-making processes can take a variety of paths. In a recent discussion, following a diagnosis of their organization, I asked a group of managers to compare their various approaches to involving people in their units in important organizational decisions. Bruce began the conversation with a fairly typical reaction to the idea of employee involvement: "I just don't think we should have to take a vote on everything we do around here," he said. "After all, if Roger [his supervisor] didn't trust me to make good decisions, he wouldn't have put me in this job in the first place."

Roger himself took the argument a step further by noting the frustration he always felt when managers wouldn't make a decision. "It just drives me up a wall when someone takes weeks and even months to talk all around a decision, when they could decide in ten minutes. I'd rather people complain about not being involved than about my not being able to make a decision." (Indeed, our diagnosis of the organization showed that lack of involvement was exactly what people were complaining about; they wanted a greater voice in what was going on in the organization.)

Other managers, however, pointed out that sharing in decision making doesn't necessarily mean giving away the store. Bill, for example, described his style as "management by walking around" or "keeping his ear to the ground." He spent hours in one-on-one conversations with people in his unit, trying to gain a good sense of how they felt. He encouraged people to cultivate new ideas. Larry, on the other hand, was much more formal in his efforts to involve people in major decisions. When faced with a difficult issue, he would call a meeting of everyone in his unit and talk through the issue in detail. Although he would not poll his employees, he was clearly guided in his decision by the group's conversation.

As the discussion proceeded, the managers began to recognize that sharing leadership can mean many different things but always involves opening channels of communication so more people can be part of the dialogue preceding the decision. None of the managers was comfortable with taking a vote on every issue, but then no one in the organization was asking to vote. Rather, they were saying, "Let us know what's going on; give us a chance to be heard. And, if you can't follow our advice, at least give us a good explanation of why you chose differently." The more the managers talked, the more they recognized that the idea of employee involvement offered a great deal. Through greater participation they could increase the information available to them, acquire new and sometimes quite creative ideas and suggestions, and prepare the way for change.

EMPOWERMENT

Many managers today are committed to a deepened involvement of lower level participants in organizational decision making. Others are going even further and talking about empowerment; that is, giving people throughout the organization not only input into decisions but the power to make decisions. The best public managers seem to be at the forefront of these efforts. Their comments reflect the many and varied reasons that a devolution of power produces additional benefits.

• Sir Robin Butler, Secretary of the British Cabinet and head of the Home Civil Service, observes that the problem of excessively centralized controls affects people at many different levels of the organization. He describes the proliferation of material sent upward to Ministers. In his words,

"Not only has this meant overnight boxes loaded with large amounts of complex and wearisom paper, which divert wearisome paper, which divert Ministers . . . from the task of setting the strategic directions which should properly be theirs. But there is evidence that it has also been reflected in excessively detailed controls at the lower levels of the Civil Service. . . . " Butler especially appreciates the irony of such a situation in an age in which modern technology moves information around so very quickly: "It is no use having information available in micro-seconds and taking three weeks to get authority from head office to act on it."

• Jim Evans was Project Director of a team that implemented the new Employee Health Tax in the Province of Ontario in a way that emphasized employee empowerment. Evans laments the traditional assumptions of managerial superiority: "In the past, we defined the input for new directions and processes as being the prerogative of a comparatively select few, typically a limited number of managers and highly specialized professional staff. We tended not to test whether there might be a broader base for participation which practically enables us to implement public policy more responsively, and at the same time ensures a high quality of program delivery. What we did in the Employee Health Tax implementation was to 'take risks' and explore some of those basic assumptions." What then occurred was a "balancing of essential controls to demonstrate the stewardship of public sector responsibility, with the application of empowerment opportunities to avoid the drag of progressive overlays of rules and guidelines."

• Allen Kilpatrick, Deputy Minister for Western Economic Diversification in Canada, is charged with the task of stimulating economic development in western Canada beyond the traditional resource industries of oil, lumber, mining, and agriculture. Kilpatrick early on decided that project officers who work with applicants for funding and other assistance should be empowered to provide quick decisions to their clients without a lot of bureaucratic red tape and confusion. In this way, Kirkpatrick connects the idea of empowerment to the idea of providing more effective service to the public, something he feels is his organization's primary goal. He told me, "Even where WD has to turn down applications for funding . . . we still provide the maximum possible assistance to clients." In providing what is called "pathfinding assistance," the bottom line is, "Don't let go of their elbow until your client gets to the right place." That goal is made possible by providing project officers with authority and flexibility to act based on their individual judgment—and then to be accountable for what they have done.

These examples testify to the importance many public managers now place on devising strategies for empowerment, but the matter is not simple. It requires vast changes in the way employees see their role as well as significant changes in the way managers see their role. On the one hand, employees are accustomed to a role of subservience in the workplace. Asking them to assume power and responsibility for things that happen around them may cause severe anxiety. Some may be skeptical of what they perceive to be a management "trick," others may fear the assumption of responsibility that accompanies greater power, and some may abuse their newfound power by engaging in trivial and unproductive actions. (Despite these potential problems, the best public managers appear convinced that empowerment is worth the effort.) On the other hand, empowering employees changes the role of the manager, especially the middle manager. If the manager no longer has all the power—which is, of course, what used to define the manager's role—then what does the manager do? What is the role of the manager, especially the middle manager, in this new system?

The answer, of course, is still evolving, but many public managers are beginning to sort out their own approaches to the issues empowerment raises. Later in this chapter, we'll examine some interesting examples of empowerment within the public sector, but it's important to understand conceptually the changes the notion of empowerment brings with it. H. J. Osborne, Vice President for Corporate Affairs for SaskTel in Regina, shared with me several ideas he considers essential to the idea of empowerment—ideas he connects to positive motivation and commitment by individuals to their jobs and by managers to the people who get the work done. He began with the benefits associated with empowerment in the workplace: "People use their skills to the maximum, and grow their skills best, in an environment which gives them freedom to act, to take initiatives, to take risks, and to use their abilities in a way that allows them to challenge themselves. This kind of work environment also fosters a much higher degree of 'job ownership' and most certainly is one in which fresh, creative ideas emerge. Petty jealousies and territoriality, to which all humans can fall prey, are less common among people adequately equipped with the skills and authority, and thus the confidence, needed to do their jobs."

At the core of the strategy of empowerment are individuals throughout the organization assuming responsibility for their own actions and being prepared to take risks in pursuit of what they believe is in the best interest of the organization. Osborne continued: "An open, flexible work environment where employees have license to take risks, along with authority and responsibility over their jobs, offers no better incubator to optimize creativity and no better platform to maximize productivity. Such an environment, however, demands that managers be prepared to take risks as well. Those include the risk of running afoul of those to whom they report, when mistakes occur, as they inevitably will regardless of the work environment, or of not managing properly those occasional mistakes. A 'no-mistake' work philosophy is likely to produce a sterile environment— people quickly realize the means to minimize mistakes of omission is to minimize tackling new ideas and to avoid change. [In the preferred work environment] errors are most likely to be those of commission and accidental, occurring in the course of employees making serious efforts to do the right thing."

Incidentally, other managers I talked with joined Osborne in stressing the importance of taking risks and encouraging employees to take risks. All reported that creativity and innovation require risk taking. Top managers and those in the legislature must be willing to tolerate "intelligent failures," even those that involve some waste of taxpayer dollars. William Talley, former City Manager in Anaheim, California, notes that "the fastest way to kill innovation and creativity in an organization is to penalize failures." Managers need to build a record of success so that their failures and those of their employees will be put in proper context, recognized as the inevitable cost of taking risks and being innovative. Talley recalls a proposal from his employees to construct a billboard in Anaheim Stadium and use the revenue it produced to pay off some transportation bonds. Unfortunately, a mistake was made. An employee failed to get proper authorization for the billboard, and it was ruled too close to the highway. Removing the sign cost the city $60,000. But Talley stuck by his employees, telling the city council that he didn't want to hear "one public word of censure for the employee [who made the mistake]."

H. J. Osborne's comments on empowerment are especially cogent as they address the role of the manager in changing relationships of power and authority. In more traditional organizations, the manager's role is defined almost exclusively in terms of control. The manager is expected to monitor employee performance and make frequent corrections to keep the organization "on course." In the empowered organization, according to Osborne, "close supervision is rarely required, and close involvement is usually only necessary because my participation is needed to prevent or remove roadblocks, to maintain communication with other senior executives, or to help deal with the sensitivities the staff should not be expected to deal with on their own." The manager becomes more of a facilitator of communications than a controlling authority, creating opportunities for interaction and helping to animate the organization. Power and the responsibility for the organization are no longer the manager's prerogative alone.

SHARED LEADERSHIP

Beyond participation, even beyond empowerment, many public managers seem to be encouraging those throughout the organization to assume a leadership role in moving the organization forward. John Gardner, whose writing on leadership has been quite influential, comments, "In this country leadership is dispersed among all segments of society and down through all levels, and the system simply won't work as it should unless large numbers of people throughout society are prepared to take leaderlike action to make things work at their level." The best public managers today and in the future will foster the capacity and responsibility for leadership throughout their organizations.

Doing so, however, requires some significant changes in the way we think about leadership. A new concept of leadership is needed to free our minds to envision new ways of working together. In the past, leadership was regarded by both practitioners and academics as closely tied to power and position. Those who sought to lead first tried to secure a position of power and influence, then to amass power resources they could use in directing and controlling others, especially those "below" them in their organizations. The key was to know where the power lay, and then to use the available power to reshape the organization in line with one's own desires and preferences. The language of leadership was decidedly authoritarian in tone, emphasizing control and directing the actions, if not indeed the very lives, of others.

Even the most progressive and thoughtful commentators on leadership could not divorce leadership from power. James MacGregor Burns of Harvard University, whose monumental work on leadership is a model for scholarship in this area, defines leadership as an aspect of power and writes that power, in turn, "is exercised when potential power wielders, motivated to achieve certain goals of their own, marshall in their power base resources . . . that enable them to influence the behavior of respondents by activating their motives." Leadership is associated with power, and power is associated with one's position in the social or organizational hierarchy.

To move beyond such a view of leadership, contemporary public managers are, even if subconsciously, creating new ways of thinking about leadership. They are no longer thinking of leadership in terms of power or position but rather in terms of a dynamic process of group development. Leadership and followership are becoming intermingled in the most fascinating ways. The change is important and deserving of more extended comment, because it represents a shift from the more rigid and controlling image of traditional leadership to a new image of leadership based on autonomy, flexibility, creativity, and responsibility.

This more contemporary view of leadership focuses not on the leader but on clusters of individuals working together and growing together. Leadership is seen as a process of development involving many people, a function that operates within a group—not a property of a single individual but an activity in which many can participate. Leadership refers to the actions of an individual as he or she interacts with others in the group. Tentatively, this new concept of leadership might be defined in this way: Leadership occurs where the action of one member of a group or organization stimulates others to more clearly recognize their previously latent needs, desires, and potentialities and to work together toward their fulfillment. Leadership is exercised by the person in the group who *energizes* the group, whether or not he or she carries the title "leader."

For a variety of reasons, it makes sense to think of leadership as connected not to power and position but to the development of the group or organization. First, power, in most of its forms, involves control—the capacity of one person to persuade another person or group to do something they otherwise would not do. Moreover, power is typically held by an individual (or vested in a position) and is exercised to achieve a particular purpose, typically one in the interest of the power holder. And, although it is obviously the case that many leaders exercise power, it is not their exercise of power that makes them leaders. Rather, there is something in the way leaders relate to the groups and organizations of which they are a part that distinguishes their actions from the actions of others.

Leadership, as it is viewed more and more, involves an individual stimulating or releasing some latent energy within the group to move the group in a new direction. Where leadership happens, something occurs in the dynamics of the group or organization that leads to change. That something need not be a display of power; indeed, as you will see later, there is every reason to believe that continued efforts by leaders to control the group are ultimately destructive of leadership. On the other hand, when the direction of the group or organization is selected through a process that gives priority to the needs and desires of members of the group or organization rather than to the formal leader, leadership is much more likely to be constructive and enduring.

Second, when leadership is viewed as connected to development rather than power, leadership is not a capacity of an individual or a position but rather is a function of the group. Unfortunately, this point is not always clear in more traditional conceptions of leadership. While Burns, for example, occasionally refers to leadership as a process, his orientation toward power inevitably focuses his attention on power holders or positions of power. Leadership becomes associated with individuals or positions rather than shifting from person to person and group to group over time. In contrast, a view of leadership as a process enables us to see leadership wherever it occurs, at all levels. Leaders are not only the "potential power wielders," the presidents, the governors, the kings, the queens, even the agency heads, but rather leadership is a pervasive phenomenon, occurring in families, in work groups, in business, and at all levels of government. Anyone can be a leader, whether for a moment, a few days or weeks, or for years. As the best public managers have discovered, the argument in behalf of improved leadership is not an argument for improved rulership. It is instead an argument for an expanded notion of leadership, for the extension of leadership—its skills, its capacities, and its responsibilities—to all levels of public organizations.

Think once more about how we recognize acts of leadership, and it's clear that leadership can occur in several ways. Certainly leadership can occur when a person desiring to move a group or organization in a particular way exercises power to do so . . . but it is not that exercise of power that in itself constitutes leadership. As the potential leader pursues his or her own interests and attempts to control the situation, the consciousness of the group or organization may be tapped and change may occur. The leader's interests may coincide with the interests of the group, or members of the group may recognize their own interests reflected in the actions of the leader. There may be an energizing effect—and here we can say that leadership has occurred—but leadership based in control may be short-lived. Typically, as soon as the leader's interests or purposes diverge from those of the group, the leader begins to close communications and resort to the exercise of power rather than leadership. Under these circumstances, leadership soon dissolves into control . . . and both the leader and the group suffer.

In the traditional view of leadership, a particular person holds the position of leader and wields the power associated with that position to bring about change. The leader is expected (1) to come up with good ideas about the direction the group should take, (2) to decide on a course of action or a goal to be accomplished, and (3) to exert his or her influence or control in moving the group in that direction. More contemporary views characterize leadership as being exercised by one who (1) helps the group or organization understand its needs and its potential, (2) integrates and articulates the group's vision, and (3) acts as a "trigger" or stimulus for group action. In the older view of leadership, only the leader is credited with the creativity and responsibility to act in the right way. The newer view takes into account the fact that no one individual can possibly fill all aspects of this role and, indeed, all persons in the organization are required to assume responsibility for leadership from time to time.

What many contemporary public managers are discovering is that leadership need not reflect the interests of the leader alone, especially as those are defined in a largely private or "superior" way. Instead, leadership must develop through an open and evolving process in which the values and interests of all the members of the group are equally valued. For the energizing effect of leadership to be felt most strongly, leadership must reflect the interests of many in the group. This way of thinking about leadership suggests a reciprocal relationship through which members of a group or organization express, in word or deed, the shared interests of all in an open and visible process. As opposed to a leader who pursues private interests, this type of leadership is quite public, involving many and open to all.

EXPERIENCES IN EMPOWERMENT AND SHARED LEADERSHIP

As you have seen, approaches to power and leadership in today's public organizations vary significantly. In some organizations, managers are seeking ways to involve more people in the decision process. In others, the aim is to move the locus of power to the field or local level; the aim is empowerment. In still others, the focus is on leadership. How can we stimulate a sense of confidence and responsibility throughout the organization so that people in all parts of the organization will take leader-like actions in pursuit of the organization's mission and values? Some examples will clarify the practical ways these programs have been implemented.

A number of public managers have launched employee involvement efforts in the past several years. Quality circles have become popular (and then faded in popularity); task forces and matrix management have tried to involve those from various parts of the organization; and, in general, public managers have simply been more attentive to what their people are saying. Some of these efforts have been hit and miss; others have been more systematic. Typical of the latter group are those programs in the U.S. federal service that were introduced under the banner of Total Quality Management (TQM).

The Defense Industrial Supply Center (DISC) of the Defense Logistics Agency, for example, received a Presidential Citation for quality improvement in 1990 based on its TQM program. That program included quality improvement efforts ranging from the automation of changes in inventory levels to a university-guided organization development program, but at its center was a new employee involvement effort. It is representative of many such involvement programs tried in public organizations around the world in the last several years, and it includes many of the standard techniques for involvement that have become so popular in the last few years. (Although these efforts are laudable, we might ask whether this is really TQM or simply use of that label for a more modest program of employee involvement.)

As an initial step, DISC's commander and deputy commander began "walking around" to stay in better touch; they also issued "commander coins" and "bravo zulu cards" (based on a Navy term meaning *well done*) for excellence in the workplace. On a broader basis, a quality circles program was begun in 1982 and has since expanded. One limitation of the circles that DISC soon recognized was that employees in the circles could not really change anything; they could only convince management to do so. To overcome this difficulty, task teams or process action teams were formed to address areas of interest to management. These teams involved not only line employees but also managers in the affected areas and, presumably, carried more weight for this reason. Another device employed by DISC was quality feedback, a short weekly meeting of supervisors and all employees in their work areas to discuss problems that inhibited quality. Finally, in addition to these group-based efforts, DISC initiated a suggestion incentive system open to all employees. Although these efforts are good examples of what a large bureaucratic organization can do in terms of employee involvement, they appear rather modest when compared with other experiments with empowerment and shared leadership. Reviewing these experiments will give you a flavor for the kinds of efforts undertaken by the best public managers, but they also illustrate some of the issues that need to be dealt with as public managers move toward empowerment and shared leadership.

REINVIGORATING THE BUREAU
OF MOTOR EQUIPMENT

The Bureau of Motor Equipment (BME) is the division of the New York City Department of Sanitation responsible for repairing and maintaining the department's fleet of over 6500 vehicles. The organization maintains a work force of over 1300 mechanics, welders, blacksmiths, machinists, and other fleet maintenance personnel; it has an operating budget of more than $65 million. When Ron Contino became head of the division in the late seventies, the division was in deep trouble. More than half the sanitation fleet was out of service at any one time, and fully a third of the trucks that did go out each day came back broken. These problems created enormous overhead costs (cleaning, collection, and waste disposal crews worked into the night to complete their routes) and obviously cut into the quality of service the department could offer the citizens of New York. At the same time, the BME itself spent huge sums on overtime for night work just to keep a minimal fleet on the streets.

Internally, the operation of the division left a great deal to be desired. Serious tension had developed between labor and management, needed tools and equipment were in short supply, and working conditions were problematic at best. The result was low morale and low productivity. One BME mechanic captured the sentiment of his fellow workers when he complained, "Because morale was low, the working environment was lousy—deplorable. I came to work with the feeling that, hell, it's a City job. I don't have to worry about producing. And our management was lousy. They didn't care about us."

Contino set about to change the organization in a variety of ways, introducing a new management team, reducing the use of overtime through changing work practices and new mechanisms for accountability, gaining a better picture of the organization through a new management information system, and establishing procedures to create a permanently reliable fleet through a new preventive maintenance program. At the heart of what he wanted to accomplish was establishment of a joint labor-management program based on the idea of giving employees more power in improving the workplace and in turn the work itself. A simple but powerful belief on Contino's part carried the program: "People will take pride in their work. They like to think that they are first rate craftsmen, human beings, and contributors to society."

Contino recognized that tapping the creativity of his work force was essential for any gains in quality or productivity to be enduring. "No quantity of sophisticated management tools can work in and of themselves. One only has to envision 1000 trades people at over 68 locations, working on 6500 vehicles from dozens of manufacturers and drawing from a parts inventory of over 87,000 individual line items, to realize that a single or even several management brains cannot expect to solve the many diverse problems which occur on a daily basis." The key was developing a climate in which people could express their natural tendencies to take pride in their work and one in which they could effectively communicate their ideas for improvements in quality and productivity. In such a process, according to Contino, the burden is on management.

Contino chose an approach that was perhaps obvious, but it was radical and far-reaching in the BME context. He established a top level labor-management committee that would have real power in the organization. In so doing Contino sent several important messages to his workers:

145

- Because the committee would report directly to me, top management was guaranteeing its own commitment and involvement.
- The committee had a definite purpose: to improve the quality of work life; to improve communication between the top manager and the workforce; and to develop operational improvements.
- The committee would have direct input into the decision making process, by playing an active role in weekly meetings with the chief executive officer.
- The union would be kept well aware of all events and have access to all information.

The union responded positively to Contino's invitation; a number of candidates were asked to join the top management team on the committee.

The first step was to make the committee visible throughout the organization. This was accomplished by having the labor membership of the committee, all of whom were now working full time on the committee, visit each of the various field locations several times. Contino recalls the importance of early and effective communications: "It was necessary to appoint a labor membership which possessed strong communications skills, knew many of the bureau's employees throughout the field, and easily gained the trust of the rank and file by virtue of their seniority with the department." Through these early visits, labor representatives began to recognize the important contributions that those throughout the organization could make to solve the problems the organization faced. A next step was to survey major groups of employees, asking their input in improvements to the workplace and the way work was being done. For example, both operators of specialized equipment and the mechanics who repaired that equipment were asked, in separate surveys, about problems they encountered and about how specifications might be rewritten to eliminate these problems. The labor-management committee then implemented those changes that were both technically sound and economically feasible.

The results achieved through this effort and several others undertaken by the labor-management committee were dramatic. After four years, BME was providing much higher levels of service while receiving 17 percent less money for materials and operating expenses. At the beginning of the change effort, only about half the trucks were available on any day; after only a couple of years this percentage was above 80 percent. Perhaps most noteworthy, however, was the changed attitude on the part of the employees of the organization.

Several important lessons can be drawn from this case, among them the importance of commitment on the part of top management to involve employees in improving the organization; the necessity of establishing clear communications and an attitude of trust and respect; and openness to new ideas, some of which may not appear to have immediate cash payoffs. Note that Contino's efforts in BME didn't follow the approach of building involvement from the bottom up, for example, as in quality circles. Rather, he started with a virtual transfer of power at the very highest level of the organization, a move Contino contends would be equivalent to a corporate chief executive officer asking union representatives to sit in on executive committee meetings first, then devolving responsibilities to the plants rather than the other way around.

EMPOWERMENT IN A LOCAL GOVERNMENT

When Robert O'Neill became City Manager of Hampton, Virginia, in 1985, he inherited a highly competent group of department heads as well as a group of city employees who took a great deal of pride in the work they were doing. O'Neill also encountered a city council open to change and interested in seriously pursuing the idea of transforming Hampton into "the Most Livable City in Virginia." These circumstances led O'Neill to undertake a series of management changes designed to capitalize on the talents and interests of both managers and employees to provide even better services to the citizens of Hampton. A major part of his effort was devoted to "freeing up" or "empowering" managers and employees to be more creative in the pursuit of quality and productivity.

At the time, the city was structured in a fairly traditional way, with several assistant city managers reporting to O'Neill, and with a number of department heads in turn reporting to the assistant city managers. O'Neill's first effort was to "flatten" the organization by asking the department heads to report directly to him and asking the assistant city managers to concentrate on larger future-oriented issues, such as quality of life, economic development, or technology. In addition, operational responsibility for most of the city's activities was delegated to a series of task forces composed of assistant city managers and department or division heads. Task forces were formed for public safety, citizen services, management resources, plant/infrastructure maintenance, economic development, and quality of life. These now appear on the city's organization chart just below the manager. Through these groups, the various managers pool their expertise in running the city. Each group is facilitated by one of the department heads and sets its own agenda to address public problems within its area. (Department heads commented that the experience has been eye-opening as it has allowed them, for the first time, to see the big picture.)

Department heads were given new freedom and new responsibility to run their own departments, but they were also given much more specific goals and objectives (in line with the council's vision of the city). In addition, they signed yearly contracts under which their compensation was based on performance. Similarly, employees throughout the various departments were awarded bonuses based on the performance of their departments, and they were given increased responsibility to solve problems and to take risks in the pursuit of quality and productivity. For example, the idea of the task force has been extended through the formation of "focus groups" brought together to address particular issues within the organization. Some departments also developed quality circle programs. Others, even more dramatically, are experimenting with self-managing work teams of professionals and clerical personnel.

The notion of empowering those throughout the organization came in part from the department heads, who, when asked where they got their best ideas, responded that their employees were the ones they depended upon. Tharon Greene, Director of Human Resources for the city, emphasizes the philosophical commitment that now guides the management of the city: "We are asking, What is management really? What is work? The role of the manager used to be to control and to dispense information. Now it is empowering employees, giving them responsibility, and letting them decide what needs to be done and how to do it." Greene told me that "what makes Hampton innovative and unique is the underlying assumption that individuals who are empowered to make decisions and to assume responsibility will make faster and better decisions; they are closest to the people and also have access to the ideas of others who are working with them, usually in teams of task forces." The result is a more active and responsive local government.

The Hampton empowerment program is clearly linked to a strong emphasis on customer service. Each year a major citizen survey is conducted, measuring the satisfaction of citizens with various city services. Bonuses for managers and employees are directly tied to the results of this survey. In addition, whenever a complaint is received by the city, an employee meets with the citizen and tries to resolve the issue, and the employee leaves a card asking the citizen to rate how well the problem was handled.

How can the city measure the success of its various efforts? First, the citizens' survey annually reports above 93 percent satisfaction with city services, a remarkably high rate. Second, over a three-year period the city saved some $3 million through employee-generated ideas. Third, and perhaps most important, city employees developed an extraordinary sense of pride and accomplishment, something that seems to carry over into other areas. For example, many staff volunteer their time and money on projects to teach other employees to read or to beautify city buildings. City employees believe they can make a difference—and they want to do so.

CHANGING HEARTS AND MINDS IN
HM CUSTOMS AND EXCISE

A. W. "Sandy" Russell described to me the transformation of HM Customs and Excise over the past several years. Russell participates in a department responsible for collecting a variety of taxes and excise duties constituting nearly half the central government's revenues, and one that also enforces import and export restrictions such as preventing the import of illegal drugs. Working with other top managers, Russell helped develop important new systems for measuring the work of the organization. In moving toward Next Steps status, objectives were more clearly stated, information systems were developed to monitor operations, and performance indicators and other evaluation mechanisms were put into place. It soon became clear, however, that management was not "carrying the hearts and minds" of the employees in the department. Many were unsure what the changes being proposed by management were all about; others were downright antagonistic to the new way of doing business in the agency.

Russell and others felt that, despite the importance of establishing the new technical systems, insufficient attention had been paid to the human side, "to what made people tick, what were their preoccupations, how they might be encouraged to ally their preoccupations with the nature of the changes that were being made." A consultant from a nearby university was hired to interview employees from many parts and many levels of the organization. The consultant asked questions that focused on how the changes being discussed related to the desires and aspirations of those throughout the organization. For example, employees were urged to think about their own circumstances and their own career aspirations.

The results were interesting in several ways. Not only did employees provide some concrete suggestions that management could act on, but the very process of interviewing opened up the organization in new ways. People were extremely frank—very forthcoming—and they appreciated being asked about their views of the organization and its future. They said that things were moving in the right direction but not with sufficient imagination. Russell read the findings as: "You simply haven't hit any buttons that inspire real commitment to these changes, but potentially you could. You're not miles off the mark."

As a result, top managers began thinking about how the creativity and innovativeness of people throughout the organization could be tapped more systematically. The result was a new system of delegation, participation, and involvement. In Russell's view, Customs and Excise could do little else. After all, the competition—drug smugglers, those who wanted to evade taxation, and those who wanted to avoid various prohibitions—were themselves becoming far more sophisticated. Admittedly, some remained rather crude; but the really big revenue frauds and evasions were highly complex, increasingly computerized, and largely white collar. Drug smuggling was a good example. Here Customs and Excise was dealing with big organizations, headed by "a lot of people who may have never touched a drug in their lives." These people did understand the business they were in, and they approached it in an extremely sophisticated way. When these complexities were added to the demands placed on the department by increased traffic and by new pressures for action to stop the flow of drugs into the country, the department simply had to improve its capacity to learn and to adapt "to meet the competition."

The new name of the game was "risk assessment," having each local or regional director examine the particular situation they faced and design a unique mix of activities that would be most effective in reducing risks to society. No longer would each customs office operate in exactly the same pattern as all others; rather, they would use their resources in a way that made sense locally. For example, in the past, certain resources were always allocated to staffing the "green channel" through which business people and tourists enter the country. In some areas, local officers determined that the risk here was negligible and that resources might be better spent on examining shipping containers. Similarly, local customs officials asked whether the time they were spending taking complaints to the local magistrate about "a few extra bottles of whiskey" might not be better spent on major drug-related issues.

In each case, the local manager now had the authority to make those changes necessary to reduce the overall risk to the region and to the nation. In doing so they were supported by national information, but the key decisions were local ones. Local managers were empowered to take those actions that fit the peculiar and rapidly changing circumstances in their particular area. Russell commented, "The symbol of it is that all our books of instruction—and they are massive—are being turned into books of guidance. There will continue to be some mandatory stuff, mainly the law and interpretations of the law, but local people will have maximum room to maneuver."

The new notion of local decision making was consistent with the logic of the Next Steps program—for example, setting standards, but then removing policy limitations so that the manager would have flexibility in meeting those objectives. Russell pointed out that these ideas were somewhat at odds with the traditional image of Customs and Excise, which is essentially a control operation—controlling revenues, prohibiting certain behaviors, and restricting others. Russell recalled that customs was historically one of the first functions of government—the first civil servant was the customs officer, then the Army captain—a tradition that included a very well-defined, hierarchical, rule-driven culture. People were accustomed to receiving extremely detailed instructions they could follow without question. Now the top managers were beginning to talk more and more about delegation and participation. The problem for Russell and others was a difficult one—how does one reconcile what is by nature a very authoritarian group with a desire to tap the innovativeness of people, to encourage them to have and to pursue their own ideas, and to develop their own approaches to the work before them?

A first step was development of a statement of vision by all members of the board, endorsing, among other things, the idea that "managers and staff at all levels should have the maximum authority to use planning and budgeting systems to make decisions in line with local assessment of risks." (Note the phrase "at all levels.") According to the statement, "The emphasis of the initiative is on the manager as leader of a team and on creating a performance-based, supportive climate in which personal development, initiative and commitment are encouraged." The next step was to define objectives "with sufficient precision to provide guidance, but not so much precision that you are tied hand and foot." Managers were encouraged to formulate new and innovative solutions to the problems they faced locally. The message to the local manager was, "If there isn't an instruction actually stopping it, go on and do it. You don't have to ask. If your idea does contradict an extant instruction, don't stop, come immediately to headquarters and there will be a presumption that—unless there is a legal point—the policy division will have to have an extremely convincing reason to retain that instruction." (Forty such inquiries have come forward since Russell made that statement. One involved a legal matter and was retained, but thirty-six followed the local lead and three others were already being implemented nationally.) According to Russell, after people finally got the message—that this new approach was not "just a mirage"— some extraordinary things began happening at the local level. "You really do start getting things zipping."

Some tension remains between the traditional hierarchy of the organization and the new local initiative—certain legal and ethical constraints must be maintained—but the resolution of that tension lies in a clear description of the legislative framework and the code of practices associated with it. There must be, for example, a precise definition of the rules of engagement, that is, what people's rights are. These are essential rules that cannot be violated. For example, "if you strip search someone, you have to follow these three steps to ensure their rights are maintained." Again, there is some tension. On the one hand, Russell and others want to promote an innovative local culture, but on the other, there are some rules that must remain. Even here, however, Russell cautions against extending these excessively. There may be a temptation at the center to add to the rule, so that "barnacles are put on it." Soon you are back where you started, with volumes of mandatory rules, many of which don't make sense at the local level. It's a delicate balance. "There will continue to be some mandatory stuff, certain things the law requires. Human rights, for example. But then you get into an area where it's much more a matter of good practice, advice, guidance, and so on, rather than instruction. That's where the flexibility is needed." Even in an organization with a quasi-military style and assignment, empowering those at the local level to take risks and to meet local needs seems to work.

TEAM EFFECTIVENESS IN B.C. HYDRO

B.C. Hydro, Canada's third largest electric utility, was the 1991 winner of the Institute of Public Administration of Canada's Innovative Management Award based on movement toward its vision of the organization as a decentralized structure with an involving and empowering culture. As in so many other cases, the original impetus for change was a vision statement hammered out by (then) Chairman Larry Bell and his top management team. After spending hours talking about the kind of organization they desired and the kind of people needed to staff such an organization, the group formulated, and personally initialed, a vision of

> a commercial, public enterprise providing energy options which enhance the quality of life and productivity of the people of British Columbia
>
> - through an integrated electric business supported by a dynamic network of autonomous business units

- with highly qualified, *empowered people who are committed to innovative work patterns and lifelong learning.*

The statement of vision was complemented by a statement of business principles (customer focused, results oriented, market competitive, excellence driven, environmentally responsible, community sensitive, and safety conscious) and a statement of corporate values (integrity, commitment, teamwork, innovation, and empowerment). Each of these values was elaborated in behavioral terms so people knew exactly what they meant, but overall the new direction was clear. It involved movement away from a dependence on centralized hierarchical structures and practices and toward a more creative and entrepreneurial culture based on the empowerment of people throughout the organization.

In the beginning, employees were skeptical about the new initiatives, so those responsible for the major elements of the change, people such as Bruce Young, Manager of Team Effectiveness, were careful to strike a balance in "letting go of outdated controls without creating total chaos." The new vision was communicated throughout the organization through a video that was viewed and discussed by every natural work group in the organization. Employees were encouraged to respond, and many did so. Quick management action on these initial suggestions reinforced the idea that employee participation could in fact produce changes in the organization. For example, a new employment security policy was established in just a few weeks.

At about the same time, the organization's structure was refocused on "key business units," and the number of layers between the chairman and front-line management was reduced dramatically. Managers were trained in the new management approach and offered contracts that involved results-based pay. They were then empowered to write their own strategic plans, leading to more decentralized decisions with respect to setting objectives, planning, budgeting, and personnel. Throughout this process, linkages were maintained between the vision and principles of the organization and the practice of empowerment within decentralized structures.

One result of creating empowered managers was that more significant dialogue took place about alternatives to traditional hierarchical structures and organizational functioning. This discussion led in turn to the concept of "empowered work teams," the centerpiece of B.C. Hydro's empowerment effort. Bruce Young related how the new system worked. "On a strictly voluntary basis, front-line managers and their people are invited to consider finding new ways to work together by reexamining the traditional boss-subordinate working contract and transferring some of the "position power" of the boss to the team. Interested managers are prepared in advance to empower their employees, and to change their [own] role from decision-maker/director to supportive coach."

The development of empowered work teams was supported in B.C. Hydro by a massive commitment to training and development by Bell and his vice presidents, a strategy they now consider to have been a good investment. Managers and employees interested in empowered work teams were given an introductory session exploring the significance of the concept of empowerment and what it means in practice. Staff who wished to go further attended a facilitated two-day session focusing on the service orientation of the unit and how managers and employees might work together more effectively. Decisions to change are voluntary, and empowered work teams define their own appropriate behavior.

Two key assumptions guide the newly empowered managers and employees: First, decisions are best made by those who are closest to, and best understand, the problems facing the group; and, second, people working in teams benefit from a certain synergy that increases the quality of the overall result. Indeed, many groups have found that empowering individuals is the easier part; getting them to work effectively in teams is harder, but eventually more rewarding. For this reason, early training sessions focus on developing a "team climate." Then managers are encouraged to emphasize the development of skills in teamwork, such as brainstorming, as they work with their various groups.

Has all this made a difference in B.C. Hydro? In traditional business terms, the answer is clearly "yes." B.C. Hydro's net income last fiscal year was the highest in the organization's history, following a record increase in net profit. B.C. Hydro now has fewer employees per customer than any other utility in Canada. A "corporate report card," developed by one of the empowered work teams, takes the story even further, measuring substantial gains in such categories as customer satisfaction, affirmative action, and energy conservation. Perhaps most telling is the excitement and enthusiasm generated by the empowerment program. Bruce Young himself summed up his feelings in a recent letter: "Personally, I feel more committed to the empowerment movement than anything else I have been involved in in 30 years of working. As a citizen and overburdened taxpayer, I feel my worklife interests could contribute to lowering the cost of governance/public administration and thereby help everyone . . . pretty motivating stuff for the average 'public servant.'"

TRANSFORMING THE FOREST SERVICE

Several decades ago, Herbert Kaufman of Yale University wrote one of the classic treatises on public management, *The Forest Ranger*. At the heart of Kaufman's analysis was an examination of the various devices the Forest Service used to control its members, especially with forest rangers scattered across the country. Kaufman spoke about the importance of developing centripetal forces that would counterbalance the natural tendencies of the organization to fly apart. His concern was how the center could maintain control over forest rangers in the field, how it could preserve their allegiance, their compliance, and their conformity.

The U.S. Forest Service today presents a strikingly different picture. Now the Forest Service is less interested in control than innovation; it is less interested in compliance than creativity; and it is less interested in conformity than flexibility. Rather than struggling to maintain the center and the hierarchy that supports it, all efforts are to push matters away from the center, to resist the powerful bureaucratic forces that draw power and authority to one place in the system. The goal now is to create many autonomous units able to achieve a higher quality and more responsive public service. Fundamental to this effort is the notion of shared leadership.

The recent and dramatic changes that have taken place in the Forest Service were stimulated by Dale Robertson, who became chief of the Forest Service in 1985. Robertson recognized that the environment within which the Forest Service was operating was quite different from that that had marked its earlier days. For instance, the Forest Service was moving away from a concern for commodity production and toward a focus on amenity resources and environmental sensitivity. Public values were changing, and those changing values placed new demands on the organization. Robertson recognized that these changes needed to be offset by corresponding changes in the way the Forest Service itself operated; he was especially concerned that the organization throw off some of its ingrained bureaucratic tendencies and "loosen up." As a longtime member of the Forest Service, Robertson recognized the stultifying effect of excessive rules and regulations. He wanted the Forest Service to become more creative and innovative, so it could be more effective in its mission of "Caring for the Land and Serving the People."

As in other cases, the changes in the Forest Service were driven in large part by events in the world outside. In the Forest Service, a major concern was to respond more creatively to rapidly changing environmental issues and demands. John Locke of the human resources staff in the Eastern Region described the changes this way: "Twenty-five years ago . . . things were relatively orderly. . . . A Region pretty much knew what it wanted to do in each of the functions and it did it because it had the experts and it didn't hear much from our customers, the public. Not only that, but there was a whole bunch of experts in the Chief's Office that pretty much set the stage for what would happen down through the organization. . . . We knew what was best for the land and the public."

Robertson began with four pilot sites: the Mark Twain National Forest in Missouri, the Gallatin National Forest in Montana, Ochoco National Forest in Oregon, and a research station in California. Later on other pilot units were added, including the Eastern Region. Cutting to the heart of the bureaucratic tradition, Robertson and his staff began by rewriting the rules, regulations, and procedures of the organization, which, when stacked one on top of another, reached seventeen feet. After reducing this stack to approximately five feet, the management group took a similar scalpel to reporting requirements, reducing them by about two-thirds. Then they gave the pilot units maximum management flexibility, including freedom to change any process or regulation as long as the change was in legal bounds, the authority to budget without the constraints of line-items, the power to eliminate personnel ceilings, and encouragement to try new ideas, even risking failure if necessary, in the pursuit of more creative solutions to local problems. Most important, the new effort, though made possible from the top, was to operate on a bottom-up basis, with management setting the stage for employee empowerment through more substantial delegations of authority, new responsibilities, and higher levels of trust.

Since the Forest Service now faces rapidly changing and highly complex public demands, it requires much more creativity and flexibility in dealing with important public issues. Moreover, those issues are often so interdependent that an integrated vision of the role of the Forest Service is needed. As Locke commented, "Timber issues are now wildlife, fisheries, or scenery issues. Hazardous materials are not only a land use issue, but a human resources, natural resource, and capital expenditure issue. The organization 'boxes' and the issues are just not in 'synch' anymore."

Under these conditions, to continue to operate through the outdated and overly centralized structures of the past simply wouldn't make any sense. Something needed to change.

In contrast, the new culture being encouraged in the Forest Service decentralizes planning and controls, giving managers more authority and discretion, encouraging innovation and initiative, and rewarding workers "based on performance rather than conformance to established norms." The effort then shifts power down through the organization, reducing barriers that kept people apart who needed to work more closely together, redesigning reward systems to encourage creativity and innovation, and demonstrating greater trust in the work force. The new spirit of the organization is captured in phrases like, "Empower employees to get the job done," "Less control, more risk," "Don't say it can't be done," and "Failure is OK!"

There are many different aspects to the organizational change taking place in the Forest Service, but at the center is the notion of empowerment or even shared leadership. In the Eastern Region, shared leadership is defined as "allowing people to become leaders according to the dictates of the work and their willingness to assume the responsibilities that always accompany leadership." In the region, the idea of sharing leadership actually began at the top, with the Regional Forester fully sharing his own power and responsibilities with his two deputies and so on down. Locke describes the shift in orientation this way: "Whereas a year ago, the daily calendars of the Regional Foresters were filled with meetings in which individual staff directors would bring forth issues for 'unilateral' resolution and decision, a majority of those resolutions are now being achieved [at a much lower level]. The Regional Foresters' calendars are much more open, providing [them] the flexibility to concentrate on the overall strategic and political matters that need to occupy their time." If the top doesn't insist on control, then benefits accrue to people at all levels.

The concept of shared leadership is being promoted not only internally within the Forest Service but also in its relations with outside groups. Jeff Sirmon, Deputy Chief of the

Forest Service, argues that the social, political, and environmental complexities of the issues facing the Forest Service today require new approaches to resource management that must be worked out with much greater attention to the "community of interests" involved in those issues. Sirmon suggests that a new mode of leadership, one unlike the earlier "authority figure" mode, is appropriate under these new circumstances.

> Leadership in this context is the act of facilitating the dialogue necessary to reach resolution. It does not mean dictating the solutions, but rather helping to create the environment from which solutions can emerge. It means taking responsibility to ensure that all interests are represented at the discussion table, that all points of view are considered with respect, that each individual can learn from the others' knowledge in a setting where each can also share their knowledge. It is within this diverse community of interests that lasting solutions will eventually be found.

Note once again how the various ideas tie together, how the idea of shared leadership brings us back around to the idea of community within/cooperation without.

One offshoot of the change in the Forest Service that is especially interesting is that so much careful thinking about management issues was encouraged during the transition. As a result, a number of Forest Service papers present excellent discussions of the difficulties encountered in bringing about such major organizational changes. One such issue, which we have already encountered but which deserves some further comment, is the role of middle managers in organizational change and their place in the empowered organization.

As in other organizations, middle managers and their support staffs in the Forest Service link the top managers with those who actually deliver the products and services on the ground. Altogether they constitute a large number

of those employed by the Forest Service. In the decades after
World War II, the responsibilities of middle managers expanded under the strain of an increasing workload to include
several important roles: overseer, information broker, expert, and rulemaker. These individuals maintained the functional integrity of the organization and offered stability to
a highly dispersed work force and, in the earlier days of the
Forest Service, that was a very important role. There was
a negative side as well; the functional interests of middle
managers often kept them isolated from one another and
tended to support a "turf" mentality.

Under the pilot experiments, the role of the middle manager changed significantly to one of creating an environment
and culture in which the ingenuity and creativity of employees throughout the organization would be unleashed. In
such an effort, middle managers had to become far more
trusting of their people, more confident that the right choices
would be made and that innovative solutions to the concerns
facing the Forest Service would be found. This new role implied much greater confidence in one's employees and required a willingness to encourage risks and endure occasional failures. Again, the idea of shared leadership was at
the core of the changes and central to the redefined role of
the middle manager. A Forest Service publication explains:

> Shared leadership across all levels of the organi-
> zation changes the traditional middle role of "con-
> troller" to one of "consultant" and "co- producer."
> Individual power, which is often fueled by author-
> ity and ego and not always in the best interests of
> the organization, is replaced by shared power across
> the organization. On the Pilot Units, the "new" mid-
> dle manager feels some loss of control . . . but re-
> member the manager is also empowered.
>
> People in the new middle routinely work together
> across staff and organizational boundaries to resolve
> issues of common concern. The agency takes advan-
> tage of the tremendous synergy and new thought

that come from a cross-section of people interacting in a team environment.

The two ground rules—use good common-sense and give high quality customer service—require the new middle to challenge rules aggressively that do not make good sense and to involve the public actively in the decision-making process.

The Forest Service, once a bastion of bureaucratic rules and intense territoriality, is now seeking new ways of operating. As in so many other organizations we have examined, the changes sought by Dale Robertson and other top managers were stimulated by changes in the world around them—changes in the management of natural resources and changes in public values. These developments required that the organization become more creative and more flexible and that people throughout the Forest Service be granted far more freedom to operate and to innovate. Managers themselves were given more room to maneuver, and in turn, they were urged to empower their employees to take leadership in pursuing the mission of the organization. Although it may be too early to assess fully the impact of these changes, all the Forest Service people I talked with evidenced a real enthusiasm—even excitement—about what was going on. In their view, it's not only working, it's working well.

A NOTE ON MILITARY-STYLE LEADERSHIP

After hearing the message of shared leadership from so many of the best public managers, I began talking with others about these emerging ideas. Over and over, skeptics responded by saying: "That empowerment stuff may be okay in certain types of agencies, maybe those in the social services or in education, but it just won't work in agencies where you need more discipline. You know, police agencies or military organizations. Empowerment or shared leadership is just too soft and mushy for organizations like that.

You'd never maintain order there." Imagine my surprise when I started talking with police officials about the approaches they were finding most successful and found them very much interested in the devolution of power, both internally and externally. Imagine my further surprise when a military audience responded to my comments on empowerment and shared leadership by saying that was exactly the kind of leadership they were now recommending.

Police chiefs have traditionally been viewed as being quite hierarchical, even militaristic, in their approach to leadership and management. (But then, in having such a reputation, they are little different from managers elsewhere.) Among a progressive group of police chiefs, however, some dramatic changes in orientation and behavior are occurring. These changes are being driven by shifting public expectations, including the need for police organizations to become more proactive rather than reactive in limiting crime, and by the changing background, educational levels, and expectations of their officers.

Some police chiefs talked about new approaches to the internal management of their departments. Larry Hesser of Longmont, Colorado, shared with me the story of his transformation in his role as chief in terms that carried almost a missionary zeal. "When I started out," he said, "I thought that responsibility and competence meant being in control. I had my own agenda and I knew I was right. If anyone crossed me, I'd cut 'em off at the knees." Hesser began to change his approach after a lieutenant who had just been disciplined came to Hesser's office and said, "I just had to come in and tell you that I think you're a jerk. I feel like a whipped dog." Hesser realized how his actions influenced others, and he wanted to change his style. Instead of bossing others around, Hesser became interested in building community. Instead of trying to accumulate more power, he realized that what was necessary was to give up authority and control. According to Hesser, the results were surprising. Not only were people more comfortable with Hesser's shared leadership, he was delighted to discover that "the level of productivity skyrockets where there is a sense of community."

Hesser agrees with another police chief, Donald Hanna of Champaign, Illinois, that leadership involves values. The leader must have a clear understanding of his or her own values and those values must be clear to all. Such an understanding requires a very careful self-examination, a self-examination Hesser undertook during a long car trip by himself. He spent the entire time trying to sort out the answer to the question: "What are the things I really believe in?" Following that experience, he was able to articulate his philosophy of policing and his philosophy of management more clearly. As Hanna frames the issue, "The greater the correlation between personal values and organizational mission and goals, the greater the understanding, effectiveness, commitment, and success of an organization."

Among police officials, sharing power internally is often complemented by sharing power with the community through an increasingly popular approach known as "community policing." John Alderson, former Chief Constable of Devon and Cornwall, is known for his advocacy of a community orientation. Decentralization of police service delivery to the neighborhood level ensures that police will become engaged with citizens in solving community problems, preventing crime, and carrying out the other functions of law enforcement. Community policing is based on the assumption that preventing crime cannot be accomplished by police alone; other institutions and individuals have to be involved. Consequently, it seeks to integrate the police and the community.

Again, there are important implications in terms of sharing power. The community policing model stands in stark contrast to the traditional hierarchical chain-of-command design of police departments; the new model involves a substantial decentralization of authority. Moreover, there is a moral commitment to ensure constitutional rights and freedoms within neighborhoods. Alderson believes that police should be "anchored" to their communities. He writes, "I believe that if they are so anchored they themselves will gain much. They will feel more secure as an institution, they will receive more public help and guidance in the delivery of their services. A way will be opened for democratic impulses in society to balance the growth of bureaucratic power."

Other police officials I talked with sought to integrate their approach to shared leadership in the community with that inside the department. David Couper of Madison, Wisconsin, has given careful thought to the way changing ideas of leadership affect his organization, both internally and externally, and now believes that the two are related. He writes:

> What does the new leadership style mean in terms of practice? First, it means a shift from telling and controlling employees to helping them develop their skills and abilities. This includes asking for their input before making critical decisions that affect them and making a commitment to listen to them and ask them about policing strategies in the community. Second, it means listening to the customers, the citizens, in new and more open ways. Third, it means solving problems, not reacting to incidents. Fourth, it means trying new things, experimenting. Risk taking and honest mistakes must be tolerated in order to encourage creativity and achieve innovation. . . . Finally, it means avoiding, whenever possible, the use of coercive power to bring about change. . . . It is only by first changing the "inside" of our police organizations that police leaders will be able to implement the new "outside" strategies of policing.

With these goals in mind, Couper developed a six-day training course for supervisors and managers that was designed to encourage a new approach to leadership—one that clearly falls in the category of involvement and shared power. Working with a quality and productivity steering committee and his top management team, Couper developed twelve points that were taught in the training sessions (see Box 4.1). These ideas would be helpful guidelines coming from any public organization; they are even more dramatic as they reflect contemporary thinking in a police organization.

Finding the idea of shared leadership so central to the thinking of some highly progressive police chiefs was remarkable, but hearing similar ideas expressed by those in

---

BOX 4.1
Principles of Quality Leadership

1. Believe in, foster, and support TEAMWORK.
2. Be committed to the PROBLEM-SOLVING process; use it, and let DATA, not emotions, drive decisions.
3. Seek employees' INPUT before you make key decisions.
4. Believe that the best way to improve the quality of work or service is to ASK and LISTEN to employees who are doing the work.
5. Strive to develop mutual RESPECT and TRUST among employees.
6. Have a CUSTOMER orientation and focus toward employees and citizens.
7. Manage on the BEHAVIOR of 95 percent of employees, and not on the 5 percent that cause problems. Deal with the 5 percent PROMPTLY and FAIRLY.
8. Improve SYSTEMS and examine PROCESSES before placing the blame on people.
9. Avoid "top-down," POWER-ORIENTED decision making wherever possible.
10. Encourage CREATIVITY through RISK-TAKING, and be TOLERANT of honest MISTAKES.
11. Be a FACILITATOR and COACH. Develop an OPEN atmosphere that encourages providing and accepting FEEDBACK.
12. With TEAMWORK, develop with employees agreed upon GOALS and a PLAN to achieve them.

Source: David C. Couper and Sabine H. Lobitz, *Quality Policing: The Madison Experience.* Washington: Police Executive Research Forum, 1991, p. 48. Reprinted by permission.

the military was even more striking. Last spring I presented some of the ideas in this chapter to a group of officers at Maxwell Air Force Base in Montgomery, Alabama. Frankly, I expected considerable resistance to the notion of shared leadership; after all, these were military people—people more accustomed than any other group to the traditions of hierarchy and command. You would think that shared leadership would be quite foreign to their experience.

To my amazement, these officers were not only open-minded about the notion of shared leadership, they were quite sympathetic to it. Their interest in the idea actually made a lot of sense, once you moved past the stereotypes of military command and control. As David Booker of the Airpower Research Institute at Maxwell explained it to me, the new thinking about military leadership "centers around the problems created by the highly fluid, high-technology, and highly lethal nature of the future battlefield, and the need for shared vision at all operational levels based on what the military calls the 'commander's concept' or 'commander's intent.'" Imagine, Booker suggested, the battlefield of the future, a battlefield described in an important report on the AirLand Battle (ALB) 2000. On this battlefield, things happen very quickly, with little time or opportunity for centralized coordination. Most of the action involves small, widely separated units, sometimes operating independently of one another, at other times needing to work together, but often with little or no communication with the commander. Field officers do not have the luxury of waiting for directions from a superior officer who sees the big picture. (Indeed, those in the field will probably have better information than the commander.)

Under such conditions, those in the field will need a high degree of flexibility; they will need to be adaptive and innovative and quick to respond. When they need to change positions to sustain an enemy attack, they will have to move quickly rather than waiting for "permission" from headquarters. When they need to join another unit to complete a particular goal, they will need to act immediately rather than going up a chain of command and down again. Certainly they will need to internalize the mission (the "commander's intent") and have the resources available to act, but in all cases they will need to maintain considerable latitude in the way the mission is executed. One expert describes the new approach this way:

> In these newer models, responsibility is delegated downward in the organization to the point at which relevant information for the decision is most available, the speed of the decision most important, and the outcome of the decision most consequential. In operational terms within an Army, this can be translated into the proposition that on the future battlefield, delegating authority downward through the structure will increase effectiveness. This can be interpreted as simply giving more authority to people lower in the chain of command, or in terms of taking advantage of emergent leadership processes outside the formal chain of command.

Or, in words I have used before, the person in the field must be empowered to act.

What is most remarkable to me is that the idea of the military "powering down to power up" is supported for exactly the same reasons strategies of empowerment or shared leadership are supported elsewhere: to respond with creativity, to adapt to rapidly changing circumstances, and to deal with uncertainty. Managers in all kinds of public organizations can learn much from the dialogue on military leadership currently under way. In some ways, these discussions reinforce arguments we have already encountered; in others, they even go beyond them. Consider, for example, the comments of a writer on military leadership:

> There is only so much energy available in an organization. The more of that energy used just to maintain the organization, the less there is available to be innovative and creative. When power is held at the top, the rest of the organization has to use its

limited resources of time and energy to feed the in-
satiable appetite of the power holders; thus, there is
no time and energy left at the local levels to do what
subordinates already know should be done.

It sure doesn't sound like the military, but it does make
sense.

CONCLUSION

Those managers considered by their peers to be at the
forefront of contemporary public management are without
question leaders in all that they do. Indeed, their work is
testimony that public organizations today cannot abide a
separation between leaders and managers, neither a separation between political leaders and appointed managers nor
between top appointed officials and those throughout the
organization. Leadership must permeate the organization;
individuals must assume a new sense of responsibility for
energizing the organization at all levels. As I said earlier,
leadership is no longer something we can associate with a
particular person in the organization or a particular position. Rather, leadership is a function or process that must
be developed and extended throughout the organization.

As you have seen, the best public managers employ a
number of different approaches to issues of power and
authority in their organizations, but nearly all contemporary
approaches are based on the assumption that public
managers must forego their preoccupation with control and
discipline, emphasizing instead cooperation, teamwork, and
sharing power. Some public managers incorporate this goal
through increased participation of employees in organizational decisions, either through formal means or simply
through "management by walking around"—though one
very clever manager wanted me to point out that simply
walking around doesn't mean you are managing. Others

seek to devolve power and responsibility in their organizations, empowering people to make decisions that are responsive to the specific and immediate conditions they face, something that makes organizations not only far more flexible but also more creative. Finally, many managers promote leadership throughout their organizations, encouraging and developing the skills and capabilities that will enable their people to act positively and forthrightly to energize the organization and move it forward.

Such changes in the way these managers think of leadership and the way they practice leadership have not come easily. They require much of the manager, not only in terms of vision and intellect—it takes a great deal of both to imagine and propose changes such as these—but also in terms of the psychological demands of shared leadership. Of course, these changes also require much of others in the organization. New expectations and new responsibilities are often placed upon employees who must adjust to these new roles. And middle managers must revise how they think about themselves and their roles.

For the employee, these changes are obviously difficult. After years of being told the way to get ahead is to "let us do the thinking" or to "shut up and do the job," having someone say "we want you to think for yourself" or "we value what you say about the job" is quite a shock. It's not at all surprising that many employees are curious if not even suspicious about this new message. They may well respond by wondering what management is really after. They may ask, "Why are these things happening to me." In a time of public sector cutbacks, they may wonder whether the whole thing is a trick to get more out of those few employees who remain. Some may simply not want to do anything that smacks of initiative and responsibility, preferring to find meaning, or at least satisfaction, elsewhere.

Middle managers also may be understandably skeptical of ideas such as involvement, empowerment, and shared leadership. Many efforts aimed at employee involvement do indeed appear to bypass middle management, thus calling into question the viability of the middle manager's role.

Quality circles, for example, are often viewed by middle managers as a way for employees to go straight to the top, a sort of "end run." Similarly, to talk of employee risk taking threatens middle managers who fear, sometimes with justification, that they will be held responsible if the employees "bomb." Finally, and quite realistically, many middle managers fear elimination of their own positions as top managers talk about flattening the organization and reducing overhead costs.

Despite these concerns on the part of employees and middle managers, the most progressive public managers seem to think that a move toward involvement, empowerment, and shared leadership is worth the risk. They have faith that employees throughout the organization, given a chance to participate in decisions and to design the most effective and responsible work practices, will not only match but far exceed previous standards. Moreover, they have faith that middle managers, given the opportunity to make decisions appropriate to their own situations, will do so with creativity, skill, and dispatch. Consistent with their caring for those throughout the organization, the best public managers have faith and confidence in their employees and their managers.

The changes I have talked about here are not easy for anyone. The agony that sometimes accompanies change is felt by those at the top as well as those at the bottom. Powerful psychological barriers inhibit any public manager from moving away from the traditional way of doing things "because that's the way it's done." There are the pressures of the bureaucratic culture—the expectation that if you are a manager you must control those who work for you and make sure they don't deviate from the proper path. There are, similarly, the pressures of the old image of leadership— that one needs to establish a direction and make sure everyone follows. And, there are the pressures of conformity and security—that you don't rock the boat, that you don't take risks, and that you don't fail.

As I have talked with public managers at all levels, I have come to believe that these are not trivial issues in terms of the public manager's self-image. These expectations constitute powerful psychological constraints on managerial behavior, tempting public managers at all levels toward the more secure solution, which is to do what has always been done, even if that means rigidity, conformity, and control. Conquering one's personal inhibitions, one's own psychological constraints, is the most important early step in transforming an organization. The public manager who would transform an organization must first transform himself or herself. Obviously, that change goes to the basis of one's persona. Change of this type is not just a matter of abstract analysis; it requires a reformulation of the way one thinks about oneself and one's role in the world. Changing themselves is basic and, for most managers, may be the most difficult step of all.

First, the manager who would lead in the modern world must overcome what seems to be an almost natural bias toward control. The manager must be willing to let go of the traditional trappings of power and authority, as attractive as these may seem from time to time. (To see how one manager did so, see Box 4.2). The manager must, paradoxically, be prepared at any moment to follow others and indeed to encourage others to take the lead. Curiously, the result is likely to be an act of leadership on the part of the manager, for by letting go the manager has energized the group, and that, of course, is what leadership is all about.

Second, the manager who would lead must be willing to shed the aura of superiority that accompanies top positions in most organizations. The assumption that the manager/leader is smarter or more clever than everyone else in the organization combined simply makes no sense today— and probably never did. Excessive control and bureaucratization also send a negative message to employees, as attested by staff participating in the U.S. Forest Service's changes. In a thoughtful analysis of the dynamics of bureaucratic behavior, the Forest Service staff recognized the many rules and regulations, and controls and procedures that surround the work of every government employee. "Government sends its employees a powerful albeit subtle message in all of this: *'We don't trust you to do the job so the bureaucracy is our way of assuring that you don't waste resources, abuse authority or defraud the government.'"* So very much of what constitutes the rules and regulations of any bureaucracy are efforts to control the behavior of employees.

BOX 4.2
Empowering an Organization

Because I like to think I have learned a few things in 25 years [in the field of urban management], hopefully there are also some things I now do differently. At the front end of my career, for example, my concern was in making sure everybody in the organization knew I was in charge. Reorganization, replacement of key personnel, and formal control mechanisms were the hallmarks of my early days. They were meant to define me as a "take charge" person and to signal that change had occurred. My guess also is that this behavior reflected a need to overcome the insecurity associated with immaturity.

In reflecting on my earlier approach, I have now come full circle. The kinds of changes I made back then were clearly visible and so probably satisfied those who wanted to see change. I have learned, however, that it is relatively simple to bring about physical, visible change but that to cause actual improvement in the way an organization functions is a far more difficult trick. It is easy to make things look different; it is not easy to make things substantially better. Obedience as the basis for organizational success has given way in my mind to the need for trust. A successful relationship is based upon mutual give and take rather than on "you give and I take." When blind obedience is the operative concept, the "boss" gathers all the power. In the trust relationship, the boss shares power with everyone else.

What impresses me as more productive now is to figure out how you get those in the organization to feel confident about what they do, to move the organization where it needs to go. The values that permeate an organization have the power to override, at least in the long run, any other changes

---

But the issue cuts another way. A manager/leader who recognizes that superior knowledge and creativity extend throughout the organization must also recognize that responsibility for success or failure does too. Far too few managers and employees in today's world really accept responsibility for their own actions, yet new configurations of leadership in public and private organizations require in-

that may be made. What is new for me now in the second half of my career is an understanding that if dysfunctional and counterproductive values do not change, not much else of importance will either. And if management is not trying to improve the organizational culture's value system, no one else will.

A related lesson I have learned, is that management cannot "order" values to change. This kind of change takes place relatively slowly, and it occurs only if management talks a lot about what is expected, sets the right example, creates the right kind of organization climate, and uses the personnel and compensation system to support the right behavior.

So I am preaching. I am talking about organizational values important to success—customer responsiveness, treating people right, supporting city policies, being a good source of information, getting and giving "more bang for the buck," and providing anticipative rather than reactive management. I reward those who join in to support these expectations and "unreward" those who do not. And, yes, here and there a little organizational change may be in order, as well.

The point of all this is to empower the people in the organization to exert themselves by their own volition, in the right direction. A manager can indicate the proper direction. A manager can encourage needed values and create the climate in which employees will choose to make the organization's success their goal. Managers used to see success as a function of the assertion of their own power. Now they see the empowerment of others as a more likely avenue to success.

Source: Excerpted from Roy R. Pederson, "Empowering an Organization," *Public Management (PM)* 71 (August 1989), pp.2–3. International City Management Association, Washington, D.C. Reprinted by permission.

dividuals to assume even greater degrees of responsibility. To encourage a sense of responsibility in themselves as well as in those with whom they work, managers who would be leaders must assume a moral task. The leadership they exercise will necessarily be moral leadership.

The tasks of leadership today are weighty indeed, but development of those inner qualities that will sustain the public manager/leader through trying times is even more difficult. Especially under conditions of stress and uncertainty, managers will be encouraged by their own psyche, and perhaps as well by the expectations of others, to pull back, to regress to older, more secure forms of management control, even those paralleling the relationship between masters and slaves. The secure path will probably not be the best path. Consequently, those managers who possess both the intellectual commitment and the psychological stamina to encourage and to empower others will become the real leaders of the future.

CHAPTER FIVE

Pragmatic Incrementalism

Change occurs through a free-flowing process in which the manager pursues a wide variety of often unexpected opportunities to move the organization in the desired direction. The manager views change as a natural and appropriate feature of organizational life and employs a creative and humane approach to change, taking into account the personal concerns and interests of members, clients, and others.

As Stephen Higgins implemented a series of management practices that dramatically changed the work of the U.S. Bureau of Alcohol, Tobacco, and Firearms, his personnel director, Joe Coffee, who was working closely with him on changing the culture of the organization, asked Higgins to describe his management philosophy. Coffee was saying, "Through training and other interventions, I can help people

177

understand your philosophy, but I need to know what it is."
The question puzzled Higgins. Although he had held a variety of administrative posts, he had never really thought of his work as involving a particular philosophy. It all sounded a little distant and high blown. One day, as the inevitable question cropped up again, he responded with a flash of brilliant though probably unplanned insight: "My philosophy is *pragmatic incrementalism.*" At the time, the answer seemed inconsequential, but it came to capture the approach that guided Higgins' revitalization efforts. Among other things, it meant that Higgins would pursue whatever opportunities presented themselves, however planned or unplanned, to move the agency in the direction of improved quality and productivity.

Interestingly, many of the public managers I talked with described a similar approach. Few had a grand strategy for organizational change in mind. Although they clearly had a vision of where the organization should be going and a good concept of the values and philosophies that should guide the organization, they rarely had in mind at the beginning a step-by-step plan for moving the organization in that direction. Although the vision was clear, the steps to attain that vision were not set in concrete. Recapturing a metaphor from an earlier chapter, it was more like the surfer who wanted to end up safely on the shore but intuitively knew that a great deal of cleverness and spontaneity would be required along the way.

The managers I talked with believe that there are many ways to realize an organization's vision. Indeed, the consummate skill of an effective public manager is exactly the ability to respond to whatever the day brings in a way that moves a body of people toward a common goal. Sometimes the manager will respond by suggesting a series of broad-ranging policies or financial rules to guide the behavior of those in the organization, but more often, as these managers suggest, the best response will be that which is more immediately sensitive to the needs and interests of the employees, the clients, and the citizens. It will rely less on cold, technical rationality and more on exciting the emotions, the passions, even the zeal of those in the organization. The steps involved are often painstakingly slow, and resistance to change can be enormous. Many of the public managers I talked with emphasized the persistence required to move an organization—not necessarily a forceful or aggressive persistence but an ability and a frame of mind. The manager must persevere despite the inevitable resistance and frustration. Although it is important for the manager to state clearly the mission, values, and objectives of the organization, much of the manager's impact on the organization occurs by chance. Some sense on the part of the manager as to what the appropriate response to any random event is may be far more revealing than any edict passed down through the organization from above. A brief conversation over drinks after work, a scheduled meeting of the executive team, or a long-awaited address to the governing body can all reinforce the aspirations of the manager and demonstrate the basic set of values he or she holds for the organization.

The revolutionary public manager works best within self-imposed constraints of appropriate mission, vision, and integrity. These constraints provide guideposts for responding to individual occurrences as they arise. They enable the manager to be consistent time after time and to keep moving in the right direction. Obviously, in the real world, sometimes it works, and sometimes it doesn't; but the best public managers have a much better batting average than others.

The idea of pragmatic incrementalism, as I will use it here, bears many similarities to the suggestion by Robert Behn of Duke University that the most successful public managers make progress by "groping along." Behn suggests that the greatest gains made are rarely the result of a fully rational planning process in which the manager considers all possibilities, then settles on a course of action that guides all of his or her future behavior. Rather "an excellent manager has a very good sense of his objectives but lacks a precise idea about how to realize them." The manager who is groping along (which is different from "groping around") has a good compass but lacks either the right general theories or the specific techniques needed in the particular situation. The successful manager has the capacity to learn along the way the appropriate responses that move the organization in the right direction. Behn suggests that the manager's behavior is similar to that of a political candidate who, in the course of a campaign, evolves a particular speech that works. The candidate gropes along, testing out one idea or even a single phrase before an audience, noting the response, then shifting just a little with the next group until the right combination of ideas and phrases occurs and "the speech" takes shape.

Many public managers approach their work in an analogous way, although the idea of groping seems to give them too little credit. They certainly are not reaching into the organization randomly or without insight. Their interventions are based on a peculiar sense of what makes large groups of people respond and change. Whether this knowledge comes from theory or experience or intuition (it is probably a combination of all three), it prepares these managers to experiment, to listen, and to learn what is necessary so they can do just the right things at just the right times. Although they are hardly groping for answers, learning only as they go, neither do they have a complete step-by-step plan for changing the organization. Although they have a good sense of the objectives they wish to achieve—what you might call a strategy—they don't follow a specific game plan. Some of their moves are calculated and under their control, but many more are the result of responding to opportunities or even creating opportunities to act.

Perhaps a musical analogy will help. There are probably some areas in which public managers are able to write and perhaps even direct a symphony that others play, but more often public managers are called on to improvise, being neither composer nor conductor but just another instrumentalist, like the leader of a jazz ensemble. By establishing the theme, the leader of the ensemble (and the manager) can chart the basic pattern and direction in which the performance will move. By setting the tone and the tempo, the leader gives focus to the spirit and energy of the group. By modeling effective and responsible performance in their own solos, leaders can energize and articulate the performance of others. But it is the performance of others that is critical. The symphony is the model of rational planning; the model of the jazz ensemble is more closely aligned with the actual experience of the best public managers.

In what ways then does the public manager improvise? First, the best public managers spend a great deal of time crystallizing a vision or a message that they want to get across, both to those in the organization and to those outside. Here Behn's reference to the political candidate's standard speech is especially compelling. The manager, like the candidate, needs to convey a message; there must be something substantive that the manager wants to communicate. Nevertheless, one of the most critical skills of leadership, at whatever level, is to crystallize the message, making it clear, understandable, and acceptable in the minds and hearts of those who listen. In this process, the manager may search out information about the audience and from the audience. The manager may try out different themes in different places to gauge reactions, and the manager may alter the wording time and time again along the way. The result is a message that is meaningful to those who hear it, a message that energizes the group and which, in the best of cases, expresses a potential already present in the group. In doing so, the manager exercises an essential aspect of leadership.

Second, the manager can establish the tone and tempo of the organization. The tone of the organization can vary tremendously, from passive to aggressive, from laid back to intense, from carefree to committed. Similarly, the tempo of the organization can vary widely, from leisurely to hectic to torrid. The best public managers seem to have a strong sense of time and timing in their organizations. They understand that age and maturity affect outcomes, that events take on different meanings based on the experience or lack of experience of particular groups. They also understand the pace at which different organizations work and that the pace of organizational life must be taken into account in any change process. And they understand that their own actions must be properly timed—or they will fall flat. The skills that managers need in order to address questions of timing are among the most important, but they are at best intuitively understood by managers and rarely addressed by scholars. Few, however, would deny their importance.

Third, and finally, the manager must model the appropriate behavior so that those in the organization can see what that behavior looks like and, hopefully, choose to act in a similar way. The manager must provide a new paradigm, not in the way paradigm is often misused to suggest a new theory but rather in a way that suggests a pattern of behavior, an approach to problems, a way of going about business. The recently appointed manager, for example, will be a source of curiosity and imitation. If the new manager no longer models the sexist stereotypes of earlier managers, people will take notice. If the new manager talks not about control but about service, many will change their own behavior in this way. Indeed, one might speculate that a drive for consistency is almost "built-in" in most organizations and provides the manager with strong reinforcement— but only if it is used correctly.

The idea of modeling applies to many areas of organizational life. If the manager wants to move the organization toward new heights of commitment and performance, the manager must evidence commitment and performance. If the manager wants to move the organization toward greater professionalism, the manager must behave as a professional. If the manager wants to move the organization toward a greater sense of ethical responsibility, the manager must be seen as virtuous in everything he or she does. The model is pervasive, affecting many aspects of organizational life, but it must be consistent with the situations in which people find themselves. A model that is too different may be rejected out of hand. A model that appears anomalous or out of place in a particular situation will be subject to intense scrutiny and may not survive. Lacking a model, the message will remain abstract and will probably change behavior only marginally.

The difference between theory and practice in the field of public administration has long been a source of debate and confusion. How can abstract theories constructed by scholars be implemented in the real world if, indeed, they should be? The theory-practice fit becomes a more personal matter here and describes not merely the relationship between scholar and practitioner but also that between two or more aspects of the individual manager's own personality and behavior. Can a manager act in a way that is fully consistent with all the various dimensions of the message that are brought forth? Can you practice what you preach? Can you walk your talk? It's a difficult question and not just an abstract one. Individuals in the organization will pick up the clues even if the manager is unaware that he or she is sending clues out at all. People will see relationships between parts of the message and parts of the model that may not be apparent to the manager. Although their observation of these clues may not be fully articulated, perhaps remaining intuitive, they will expect agreement among the various parts. Enough inconsistencies between the message and the model will have important, negative ramifications.

The phrase *pragmatic incrementalism* means several things. First, it signifies that the best public managers bring about changes in the quality and productivity of their organizations one step at a time. Although these managers have a picture of the direction they want to move, there is no grand design, nor is there typically one major event that signifies the change. Changing the organization is accomplished in a series of small steps, hopefully all or at least most being steps in the same direction, but small steps nonetheless. Karl Weick of Cornell University refers to this strategy as one of achieving "small wins": "A small win is a concrete, completely implemented outcome of moderate importance. By itself, one small win may seem unimportant.

A series of wins at small but significant tasks, however, reveals a pattern that may attract allies, deter opponents, and lower resistance to subsequent proposals." Obviously, with each win the odds of succeeding in future situations is improved, so the strategy builds on itself. Although each step by itself is small, the accumulated journey can be quite significant.

The best public managers seem comfortable trying to influence the organization in a variety of ways, sometimes trying several different approaches simultaneously. Some public managers engage in strategic planning efforts, others become involved in organization development activities, still others create important new training and development programs—some try all these and more. Whatever the combination, even while these efforts are going forward, other things are happening. Standards for performance are discussed, changes in key personnel are made, new ways of thinking about authority and responsibility are formulated. All the while, these managers talk about their vision of the organization with anyone who will listen and, little by little, the message gets through. These are small steps, some even very small steps. The changes made from day to day are incremental at best, but over a period of time these changes made a dramatic difference in the way these organizations worked.

Second, these public managers are pragmatic in their efforts to move their organizations forward. By describing them as pragmatic, I don't mean to imply that they are insensitive to theory or to the "big picture," for as a group, these managers struck me as extraordinarily perceptive with respect to both theory and to seeing the big picture. They were very interested in the context, how things fit together, but their interest in understanding both the theory and the context focused on using their knowledge to take practical and immediate steps to change things. Some of the discussions we had were highly theoretical. Managers I talked with were extraordinarily sophisticated in their treatment of topics that often leave management scholars baffled. But what moved these managers was not knowledge in the abstract but the way ideas could be brought to bear on specific problems in specific situations.

These progressive public managers were pragmatic in another sense—they were willing and able to respond to whatever opportunities presented themselves to move the organization along. Many of the changes they instituted were planned, but others were impromptu reactions to particular events or even particular conversations in which they found themselves. These managers seemed comfortable with a view of public organizations that I have never found fully reflected in the academic literature on public management. They clearly understood the limits of their control over what happened in their organizations. They understood the limits of how much they could affect the actions of others. Interestingly, their response was not simply to "go with the flow"; rather, it was to "catch the flow and redirect it." They understood that the image of the organization that was in their heads would never be fully reflected in the minds of others. Instead of finding that frustrating, they reveled in the opportunity to move with the organization in order to move the organization. Consequently, from the biggest and most dramatic restatements of mission and philosophy to the most casual talk in the halls, the actions of these managers were opportunistic, taking advantage of whatever came along to move them closer to their goal.

APPROACHES TO
ORGANIZATIONAL CHANGE

In other chapters, we have focused on particular components of the change process. In this chapter, we'll look at the work of a limited number of successful public managers to see how each one put the various pieces together in a combination that advanced his or her organization in a positive direction. Obviously, the particular mix of activities varies from organization to organization, although many of the same themes run throughout. What is most important is how all the threads are combined into the fabric of successful public management practice, and how particular managers pursued an opportunistic, broad-ranging, sometimes free-form, and often intuitive strategy called pragmatic incrementalism.

ALISON CROOK, STATE LIBRARIAN OF NEW SOUTH WALES

Many people think of libraries as stodgy, slow-moving relics of a quieter time. Few think of librarians as being on the cutting-edge of management thinking. Alison Crook, however, defies both stereotypes, running a very complex, technologically driven information communication organization with a clear understanding of contemporary directions in public management. Without question, she prefers a multifaceted, incremental approach to changing an organization, a practice she describes not as "guerilla warfare," which should be reserved for organizations that are in real trouble, but as "a persistent gentle shaking." As you will see, Crook's persistent gentle shaking dramatically changed the way the State Library of New South Wales operates.

A decade ago, the State Library was ill-equipped technologically, with an antiquated batch serials system and a shared system of cataloguing. The organization itself was traditional, run very formally, rigidly structured, with considerable divisiveness between sections of the organization. Today, in contrast, the library provides a wide variety of information products and services, ranging from answering inquiries personally or electronically, to running an Australia-wide electronic mail and data base access service for libraries, to running a for-profit industrial information business. The goal is to be able to deliver information rapidly from anywhere in the world to anywhere in the state. The State Library has a budget nearing $35 million.

Crook was the first chief executive of her organization from outside the library establishment and, partly for this reason, she worked hard early on to gain the confidence of senior management. At the same time, she sought to improve the public's image of the library and to build credibility with important external constituencies. In those early days, Crook moved very carefully, recognizing that the staff would ultimately make or break any effort to change the way things had always been done. Ironically, Crook reports that "the main problem now is overload and too many good ideas."

One of Crook's early efforts, like that of so many of the managers I talked with, was to develop a statement of mission, which she molded through a strategic planning activity. Through a process involving people throughout the organization, Crook asked her staff to focus on goals and strategies and to begin to work toward common purposes. This activity was paralleled by a staff development program, initially designed to build the management skills of those running various departments and sections. (Like many other organizations, the library tended to promote the best professionals or technicians into management jobs for which they really were not prepared.) It was essential for skilled librarians and technicians to have the management skills necessary to bring their ideas to fruition—skills in problem solving, decision making, and action planning. Crook now sees the organization's ongoing planning activities as dovetailing with an enhanced staff development effort, and considers both well worth the effort. "It's always difficult to assess the concrete benefits of staff development, but to my mind it constitutes one of the most effective means of getting new ideas and views aired in an organisation, and as such is an essential element in loosening up and getting change started."

The particular changes Crook wanted to see in her organization focused on providing better service to those who used the library and on the involvement and empowerment of staff to provide improved service. She is clear about the distinctions between her approach and the traditional approach to managing public and private organizations. In those established groups, the manager's role is to conceive good ideas—to think. The workers do as they are told, then the manager reviews the work to see that it's carried out correctly. Crook describes two experiences leading her to seek an alternative. One occurred during a period in which she and her husband were working in a small mining town in northwest Queensland. Alan arrived home one night filled with anger because he had made a suggestion about how things might be done better and was told, "You're not paid to think, you're paid to do what you are told." Similarly, Crook recalls a fellow worker who commented that she never expected to enjoy or to get satisfaction from her work; she was just grateful to have a job. These experiences led Crook to think about better ways to organize work.

Such feelings were intensified as Crook came to understand the environment in which public organizations operate, an environment filled with strain and volatility. Under these conditions, she recognized that the old formulas for success were no longer workable and that public organizations and public managers had to change. The change required was one that focused on service to customers and support to staff. "When we've recognized both that the environment is tough and rapidly changing, *and* that if we want our organisations not only to survive but to thrive, we must get close to the customers, understand their needs, and meet them—then it becomes crystal clear that we need *thinking, committed staff.* Without this, you and your managers may talk service till you're blue in the face—you may even succeed in changing the symbols, changing publicity, and changing some external perceptions for a while, but the changes won't happen on the ground where they count, and where the customer feels them."

Crook articulated her commitment to service but also took a series of practical steps to demonstrate that commitment. She recognized that the building in which the State Library is located was somewhat confusing to library users. Crook felt that an inquiry desk should be placed in the foyer;

moreover, she felt that the desk needed to be staffed by persons with a sufficiently broad understanding of the organization to answer questions, point customers to the right areas, and tell them of other facilities where they might find help. So the Foyer Inquiry Desk was created and staffed on a rotating basis by people from the supervisory level and above. Complaint forms were also available so that library staff could either respond or explain the problem in more depth. Crook, who takes her turn at the inquiry desk, reports that the experience is a positive one, helping her stay aware of what's going right and wrong at the library.

Other areas of direct customer contact were targeted for improvements as well. For example, the switchboard position was upgraded in terms of salary and staffing. The security staff were given new uniforms and attended staff development courses that focused on public relations. These somewhat cosmetic changes were supported by a change in management approach that recognized that a service orientation needs to be supported by a degree of autonomy in anticipating customer needs. Crook explains: "A truly service oriented organisation may be different in a great variety of ways from one which is not. For a start they will need organisational structures which allow for flexibility and fast response to changing customer needs, and which encourage innovation to meet those needs."

Crook describes herself as "a great believer in small is beautiful when it comes to structures for meeting customer needs." She claims that department stores have long understood this logic, using a departmentalized approach to giving their customers an impression of boutique service while enjoying the benefits of shopping under one roof with reduced prices from volume buying. At the library, this meant one small section dealing with services to people with disabilities, another dealing with multicultural services, another with inter-library loans, and so on. Nine small groups raise funds for the library, each with its own target group, to which it offers specialized services. Even within the reference library, where all seventy professionals are "cross-trained" to do all the basic jobs, there are subject matter specialists. The idea, in all these cases, is for each small group to meet specialized needs, find better ways to deliver their services, and promote more effective service delivery.

This same approach has guided other efforts in the library. For example, Crook has pursued a highly participatory approach to the introduction of new information technology. Recognizing that merely automating existing processes may not actually lead to improvements, each experiment with new technology has been accompanied by a participative job redesign effort involving joint steering committees that include elected representatives of all staff whose jobs are affected by the technology. The idea is to rethink work flows and the design of various jobs so that the greatest productivity *and* job satisfaction are derived from the change. Another manager summarized it this way: "You should straighten the cow path before putting in the road. You don't want to just automate the same way of operating. You want to make it better."

The philosophy is now familiar—an effort to connect a concern for improved service with empowerment of service level personnel. For a service orientation to succeed, a great deal of freedom to act at the point of customer contact must be built in. In Crook's view, the organization needs to have shared values, a strong customer orientation, and tight financial controls. "But within those parameters it should be loose, fluid and flexible enough for the front-line teams to be able to feel that they can go for it and to feel the excitement and enthusiasm that flows from accepting responsibility for results."

The combination of a strong service orientation and empowerment of those on the front line who deal directly with customers is essential to Crook's strategy. She believes in an orientation that is considerably at odds with standard management practices. So much of what occurs in modern organizations promotes the view that those at the top, the senior managers, are the most important people in the organization. And when those managers actually start to believe this themselves, they expect compliance with their own desires rather than responsiveness to those of the customers. Crook sees this as a formula for failure.

In her view, managers must be sensitized to the importance of the customer through staff development and constant reminders. They must also come to understand the different role they must play. Crook explained:

> Now we are suggesting that, with the interests of the customers in mind, we should be empowering the front line staff member to solve the problem, and to be contributing mightily to decision making about how we can best provide a service. Middle management now has to learn to be leaders who contribute to building the shared values of the organisation; who assist in resolving inter-departmental or inter-branch difficulties; who are working to ensure that the customer messages are getting through clearly to senior management; and to see that their front line heroes are getting adequate recognition and encouragement.

Adequate recognition is important, something the manager can attend to through small gestures of appreciation but also through more formal award programs. In Crook's case, the first two award winners were library technicians who were asked to check on the availability of microfilm readers designed for left-handed people. When they discovered none were made, they took the initiative to convert a couple of machines over, so the library can now serve left-handed people as well as right-handed people!

Alison Crook has made significant changes in the State Library of New South Wales. Her interests in a strong customer orientation combined with empowerment of front-line people to service customers more effectively have changed the way the library operates. But, again, these changes didn't come about overnight. Crook orchestrated the changes by combining a clear vision and a lot of opportunities seized upon—and, of course, some persistent gentle shaking.

JAN PERKINS, CITY MANAGER
OF MORGAN HILL, CALIFORNIA

When Jan Perkins became city manager of Morgan Hill, a northern California city of approximately 25,000 population, she thought she was moving to a community in good financial shape that was ripe for change and innovation. There were certainly some challenges, especially in restoring morale among city employees and developing an adequate planning process, but things looked pretty good. After only a few weeks, however, the picture changed dramatically. Lower level employees in the finance department alleged financial mismanagement, allegations that eventually resulted in the resignation of the finance director and the revelation of a $1.8 million deficit that no one had known about before. The elected city council soon acted to restore financial stability by passing a new utilities tax, but that action triggered an antigovernment movement that was successful in removing from office all those members of the council who voted for the tax. At the time of our first interview, Perkins reported that the city council didn't even have a quorum to conduct business.

In the midst of this political chaos, Perkins was responsible for managing the city staff efficiently and responsibly. She began by listening. A series of budget workshops were conducted in the community, providing Perkins with a chance to let people know what was happening with the city budget and to hear citizens' suggestions for solving the budget crisis. Internally, she talked with lots of people, asking them about the strengths and weaknesses of the city government and their concerns about their own work. She followed a fairly systematic game plan, going to their work areas, talking in fire stations, riding with police officers. The key question she asked was, "If you were city manager for a day, what would you do?"

Listening to the city employees provided helpful information to the new manager, but it also provided her an opportunity to model an important behavior for supervisors and others—listening. Perkins felt that if managers didn't listen to the employees and provide chances for them to suggest improvements, "We're going to miss out on good ideas, things that will keep us out of trouble." At the same time, Perkins began providing a new language; she started using some words they hadn't used before—words like "customers" and "values" and "continuous quality improvement." Whereas previously there had been no theme or continuity in the work of the city, Perkins began offering a common language and a common direction.

The message was soon given broader expression at a day-long workshop Perkins organized. All the city's managers and supervisors were there, along with a few others whom department heads recommended as "having something unique to offer." Perkins describes the group that came to the workshop as "hungry for direction" and very much in need of long-range planning. At the workshop, some time was devoted to effective communications and team building, but the primary focus was on values. Some issues that emerged were specific, like "Why aren't some people putting in a full day's work?" Others were more general, like responses to the question, "What does this organization stand for?"

The result was a statement of values (see Box 5.1) drafted by a group of six or seven employees following the meeting. (The draft document was widely circulated for input, including that of the city manager, but was actually the product of the group.) The statement was posted in department offices and the lobbies of city buildings, included in pay envelopes, and the subject of discussions in groups ranging from those in city offices to local civic organizations. All seemed to appreciate the commitments being made by the city staff and the direction provided by the manager.

Though the budget crisis intervened, some months later the next step in the planning process was undertaken—development of a five-year business plan for the city. This plan was again primarily the product of the city staff, although workshops with members of the city council and other groups were held as well. (A local businessman volunteered to facilitate the meetings.) The result of these meetings was a business plan that is now being circulated in draft form. The plan contains information about "key issues and trends affecting local government, five-year financial forecasts for the major City funds and departmental profiles which summarize the factors impacting City departments." In its final form, the document will provide a framework to help the city council define specific objectives they would like to accomplish.

The business plan does not paint a rosy financial future for the city, suggesting that new employees or major new pieces of equipment are not likely any time soon. To Perkins

---

BOX 5.1
City of Morgan Hill
Corporate Values Statement

THE CITY'S MISSION IS TO FOSTER A SAFE, ATTRACTIVE COMMUNITY THROUGH QUALITY MUNICIPAL SERVICES.

Integrity and fairness are basic to the accomplishment of the city's mission. Personal and organizational integrity is essential. This means we:

- Promote and recognize ethical behavior and actions.
- Value the reputation of our individual professions and departments, but we promote honesty and fairness over loyalty.
- Openly discuss both ethical and fairness issues.

The City of Morgan Hill values leadership. This means we:

- Reward and recognize those who contribute to the development of more effective ways of providing public service.
- Listen to and promote suggestions emanating from all levels of the City organization and from the community we serve.
- Encourage prudent risk taking and innovation and recognize that growth and learning may be spawned by honest mistakes.
- Demand leadership by example.

this means that everything must be done to assure that the fullest capabilities and creativity of the city staff are exercised. In this regard, Perkins feels blessed, for the employees of the city are an exceptional group. The key, in her mind, is to give them all possible opportunities to do what needs to be done. In part, this means stripping away the constraints of traditional hierarchy; in part, it means empowering employees to act.

This has come about in several ways. Perkins now relies heavily on employee task forces to do some of the major work of the organization. For example, task forces have been

---

Providing city services is a substantial expense to the taxpayer. The City is committed to providing quality service for the resources expended. This means we:

- Regularly assess the cost vs. the benefits of all City programs.
- Require a standard of professional performance for all personnel.
- Administer City funds in a cost effective, prudent, manner, and seek economy in everything we do.

We value our human resources, which includes the City Council, Boards and Commission, City personnel and volunteers. This means we:

- Recognize the daily contributions of employees who have dedicated their lives to public service.
- Publicly acknowledge and praise individuals that excel at their job.
- Support and encourage individuals in their pursuit of professional development.

We value a partnership with the community. This means we:

- Foster an orientation toward "the citizen as customer."
- Solicit the faith and trust of our residents and continually work to deserve their confidence through our attitudes, conduct and accomplishments.
- Place a high value on treating everyone with respect.

---

formed to deal with issues of data processing, training and development, and sexual harassment. These task forces are not controlled by management nor created merely to report to the manager; they are task forces empowered to act. The data processing task force, for example, is headed by a police officer and includes a planning engineer, a fire fighter, and a data processing technician, all people recognized for their skill and interest in this area. The group has been authorized to approve or disapprove hardware and software purchases and will have a budget at its disposal to implement what it sees as the city's data processing needs. Perkins is available to meet with the group, but her only request is that it keeps everyone informed and makes sure everyone has access to the group. There is no question that this group has been empowered to make changes—even to pay for them.

Employees are also empowered on a more individual level. Perkins described to me the work of the park maintenance people, of which there once were six and now are three. They have complete authority to do whatever it takes to present the city's parks and other city lands at their best. These people are dedicated to making the city beautiful and, given the power to do so, have been enormously creative in pursuing their task. For example, they are able to obtain free flowers from local nurseries and, in turn, the medians look great. Perkins meets with the group occasionally and says, "If I can help, I will, because I know the results will be there." Leadership resides with the employees rather than with the manager.

Perkins feels that the old paradigm of the boss knowing what's best and telling others what to do simply won't work anymore. Within the financial limitations of the budget, existing staff must be given every opportunity and every motivation to get the work done. Opportunities come through participating in task forces, being close to the customer, and by having the authority to act. Motivation comes from the intrinsic rewards of being involved, working outside one's normal realm, and being recognized as an important and contributing individual. Perkins repeatedly stressed to me, as she does to the council and the public, the value and competence and creativity of her employees.

In fact, when we talked about what keeps her going in a situation that is curious at best, turbulent at worst, she remains highly optimistic and very committed to the city. What's the key to that optimism and commitment? It's seeing an organization and its people take responsibility. "Employees now are expected not only to report a problem but to say what we should do about it. They are expected to think about what they can do. That's what keeps me motivated. Seeing them succeed."

What is so striking about Jan Perkins' recent work in Morgan Hill is that the extraordinary managerial changes she initiated have occurred in a highly charged political environment. As many public managers have discovered, bringing about organizational change is difficult enough in a stable environment or even one that seems to support the changes you are making. Yet Perkins has accomplished substantial changes in the management of her city in extraordinarily turbulent times. Notice the glue that holds it all together—not the old glue of power and control but rather the faith of the city manager in the capabilities of her employees and their achievements. That's a substantial difference today from yesterday.

MIKE FOGDON, CHIEF EXECUTIVE, BRITISH EMPLOYMENT SERVICE

In some ways, Mike Fogdon's story appears to be at odds with the strategy of pragmatic incrementalism. In anticipation of his agency's becoming a Next Steps Agency, he planned a series of changes, many of which were implemented on the first official day of the agency's new status, what Fogdon refers to as "Day One." These changes, however, had been the subject of intensive dialogue and tireless work for some time previously and, indeed, their implementation was a signal that new things were happening in the agency and that other changes could be expected.

The Employment Service was created in 1987, at which time Fogdon was called from his post in manpower policy to head the agency. The idea of the new agency was to bring together the Job Centre Network, then run by the Manpower Services Commission, and the Unemployment Benefit Service, a network of unemployment benefits offices. The rationale of ministers in making such a move was to merge job placement activities and benefit payment services in one agency so the needs of the unemployed would be served by a single organization. At the time there were approximately 1,000 Job Centres and an equal number of Benefits Offices, with a combined staff of some 40,000. Benefits totaling some £4 billion were dispensed by the agency.

Fogdon and the Employment Service reported to the Secretary of State for Employment but enjoyed some degree of autonomy from the start, operating almost like a discrete business. Consequently, when the Next Steps Agency concept was announced, the Employment Service was a natural candidate. As you will recall, the Next Steps program created new executive agencies, each headed by a chief executive, that were given both specific performance objectives and increased flexibility in meeting those objectives. In each case, a "framework document" was created, spelling out the aims and objectives of the agency, its specific responsibilities, and the management process under which it would operate. For example, the framework document establishing the Employment Service provided a mission of helping to "promote a competitive and efficient labour market particularly by giving positive help to unemployed people through its job placement service and other programmes and by the payment of benefits and allowances to those who are entitled to them." More specifically, the objectives of the agency included providing unemployed people with job search skills, opportunities for self-employment, or access to training; paying benefits "promptly, accurately and courteously"; and encouraging unemployed claimants "to seek work actively."

Fogdon described the trade-off in fairly straightforward terms: "We are told that we are to improve quality of service to our clients, enhance job satisfaction to those in the staff, and provide better value for money for the taxpayer. We are then given a range of flexibility in finance and personnel." The flexibility, however, was not trivial. On the financial side, Fogdon was, for example, given carry forward ability, up to a certain amount, thus enabling him to avoid foolish year-end spending. On the personnel side, Fogdon was allowed to change the minimum educational requirements for employees, his thinking being that the key issue was not education but interpersonal skills. Similarly, the normal personnel requirement for a twelve-month probation period was eliminated to reduce uncertainty and boost confidence among new employees.

The Next Steps program was established in 1988. Fogdon soon volunteered his agency, but the Employment Service was not designated a Next Steps Agency until April 1990. The delay in making the Employment Service an executive agency occurred because a number of reviews were necessary. In keeping with the political tenor of the time, certain questions were asked: "Why is the government in this business anyway? Could we sell the Job Centres? Could we contract them out? Could the banks do the work?" Once these issues were settled, the impending status of the agency was announced, and the Employment Service was "launched." Fogdon was "in post" at the time and was asked to continue as chief executive, something that pleased him a great deal. He told me, "At last I had my own train set and could make it run the way I wanted it to run. It gave us a powerful impetus."

A variety of things happened almost immediately. A new mission statement was prepared, tested throughout the organization, then implemented on Day One of Agency status (see Box 5.2). Issuance of this statement was accompanied by a series of pragmatic and often slightly more than incremental steps. For example, in merging the two earlier organizations, the government had provided some extra money for "estate rationalisation" or improvement of facilities. Bringing the Job Centres and Benefits Offices together provided an opportunity to change the face of the agency in a dramatic way. Whereas the older offices, especially the Benefits Offices, tended to be very severe, with "high counters, linoleum on the floor, and ashtrays screwed to the floor," the new look featured an open environment, with good quality carpeting and furniture, potted plants, curtains, and "things you don't traditionally associate with public sector squalor." A new logo was adopted and, along with key phrases from the mission statement, was displayed on a desk calendar found on every desk. "It didn't cost very much, but the impact was tremendous."

These changes were only the beginning. Fogdon set about to change the way the offices operated as well. "Prior

---

BOX 5.2
British Employment Service
Our Mission Statement—Into the 1990s

The ES. The ES was created by the Government to provide an effective and high quality public employment service. We are well qualified and equipped to do this through our committed and trained people and our nationwide network of local offices.

Our Purpose. Our purpose as a public employment service is to help people into work, thereby filling employers' vacancies, and to pay benefits to those unemployed people entitled to receive them. Our continuing priority in the 1990s will be to help unemployed people, and particularly the most disadvantaged, to find work, and to ensure that in the meantime we pay them benefits accurately and on time. However, our role may need to broaden and develop in response to new policies and programmes introduced by Ministers. The ES has earned a good reputation in responding to new opportunities. We must be ready to meet fresh challenges.

Our Values. The ES serves people through people. We must all work together in close cooperation to provide the best possible service for our clients. We will ensure that the ES to Day One, if you went into an office, you would be given a claim form by a low grade clerical officer and told, 'There's your form, fill it in, come back, and I'll check it. Next please.'" Recognizing that clients of the Employment Service don't want to be there in the first place, and shouldn't be treated rudely to boot, Fogdon insisted on respect for customers and consistent good service. Beginning with Day One, the clerical function was replaced with an executive function. A newly created "client advisor" went through a structured interview of up to forty-five minutes with each client, analyzing strengths and weaknesses and checking available positions. If suitable jobs were open, the client

is a well managed organisation, where people want to work and where they can realize their potential.

Our Vision. We will become a business-like agency, respected for the quality of our customer service and people. We will make good use of agency flexibilities in meeting our targets, and deliver programmes and services cost-effectively through a unified local office network.

Our Aims. To achieve this vision for the ES, we have set for ourselves the following key aims for our organisation:

- to improve the effectiveness and quality of ES programmes and services;
- to foster relationships with people and organisations outside the ES who can help our clients;
- to develop a strong culture for the ES as an agency with greater emphasis on effective management and on the achievement of positive results from our efforts;
- to integrate the ES local office network across the country;
- to ensure that all of us in the ES have the capability to deliver the programmes and services required in the 1990s.

By achieving these aims we can build an Employment Service for the 1990s valued by our clients and by us all.

might be placed right away. If not, the advisor and client moved to a claims situation.

On Day One Fogdon also introduced a new booklet, "Helping You Back to Work," which contained information about job hunting as well as claims. The advisor and client would agree on specific action steps that should be taken and this "Back to Work Plan" was inserted in the book along with information about when the client would return. Fogdon wanted people to keep this information, so he came up with the ingenious idea of sticking the UB40 form on the back cover. (The UB40 is the basic "passport" to benefits, as well as the name of a well-known rock group.) The entire package was placed in a plastic wallet and given to the client (some 4 million last year). When the client returned, he or she was asked to produce the booklet so that an advisor could review the individual's progress in finding work as well as the client's right to benefits. In all these ways, Fogdon sent powerful signals throughout the organization emphasizing the importance of service to the agency's clients. As a result of these and other efforts, there was a dramatic increase in customer satisfaction with the work of the agency (as measured in customer surveys)—in Fogdon's words, "sometimes almost embarrassingly high levels of satisfaction."

In addition to changing the service orientation of the agency, Fogdon made some internal management moves as well. These moves were somewhat more incremental in nature. For example, Fogdon developed a new approach to measure the work of the agency. "We used to measure how many we interviewed, not what happened to them. Now we're interested in outputs. We want to establish visible targets, both for quantity and quality. I ultimately want to get down to a handful of key performance indicators— numbers of people placed in jobs, speed of handling benefits, and accuracy of benefits. The organization knows these are the ones I'm interested in." (Note that these objectives reflect the mission set out in the framework document.)

These targets as well as the mission statement and the changes it portended were the subject of a major conference of all the middle and senior managers, some 230 in number. Although the conference was helpful in broadcasting the new message, Fogdon realized that if he were going to improve the image of the service, he would have to network beyond this group. So, he decided—against the advice of some senior managers—to go directly to the local office managers. "We have a thousand local office managers up and down the country, in small towns, in inner cities, all over the show. They are the visible face of the Employment Service. So we thought it was very important to touch base with every one of these local office managers."

Fogdon and his executive board of six people divided up the thousand and started to work, contacting every one individually or in small groups. "What we found was a tremendous untapped vein of goodwill. We decided on a policy of being completely frank and honest, completely open, no holds barred. Let's be up front with the issues; let's get it all out on the table and talk about it." This was the first time someone from the center had gone out to talk with the key people, those at the local office level, with the result that even those local office managers who were waverers or cynics came to understand the changes and, in most cases, to buy in.

The "buffering" between the organization's center and the local offices caused by middle and senior managers might have led others to change the organization chart. Fogdon, after all, had inherited a somewhat "tall" structure, and he felt there was at least the potential to eliminate one level. After some reflection, he chose not to restructure but to refocus. He wanted his managers to be more active and creative than before. "I've heard it said that organizations that don't know where they are going reorganize," Fogdon later reflected. "That rang a bell with me. We were quite clear about where we wanted to go. I didn't want to create a lot of insecurity among managers, when the key thing was to change the local perception and to improve the quality of the delivery, the job satisfaction of the staff, and the value for money." Pragmatic incrementalism includes knowing when *not* to act as well as when *to* act.

As more and more changes occurred in the Employment Service, Fogdon came to recognize more clearly the essential nature of the local offices and began a strategy of devolution, pushing decisions down and giving local managers more flexibility. This move was motivated by the recognition that the Employment Service deals with issues that vary from place to place. There is not a single national labor market that the organization must respond to; rather, there are different labor markets in different parts of the country, and each must be attended to. If there are vacancies to be filled, you need one kind of program; if a major industry is going out of business, you need another. Consequently, Fogdon sought to move as many decisions as possible to the local level. On this issue, Fogdon confided, "We have a long way to go; this is a road that will never end. But we are pressing all the time to get that concept over. The local office is where the delivery happens and that's where you should give as much enabling power as you can. That's the key level, and all above is superfluous if you don't get it at the local level."

Earlier we encountered the notion of inverting the pyramid, but I pointed out that in most organizations such a move is purely symbolic, with few changes in power or pay. Fogdon is actually examining both these issues. He points out that "in the past the local manager has been seen culturally at the bottom of the tree. People said, 'If you want to get on, lad, get into an area office, a regional office, the head office.' What happens then is that all the talent drains out from your key delivery area." Currently, all local office managers receive the same pay; yet some are clearly in more difficult posts than others, especially those in the inner city areas. One way to approach the pay issue would be to classify the offices based on difficulty and pay those in the more difficult areas more money. Similar changes could be applied to management positions on up the ladder.

Near the end of our conversation, I asked Fogdon whether there was a particular philosophy or commitment driving his management of the organization. His response, very much like that of others I talked with, was simple, yet extremely compelling: "I work from the premise that if you can get people interested in their jobs and satisfied with the work they are doing, the commitment that they give will be greater and you will get added value from that. One way you do that is to create worthwhile jobs. I want people to be able to say they work at a Job Centre and to be proud to say that they do." The combination of pride and commitment that Fogdon described seems to me very basic to the work of successful public organizations, indeed to a successful public service more generally.

IAN LEMAN, GENERAL MANAGER, B.C. HOUSING MANAGEMENT CORPORATION

A big, somewhat burly Scotsman, Ian Leman became general manager of the British Columbia Housing Management Corporation after a long career in the public service, one that took him from a starting position as a very junior official in the park system to directing a major agency of provincial government. Although he progressed remarkably through the ranks, according to one friend and colleague "he never lost sight of where he came from." Consequently, Leman continues to express a genuine concern for every individual in his organization. Moreover, he really feels that a spirit of teamwork and cooperation is essential to the development of a high performance public organization. Not surprisingly, Leman was quite concerned when he discovered that the organization appeared to be going in several different directions at once. He felt something needed to be done.

In his efforts, Leman was aided, encouraged, and complemented by Sylvia Porter, his director of personnel. Porter had, at one point, been the business agent for the clerical/administrative union; indeed, she negotiated the collective bargaining agreement under which the union currently operates. An opportunity in personnel presented itself and, after a few years, Porter found herself directing the personnel operation. Even in this position, which one might see as being "on the other side," Porter continued to listen carefully to what employees were saying. All kinds of people, from janitors to architects, came to her with their concerns. One thing that became clear to her, as it had become clear to Leman, was that the organization definitely wasn't filling the needs of its people.

After considerable discussion among the organization's five directors and in a slightly larger management committee, Leman decided to hold a two and a half day retreat to assess the strengths and weaknesses of the organization and to develop a clear statement of the mission of the organization and the values that would sustain that mission. Twenty-four people were selected to attend, based in part on their roles in the organization. An effort was also made to include people from all levels so that input was obtained from everyone. Although many participants were enthusiastic about the idea of a retreat to talk about mission and vision, others, including some of the directors, were openly skeptical. With Leman's encouragement, everyone went along.

Going into the session, Leman set three goals for the strategic planning exercise the group was undertaking. First, build teamwork, so that people would not only be productive but would enjoy their work and understand their role in the organization. Second, strengthen communication and empower each staff member to help shape the culture and values of the organization. And, third, identify the tools that people needed to do the job, including not only "paper and pens, hammers and nails," but also training, development, and recognition.

The retreat got off to a stormy beginning, with heated debates arising between the more traditional finance and administration group, who some described as "entrenched bureaucrats," and a newer more entrepreneurial housing construction group, who some described as having a "free-wheeling, cowboy style" of management. (Porter saw the conflict as one "between those doing the building and those paying the bills.") After two days in close proximity, some communication began to occur. All differences were not resolved, but there was basic agreement on a new statement of mission—to deliver quality housing services to those in need—and an accompanying set of commitments to a customer orientation, to cost-effectiveness, and to creative and innovative solutions to housing problems. Finally, a statement of values for the organization was drafted and finalized (see Box 5.3).

BOX 5.3
British Columbia Housing Management Corporation
Defining a Vision for the Future—Our Values

Respect. An atmosphere of mutual tolerance and understanding is of critical importance to us. We believe in treating our clients and our colleagues with dignity and respect.

Communication. We value direct and open communication and encourage the sharing of information and ideas. We know that good internal communication shows in the quality of our service, and we are working together to make this a reality at all times.

Initiative. We encourage a positive, flexible attitude to getting the job done. We know that the real power to improve lies not in management directives, but in the initiative, drive, and imagination of each employee.

Recognition. We believe in recognizing the contributions of all, rewarding outstanding performance, and in celebrating special achievements.

Teamwork. We know that teamwork produces the best results.

Cost-Effectiveness. We believe in prudent, cost-conscious management.

Empowering Our People. We are committed to fostering innovation, and encouraging staff to develop their potential. We support our employees in developing the communication, leadership, and technical skills to fully participate in our organization with confidence and vigor.

The following Monday the new statements were circulated throughout the organization and supervisors called in to begin talking about them. For everyone to buy in, Leman felt that something more significant was necessary so he agreed to a second retreat, this one involving all 300 people in the organization. Simply to keep the offices open, the staff was divided into two groups, one which met Monday through Wednesday morning, the other Wednesday afternoon through Friday. In advance of these sessions, the original twenty-four were trained in group problem solving so they could act as facilitators during the retreat. Many of the sessions were conducted in small groups of ten or less, each with a facilitator from the original twenty-four.

Leman's predilection toward inclusion and equality ensured that everybody in the organization was present, which meant that in any particular group there might be a janitor with little proficiency in English, an architect with several graduate degrees, and one of the directors. As you might expect, employees resisted initially. Some upper level personnel thought the retreat was demeaning; some lead hands (supervisors) were uncomfortable sitting next to their branch chiefs. Despite the concerns, they stayed together, they had coffee and lunch breaks together, and they began to communicate.

The retreat was useful in several ways. First, it began the process of team-building, confirming the single vision that would guide the organization. Second, it opened new channels of communication, including communication among those in different areas of the organization and those at different levels. Third, it modeled a pattern of behavior that said, "We are a nonelitist organization. We want everyone to participate and to be involved." Of course, there was still plenty to work on.

At the end of the retreat sessions, each participant was given a questionnaire to take home, fill out, and return. The questionnaire indicated areas of continuing concern; this formed the agenda for the next round of activities. For example, the survey demonstrated once again that the managers, from the top on down, were not communicating very well with the staff. In response, an internal newsletter was begun, and training sessions focusing on communications were conducted. People from all levels were involved, and the message was one of "coaching employees" rather than "ordering people around." Similarly, concerns were expressed about the difficulty of moving up the ladder in the organization. In response, new programs were developed to give people experience in higher level positions for which they might later apply. During one manager's maternity leave, for example, a lower level employee was temporarily placed in the position; someone below filled that employee's position, and so on. All these people were able eventually to move to higher level positions in the organization.

The broad-based strategic planning activity Leman initiated created a mission and a set of values that have given new focus and guidance to those in the organization, and every effort is made to assure that they are really meaningful. Porter described the mission statement to me as "not just words on paper; it's the way we do business." As an example, she spoke of the recruiting process, in which new employees are selected based on a personality profile consistent with the mission and values of the organization. A potential employee might be asked to describe specific instances in their past experience where they had gone out of their way to help a customer. Or, to assess the potential employee's concern for the dignity and worth of individuals in the organization, the person might be asked what they would do if they encountered a situation in which derogatory remarks were made about a particular ethnic group.

Porter expresses a view shared by many other managers whom I talked with: "The employee of the 1990s is simply not the same as the employee of the 1950s. People just can't be ordered around and told what to do." But Porter adds an interesting twist to the argument, stating that the quality of an individual's work life *and* home life affects that person's contribution at work. Porter feels this is especially true with more and more women joining the workplace. "Giving orders may have been okay for men, who were able to go home and the wife had dinner on the table, but that's just not the world we live in." To accommodate some of the pressures of modern home life for both men and women, Porter introduced a flexible work schedule, extending daily hours and providing an extra day off every three weeks. Some executives objected to her logic, saying that the employees were lucky to have jobs and should adjust their lives to the demands of work. Porter insisted, however, that the work force has changed. Just to press a little, I asked how she could demonstrate increased quality or productivity. The answer was easy, she said: "Since the flexible schedule was introduced, sick leave has been reduced by over 50 percent, with major cost savings to the organization." Meanwhile, the organization continues its process of change, with Ian Leman's inclusive approach affecting so much of what the organization does.

STEVE HIGGINS, DIRECTOR, U.S. BUREAU OF ALCOHOL, TOBACCO, AND FIREARMS (ATF)

Steve Higgins has two newspaper clippings on the wall of his office. The first, from the *Washington Post*, November 13, 1981, is titled, "ATF Gets the Pink Slip." It reads in part, "After months of rumors, formal notices were sent out last night to field offices of the Bureau of ATF that the Treasury Department has decided to eliminate the agency." The other, from the *Cincinnati Inquirer*, carries a headline that says, "Proven Worth Keeps an Agency Alive Past Its Scheduled Execution." The article concludes, "Now apparently, the bureau will survive. But unlike other bureaus, its survival is not due to powerful and influential friends in high places. It survives because it does what all good agencies should do: it proves its worth through hard work."

When Steve Higgins became Director of the Bureau of Alcohol, Tobacco, and Firearms in 1982, the agency was in considerable trouble: An Alcohol, Tobacco, and Firearms executive was implicated in Watergate, the agency's leadership was fragmented, and the Reagan administration had tried to eliminate it. There were serious doubts about the agency's ability to survive. Moreover, tension between the two main functions of the bureau—tax compliance and law enforcement—was becoming increasingly destructive, as was the relationship between the administrative services and these two functions. The agency Higgins inherited was, as he told me, "in trauma."

Moving Alcohol, Tobacco, and Firearms from that point to the highly effective organization it is today required a great deal of skill and tenacity and an approach that, as we saw earlier, Higgins refers to as pragmatic incrementalism. Higgins began the changes in the agency with a three-day retreat for his top twelve executives. As these meetings began, Higgins didn't have a comprehensive plan or specific timetables for reforming the agency, nor was one produced during the retreat. Rather, consistent with the notion of pragmatic incrementalism, a vision was articulated, a direction was set, and a limited number of "first steps" were agreed on. Higgins built a framework in which lots of other small changes could meaningfully occur. He describes this approach carefully: "In my view, the best and most lasting way to change an organization is by being alert to the many small things that need to be changed and then changing them as quickly as circumstances allow."

The retreat and work done in the following three months produced a mission statement, a statement of management values, a set of management qualities, competencies, and expectations for those in the bureau, as well as a plan for managerial and supervisory training that would reinforce these values. The values selected were intended to transform Alcohol, Tobacco, and Firearms from a hierarchical and authoritarian chain-of-command organization to a highly participatory one valuing teamwork and innovation. These concepts are captured in a single statement that describes the organization: "A team of professionals who value and demonstrate a clear sense of mission, concern for people, supportive and cooperative attitudes, and openness to change and progress" (see Box 5.4). Merely stating the values, however, was not enough. In addition, the executives who were present made a commitment "not just to talk about and relay the values, expectations, and competencies, but also to model them through (their) own behavior and reinforce them whenever and wherever the opportunity presented itself.''

The new values of the organization are communicated in many ways, some formal and some informal. A key effort is the agency's training program for managers and supervisors, a training program directly tied to the organization's

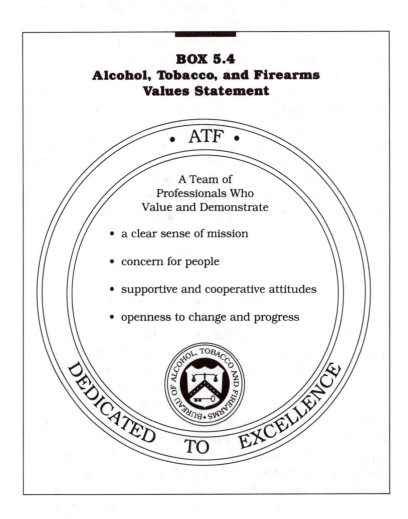

BOX 5.4
Alcohol, Tobacco, and Firearms
Values Statement

• ATF •

A Team of
Professionals Who
Value and Demonstrate

• a clear sense of mission

• concern for people

• supportive and cooperative attitudes

• openness to change and progress

DEDICATED TO EXCELLENCE

values. Through training sessions, managers and supervisors work to improve both their technical understanding of management (financial management, automation, and so forth) and their interpersonal skills (communications, motivation, and so forth). Significant attention is also paid to the management values of the agency. Each component of the values statement (such as "concern for people") is elaborated in terms of management qualities, management practices/expectations, and management competencies (see Box 5.5). These are emphasized in all the training sessions.

One early decision was not to hire outside consultants or even maintain an internal training staff to conduct the training. Instead, the courses were designed and staffed by other Alcohol, Tobacco, and Firearms managers and supervisors, including the top executives. Higgins himself attends the opening and closing of each basic management course, usually focusing his remarks on the values of the organization.

One interesting twist that has been added to these courses is an emphasis on team problem solving using real problems in Alcohol, Tobacco, and Firearms as case studies. After the program participants have worked on a particular problem, they present their recommendations to the top executives. This exercise not only models the sense of teamwork desired in the agency but provides specific recommendations for organizational improvements. For example, one group suggested conducting exit interviews with employees leaving Alcohol, Tobacco, and Firearms, a suggestion that was implemented and has provided another important feedback mechanism for top executives. To date, some 80 percent of the recommendations generated in this way have been accepted by top management.

Top executives also try to "listen" to the organization in other ways. As many as ten times a year the executives meet with managers and supervisors who are asked to comment on the continued appropriateness of the Alcohol, Tobacco, and Firearms values and on forces that are either helping to promote the values or getting in the way of their

BOX 5.5
ATF Management Values:
"Concern for People"

Management Practices/Expectations

You are expected to develop and maintain a managerial climate within your operation which encourages open communication, fairness, a consideration for the importance of subordinates, and an involvement by all who are affected by, or have a legitimate role in, the decision-making process. Mistakes of action should be seen as opportunities to grow and learn.

Management Competencies

- Mission goals in ATF
- Career counseling/ mentoring
- Self-development/ awareness
- Group problem solving
- Gaining understanding
- Providing constructive criticism while maintaining self-esteem
- Managing differences
- Client relations skills
- Skills to help people move in new directions

Management Qualities

- Seeks to understand subordinates (for example, strengths, weaknesses, ideas)
- Is flexible and adaptable when needed
- Is responsive to needs (of peers, other ATF organizations, subordinates)
- Demonstrates fairness (in pay, EEO, grades, discipline, advancement)
- Demonstrates open, honest communications

214

achievement. Another way that executives get direct feedback from employees is through formal surveys of the views of all employees or specifically those in supervisory positions or above. The results of both surveys are distributed to all employees and have been the basis for some specific changes, for example, offering more team-building activities.

Although the primary emphasis in the early years of change was on managers and supervisors, increasingly these people are involving nonsupervisory personnel in similar activities. These events have led to a great deal of attention to total career development, an openness on the part of top executives to strategies for improving the work and the careers of people in the organization from their first orientation to their exit interview. One initiative that Higgins views with special pride was initiated by the executive secretarial staff. This group worked hard, leading the division in developing new programs for clerical and secretarial people aimed at improved performance and improved career development.

I described Higgins's use of the term *pragmatic incrementalism* as a brilliant but probably unplanned insight, and indeed it was. But over time the phrase came to characterize much of the agency's approach to change. Two charts have been developed within Alcohol, Tobacco, and Firearms to illustrate the "one thing follows another" nature of organizational change. The first chart (see Box 5.6) illustrates the outcomes of various activities and commitments established at the original retreat. For example, executive role modeling might lead to other outcomes that in turn would be the basis for still further changes. The second chart (see Box 5.7) more specifically illustrates the chain reaction of events that actually occurred along a couple of paths between about 1983 and 1988. The point is that no one attending the original retreat envisioned a set of events or outcomes that would look like this—but the participants set in motion a process that eventually led to interesting and positive results.

Joe Coffee has participated in all aspects of the Alcohol, Tobacco, and Firearms change process and has commented

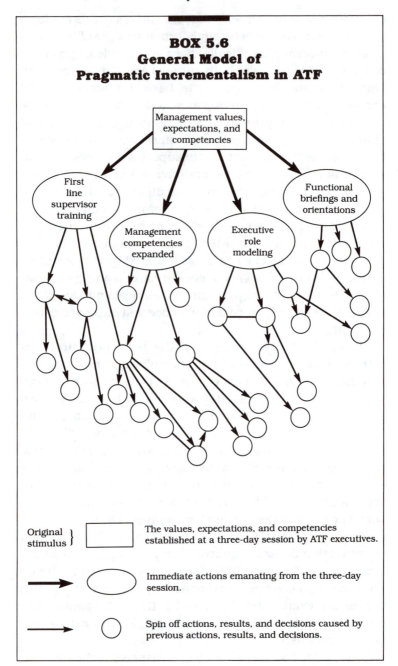

BOX 5.6
General Model of
Pragmatic Incrementalism in ATF

Management values, expectations, and competencies

First line supervisor training

Management competencies expanded

Executive role modeling

Functional briefings and orientations

Original stimulus } — The values, expectations, and competencies established at a three-day session by ATF executives.

— Immediate actions emanating from the three-day session.

— Spin off actions, results, and decisions caused by previous actions, results, and decisions.

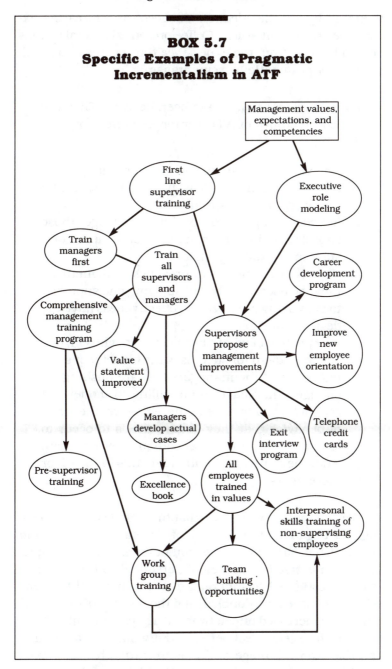

BOX 5.7
Specific Examples of Pragmatic
Incrementalism in ATF

thoughtfully on the Alcohol, Tobacco, and Firearms experience. In a recent article, Coffee presented several lessons he had learned from the experience that express very well the idea of pragmatic incrementalism:

> Four basic principles have been derived. They are the cornerstones of ATF's improvement effort. . . . They are:
>
> 1. Knowledge of management approaches has limited usefulness unless they can be applied by *managers* in real situations.
> 2. In order to apply any of this knowledge, those choosing to do so must have an accurate understanding of the organization.
> 3. Usually an array of approaches and methods must be used. Rarely will applying one approach to increasing organization effectiveness have the desired effect.
> 4. Irrespective of what approaches are chosen, one key ingredient for success is the tenacity or staying power of the managers that are pushing for change. They have to be willing to model and reinforce, in a hundred different ways, the kinds of behavior that they believe needs to occur to create the kind of organization they envision. And, they must be willing to do this for 5, 10, or more years.

Several indicators suggest that the change process Steve Higgins began in the Bureau of Alcohol, Tobacco, and Firearms has had some important outcomes. For example, even with a steady number of personnel, the number of cases investigated has increased, the number of firearms seized has more than doubled, and the number of explosives seized has increased fifteen times. Perhaps more important, those in the agency feel better about what they are doing, and the external image of the organization has improved considerably. And, remembering the history of the agency, it's significant that eliminating the bureau is no longer really an issue.

Clearly, the public manager who wishes to change an organization must develop a certain persistence, for change does not come easily in large organizations. On the other hand, change does occur.

CONCLUSION

As a strategy for organizational change, pragmatic incrementalism suggests that the public manager needs a clear vision but may not have a specific plan for getting there. Instead, the challenges and opportunities that arise every day must be responded to in a way that moves the organization in the right direction. In contrast to some theoretical views of the change process, the real world of public management rarely presents the option of designing a fully rational plan for changing an organization. Even if this were possible, the plan designed for one organization would most likely be inappropriate for any other. Events unfold too quickly, both within the organization and outside. Too many people and too many interests are involved. Information is limited and communication is haphazard at best. If these conditions were otherwise, public managers could plan the future of their organizations more rationally. They might even control their own destinies and those of others. But in today's world, that's simply not possible.

In any case, the idea of rationally planning an organization's future and exercising unilateral control in moving the organization in that direction doesn't make sense today. Public organizations are far too complex, the demands placed on them by elected officials, by citizens, and by clients are far too great, and the need for creativity and adaptability is so crucial that for anyone to pretend to the omniscience implied by the old notion of hierarchical control is ridiculous. What is needed instead is an approach to change that suggests a clear focus, but one that in turn opens it to the ideas of many different people throughout the organization who see all its activities. This kind of approach capitalizes on the creativity and adaptability of everyone in the group. The manager successful in bringing about change in this way must not merely be a visionary but someone fully involved in the organization—someone whose activity reflects not only a commitment to that vision but the understanding and flexibility to recognize that there are "many roads to the summit" and that the right road may change from day to day.

Let's be a little more concrete. As I have brought together the stories and experiences of many different managers, all considered by their peers to be models of contemporary public management, what has been most striking is the similarity of their approaches. Talking with managers from several different countries, I have found that many of the same ideas and approaches are being employed. Strikingly, these approaches are very much at odds with the standard patterns associated with bureaucratic organizations in the public sector. Although I have talked extensively here about shared leadership and empowerment, we all know managers in public organizations (and elsewhere) who are highly authoritarian, even tyrannical in their work. In my view, the more progressive managers discussed here are precursors of a new approach to managing public programs. This approach is not yet clearly understood, but it will significantly change the way we approach public organizations (and perhaps even private organizations) in the future.

A first element of this new approach is a commitment to values. The managers we have considered here may make changes in the structure of their organizations, but those changes are incidental. Unlike traditional managers who often seem preoccupied with structure, these contemporary managers are more concerned with changing the values of their organizations. Frequently, they approach this task by involving many others throughout the organization in articulating a new mission, a new set of values, or a new management philosophy. Not surprisingly, since we are talking about public agencies, in many cases, those values are centered around serving the public, either the clients or customers of the organization or the larger body politic. Parallel to these concerns are the frequently voiced concerns for improving the quality and productivity of public organizations.

Obviously, leadership is required to move any organization, but the type of leadership advocated and modeled by many of these very special public managers is quite novel. Rather than seeking to dominate others, these managers seek to involve them. Rather than seeking to control others, these managers seek to empower them. Rather than seeking to restrict others, these managers encourage others to be creative, even if it means taking risks. In their approach to leadership, these managers are moving far beyond the older hierarchical chain-of-command approach to organizational leadership. Their idea is that leadership must extend throughout the organization, that all must lead and all must be responsible for doing what they can to improve the organization.

Closely allied to this idea is the idea that people working in public organizations have a basic desire to do their work well and that their work can be improved through sharing ideas and obligations. Thus, these managers talk about the importance of teamwork and group interaction in problem solving. Working smarter means working together. They also talk about community, because they sense that persons who feel a sense of solidarity will work together more effectively and more responsibly. In part, they also acknowledge that the idea of community just feels right. Community is very much needed in society, and these managers recognize that need. They also intuitively recognize that, ethically, a sense of community is something that public organizations should model for the society as a whole.

What's so striking about these approaches, in addition to their being found so often among the most highly regarded public managers, is the way they all fit together. Without a sense of vision and direction, for example, the idea of shared leadership dissolves into anarchy. Conversely, without a concept of leadership truly and regularly shared, the vision of the person at the top of the organization remains distant and remote, unlikely to change much at all. The same kinds of connections appear elsewhere. The idea of customer service, if taken seriously, requires that those who serve customers be empowered to make decisions that enable them to serve. The idea of community suggests that life in these public organizations should not be manipulated from above, but that all should be free to participate in defining and redefining the basis of the community. And that closes the loop, or at least nearly so, for the act of redefining the community involves creating a new vision for the organization.

As we have seen previously and as the examples of pragmatic incrementalism demonstrate further, the concepts and approaches discussed in the three previous chapters are fully interdependent. It seems you just can't have one without the other. Within any particular organization, given its own peculiar mission, composition, or circumstances, the mix may be unique; but achieving some mix of these ideas is a recurring theme among the best public managers. They pursue many of the same ideas, and they pursue them in a similar manner—having a direction clearly in mind, then capitalizing on whatever opportunities time and chance provide.

I would certainly not say that changes such as these come easily in public organizations; they require tremendous dedication and hard work on the part of the managers involved. There can certainly be roadblocks along the way. In some cases, managers find it difficult to "sell" these new management values to elected officials schooled in more traditional management approaches. Especially when a proposed management improvement requires some investment in terms of new staff positions, funds for training and development, or support for an outside facilitator, elected officials may balk. Other barriers to change may come from within the organization, through middle managers concerned about their new roles or from staff not willing to assume greater responsibility for their own work.

Managers seeking major changes in their organizations also recognize the psychological demands of such efforts. In part, these pressures on managers arise from the fact that encouraging change in public organizations today requires some different skills from those required of managers in strictly hierarchical systems. Certainly the manager's ability to envision an appropriate future for the organization remains a part of the manager's work, yet coming up with that personal vision is much less important for many public managers than *evoking* a vision, drawing forth the very best possibilities that lie within the organization and involving many people in choosing and committing themselves to a new direction. In any case, the process of creating a vision of the organization's future requires the manager to be able to deal with complexity, uncertainty, and stress better than colleagues of previous generations. I have noted time and again the turbulent environment of modern public administration; to move successfully in that environment requires that the manager have the maturity and self-presence to deal with the peculiar pressures of contemporary public management.

Note that the issues here go beyond the traditional technical areas of knowledge required of managers, whether it be their knowledge of a particular substantive area (such as social welfare or transportation or criminal justice) or their knowledge of management itself. These issues even go beyond the traditional behavioral skills associated with public management: communications, motivation, and group dynamics. These more traditional areas of knowledge or behavioral skills are still extremely important, indeed absolutely essential to managerial success, but today's managers must be prepared psychologically to deal with the more contemporary pressures of complexity, uncertainty, and stress. Today's public manager must take risks and withstand the fear of failure. Today's public manager must release power and, through trust in his or her subordinates, be prepared to stand accountable. Today's public manager must face a highly uncertain future, yet have the confidence to move forward.

At the very basis of this psychological preparation for contemporary public management are issues of maturity, aspects of the human psyche deeply rooted in the capacity for self-reflection and self-esteem. These skills, it seems to me, are at the very heart of what enables the best of today's public managers to do their work and to do it so well. The sense of balance they reflect may be seen in many ways: through a lighthearted attitude, through a genuine concern for others, or through the capacity to juggle many things at once. Basically, they reflect the sense of personal security that comes from knowing where one stands and having the personal courage and integrity to do what one's commitment requires. That brings us to one final item.

We have seen how the best public managers pursue their efforts at organizational change and how these various efforts must inevitably fit together. But there is still one element to consider and, indeed, it is the glue that holds the whole puzzle together. Pervasive among the managers I talked with was a deep commitment to public service that manifests itself in many ways: a concern for serving others; a concern for democratic governance; and a concern for the highest standards of ethics and integrity, both personally and throughout their organizations. These commitments to public service run deep. Although some managers may move in and out of the public service, and some may even stray from their high ideals, overall these managers find an incredible sense of purpose and meaning in public service. Indeed, it is this same sense of purpose and meaning that these managers seek and very deeply appreciate among those within their organizations. In the next chapter, we turn to a consideration of the ethics of public service.

A Dedication to Public Service

Individuals throughout the organization understand and appreciate the special character of public service, especially the role of public organizations in the process of democratic governance. The manager insists that members of the organization maintain high ethical standards and encourages them to make their organization a model of integrity for similarly situated groups.

Throughout the preceding chapters, I have spoken often of the commitments and values of highly regarded public managers—commitments to service, to quality, and to change. But one overriding commitment comes through loud and clear in talking with the best public managers, and that is a commitment to public service. Many, if not most, of these outstanding public managers have had opportunities to work in the private sector, often at salaries considerably above what they make in government. Some spent part of their careers in the private sector but found that experience unfulfilling. There is something special that keeps drawing them back to the public service. Despite the fact that their salaries are lower, that the demands on their time (and the publicity given their activities) are greater, and that the "rules of the game"—rules that are both legal and ethical— are more strict, these managers are compelled to return to the public service.

The dedication of these managers to the idea of public service is not only striking in a personal sense but is pervasive in their attitude toward their work and toward their organizations. Indeed, it is absolutely central to the changes in management philosophy examined here. Some of the approaches to successful management practice we have explored here may seem merely to involve adoption of recently popular business practices, but where the very best public managers are concerned, such a view is not merely simplistic but incorrect. Although some in government may uncritically adopt ideas such as "a customer orientation" or "total quality management" just because they seem to have worked in business, these highly regarded public managers are far more careful in their application of ideas such as these. They know, for example, how much more complex the idea of "customer service" is when it is used in the public sector. They know that "empowerment," used in a government context, is an idea that goes to the heart of the governance process. Indeed, where the best public managers have adopted these ideas or any of the others considered here, they have not done so just because they wanted to copy something that had apparently worked in the private sector. Rather they found these ideas compelling *because the contemporary demands of public service made them so.*

This distinction may be subtle, but I think it has profound implications for the future of management reform in public organizations. It suggests that there are "right" reasons and "wrong" reasons for undertaking any particular management reform and that only those reforms undertaken for the right reasons will ultimately be successful.

Interestingly enough, that closely parallels what Michael Stahl of the U.S. Environmental Protection Agency wrote to me several years ago in response to a question about his advice for people considering a public service career:

> If you are considering a career in the public service, take the time to reflect on your motivation for entering the public service, because there are "right" reasons and "wrong" reasons. You are entering for the right reasons if you want to make a contribution to the solution of social problems, promote democratic values and ethical standards in using the powers of government, and if the concept of serving the public is a passion. You are entering for the wrong reasons if you are looking for public adulation and recognition for your accomplishments, seeking material or financial rewards as compensation for your hard work, or expecting to acquire levels of power and change the world according to your own plan. Those entering the public service for the wrong reasons will be bitterly disappointed. . . . Yet, for those whose passion is to contribute to the public good, government service can represent the single most satisfying way of translating your passion into ideas and events for improving the quality of life for scores of people.

These comments state most eloquently some of the enduring reasons people are drawn to public service. But, looking back, it now seems to me that they have meaning for those already in the public service. There are right reasons and wrong reasons for almost everything you do as a public servant, including those things you do as a manager. The revolutionary management approaches examined here, at least in their very best expressions, grow out of a passion for integrity in the public service, a concern for democratic governance, and a commitment to ethics in all areas, including management itself. However subtle the distinction between those efforts undertaken for the right reasons and those undertaken for the wrong reasons, the connection between the various management approaches we have already reviewed and one final commitment shared by the best public managers—a real dedication to public service—is worth exploring in more detail.

A CONCERN FOR INTEGRITY IN THE PUBLIC SERVICE

In talking about ethics and integrity, public managers from different countries wished to make clear the differences they thought existed in their different settings. Their point of view on this issue was interesting, for when we talked about other approaches and philosophies, parallels with the work of their counterparts inevitably arose. Mike Fogdon, for example, was surprised to find that an approach he had "invented" for the British Employment Service had been tried at almost exactly the same time by someone in Missouri . . . and someone in New South Wales . . . and so forth. The comparisons with respect to management practices, such as setting a mission and values, seeking improved service quality, promoting community within/cooperation without, and encouraging empowerment and shared leadership, are striking but understandable.

However, on the closely related issues of ethics and the public service, managers in different countries were more adamant. They felt that the history and political cultures of the different nations placed different pressures on public servants, whether in terms of public respect for those serving in government, in the relationship between elected and career officials, or in standards for ethical conduct. In some countries, ethics are seen as so endemic to the public service that little discussion is needed; in others, no topic is more current or popular. Indeed, there are differences in history and culture.

At the same time, similarities abound in the experiences of the most highly regarded public managers. The best public managers in all of the countries I visited share some basic concerns. For this reason, I will outline briefly some of the political and cultural forces that have recently affected the public service in each country, then try to identify some of the main ethical issues that these public managers face. What is critical to understand is that these questions, and the responses of the best public managers to them, while growing from different histories and different traditions, are fundamental to the public service and can't simply be dismissed in any discussion of improvements in the management of public organizations. Just as it is difficult to conceive of a strong public service or "customer" orientation without paying attention to devolving power in one's organization, it is difficult to think of any of the approaches discussed here being successful without attention to the ethics of public service. As I said before, a dedication to the public service is the glue that holds it all together. This dedication, however, has been severely tested in recent years.

THE ABUSE OF PUBLIC SERVICE

Over the past decade or more, one of the most common experiences of the public managers I talked with, as well as all others working in the public service, has been a fairly sustained attack on those in government. Public sentiment questioned the expansion of government that occurred through the sixties and seventies and, in turn, politicians of all political stripes have found it advantageous to denigrate the agencies of government, the "public bureaucracy." Although the nature of the assault varies from country to country, and from jurisdiction to jurisdiction within each country, in almost every case a common characteristic of the national mood is a strong feeling of doubt and resentment with respect to public organizations. Bureaucrat bashing, as it is often called, continues to be in vogue. Consequently, managers in the public sector have labored under very difficult conditions and dealt with work forces demoralized through no fault of their own.

These conditions are not completely unique to this decade, for questions concerning the trustworthiness and competence of the public service seem to arise in every generation, but overall the public service had been held in high regard in most of these countries until recently. Indeed, in some periods, the dignity and worth of public service have been expressed in glowing terms. In these times, no other pursuit has held as much respect as the pursuit of the public good. Certainly, the grand tradition of public service in the British Commonwealth was sustained over many years and in many different contexts, while in the United States, of course, one only need recall the familiar declaration of John F. Kennedy's inaugural address: "Ask not what your country can do for you; ask what you can do for your country." Those Americans who responded to this call, and those in other countries who similarly came forward, did so for the "right reasons," and they did so because they lived in a society and in a time that placed a high value on service to others.

Although the bright and passionate message of the early sixties may have dissipated, the long tradition of public service in each of these four countries has been sustained through the years and remains strong even today. Despite recent attacks on the agencies of government, many people still hear the call to service and respond. Although their expression of what I will call the "public service motive" may vary from a desire to help other people to wanting to make a difference to being on the cutting edge of positive change, these people have made a commitment to contribute in whatever way they can to build a better society and a better life for others. Public service, for them, is a compelling and rewarding vocation, a calling worthy of a lifetime.

For some people this commitment to public service remains abstract, even naive, but among the best public managers the idea of public service is both complex and profound. It undergirds everything they do. Issues of ethics and governance are not distant philosophical matters; they arise almost every day—in the response to an elected official seeking advice on a proposed policy, in a conversation with an employee uncertain about the proper way to conduct an investigation, and in those lonely moments when the manager contemplates whether to go along with a questionable instruction given by a "superior" or to object. In these and many other ways, public managers are placed daily in the position of resolving important dilemmas, and at the base of their resolution of such issues is their understanding of and commitment to the ethics of public service. That's as it should be. However, a question remains: How can such an understanding and commitment be sustained in a world that seems to constantly question the efficacy of the public service?

The attack on the public bureaucracy during the eighties was intense, perhaps most so in the United States. Presidents Carter and Reagan, for example, both ran "against the bureaucracy," holding government responsible for considerable ills and misdeeds. In some measure, their attacks were directed at the size of government and at specific policies they opposed, and, to that extent, their concerns were perhaps understandable. After all, government in the United States had grown tremendously in the 1960s and 1970s. Federal spending multiplied from $92.2 billion in 1960 to $576.7 billion in 1980 (in actual dollars). Government also expanded in scope with the passage of major civil rights legislation, new programs in employment and training, environmental protection, and workplace health and safety, to say nothing of Medicare, Medicaid, and a myriad of other programs. By the late seventies, even some supporters were wondering if government had grown too big and cost too much.

The problem for the public service came as these concerns about the growth of government and about specific policies spilled over into charges leveled against those who staffed the agencies of government themselves. Nowhere was this more evident than in the Reagan administration. Authors of a Heritage Foundation report, for example, assigned responsibility for "the mess in Washington" to "the bureaucrats," persons for whom political executives should feel "legitimate hostility." About the same time, Donald Devine, Director of the Office of Personnel Management, spoke of the relationship between political and career executives in a way that assigned civil servants the role of automatons. Finally, the Grace Commission, ostensibly created to ferret out waste and inefficiency in the bureaucracy, chose civil servants as a prime target. All these examples and many others suggest that a generalized discontent with the massive growth of government in the 1960s and 1970s was converted by the Reagan administration into an assault on the public service. It is no wonder that morale among federal government employees reached all time lows during this period.

The situation was aggravated, in my view, by the ethical insensitivity of the Reagan administration. Ideologically, of course, the Reagan administration supported the free market idea of expanding individual autonomy in the pursuit of self-interest. But, in contrast to previous conservative administrations with similar tendencies, the Reagan administration permitted, if not encouraged, these same values in government. "The result [was] an implication that the same standards that are appropriate in business are appropriate in government . . . , that whatever practices are acceptable in the private sector are acceptable in the public sector. For example, as long as one operates within the bounds of the law, the use of public office for personal gain is perfectly reasonable. In this view, the public service is merely the pursuit of private interest through the mechanisms of government." Obviously, such a posture strips the public service of its central ethical precept, the idea that there is a public interest that somehow transcends the pursuit of personal interests. It tears at the heart of the notion of public service.

Although the Bush administration failed to endorse strong efforts to restore a greater sense of pride and responsibility in the American public service, there were some encouraging signs. President Bush, of course, personally worked at various posts in the federal service during his career and seemed to respect those professionals in government with whom he interacted. Indeed, he consciously avoided criticism of the bureaucracy and even made several very laudatory statements about the work of government employees. Moreover, his top-level appointees tended to be far less ideological and far more pragmatic in their orientation toward the bureaucracy. The tension between the administration and the bureaucracy considerably lessened, though a reinvigoration of the public service has hardly become an item at the top of the political agenda.

The experience of American civil servants under the Reagan administration was closely paralleled by the experience of British civil servants under the Thatcher regime. Certainly, the Thatcher government was also highly ideological in its pursuit of conservative policies and, like the Reagan administration, conveyed from the outset that the civil service was a potential roadblock to its progress. One new minister, for example, commented that "unless we break out of the civil service straightjacket now we'll never get another chance to rule. It is beginning to look to many of us that civil servants are a breed who really believe they run the country and that all they've got to do is to knock a few ministers into shape." Moreover, consistent with her desire to reduce the role of the state in national affairs, Thatcher took direct aim at the size and constitution of the civil service, abolishing the Civil Service Department, severely cutting government, and even directly attacking particular civil servants with whom she disagreed. Not surprisingly, "the constant reiteration by the government of the theme that public service was not as praiseworthy and patriotic as high civil servants had supposed but a drag on the private sector and the true heroes of British society, the entrepreneurs, combined with Thatcher's criticism to produce a major morale problem in the civil service."

Thatcher's resignation in November of 1990 and her replacement by John Major signaled the end of the conservative ideological movement that had so dominated British politics in the 1980s. Although Major is also a Conservative, he, very much like George Bush, is far more pragmatic than ideological, more concerned with making things work than with forcing a clear and specific policy agenda. Consequently, Major seems more attentive to the advice and counsel of senior civil servants and is more willing to work with them to implement those policies that are adopted. Also, as a matter of personal style, Major seems more comfortable relying on senior civil servants as opposed to researchers from the "think tanks" or the universities. This is not to imply that Major will curtail management efforts such as the Next Steps initiative, which, though having roots in an antigovernment critique of the civil service, is now widely regarded as a hopeful experiment by those of many political stripes. Certainly, a more positive tone is now present, although it is likely that the British civil service will never again be quite the same.

Although the public service of both Australia and Canada did not escape the 1980s critique, at least in these countries it didn't carry quite the same ideological fervor as in the United States or Great Britain. In Australia, concerns were expressed early in the decade that the public service had become too independent, too entrenched, and largely unresponsive to the political will. At the same time, fiscal limitations raised questions about the efficiency and productivity of government. A set of initiatives resulted, loosely thrown together under the banner of "managerialism." These efforts have been heralded by some as bringing new order to the administrative mechanisms of government, but decried by others as heartless techniques for institutional control. As we saw in Chapter One, managerialism grows out of an economic perspective that gives priority to market factors rather than social and political concerns. Paradoxically, it urges increased managerial controls and a highly quantitative approach to managerial decision making at the same time that it urges privatization, corporatization, and market-driven management practices.

Although many have denounced the value (and more important the *values*) of this approach, there seems to be little question about its ascendence in Australian government. Michael Pusey of the University of New South Wales conducted a major study of the public service in Australia and concluded that the economic rationalist position is already becoming entrenched, especially in agencies such as Treasury and Finance. These and other agencies, according to Pusey, are now "dominated by New Right/economic rationalist ideology, including the belief that public policy must be cut loose of any criteria that is not economic and that 'the market,' rather than social needs, should determine what happens." As noted earlier, employing certain managerial strategies used in the private sector has been beneficial, but adopting the values of business, for example, making decisions based solely on economic criteria, is much more problematic. What becomes increasingly clear is that the choice of one or another approach to management carries with it important value implications. In any case, in Australia, in ways quite different from the United States and Great Britain, a business-oriented ideology created ethical dilemmas for the public service that have yet to be resolved (see Box 6.1).

The Canadian public service suffered many of the same attacks during the 1980s as we have seen elsewhere, however, there are at least some signs in Canada today that signify a renewed sense of confidence and support. Again, the story is much the same. Early in the decade, the public service was portrayed by many as elitist, isolated, and out of control. Political leaders sought to divert criticisms of their own policies to the government organizations that administered those policies—and did so with great success. Of course, there was considerable talk about reducing the size of the public sector. Consequently, two important surveys of Canadian public employees in 1986 and 1988 revealed a public service in considerable trouble. "Public servants were demoralized; they were losing confidence in their public-service leaders and in themselves; they were unsure of their roles and their futures; and they were overburdened with work, chafing under perceived unfair criticism, and lacking the tools and skills to face new challenges."

Several studies internal to the public service pointed to the need for management reform. In December 1989, Prime Minister Mulroney announced "Public Service 2000," a review that would eventually recommend a professional

---

BOX 6.1
Accountability at the Coalface

David Bunn, of the Public Sector Union, graphically described at the Brisbane public sector ethics conference the accountability quandary at the coalface.

Although public servants have to implement policy, "over the counter, on the phone, through bullet proof glass," citizens give you a very strong message that you work for them.

It doesn't help to say that a citizen has totally misunderstood the constitution, and that you are totally responsible to the minister and they can bugger off.

When relations go wrong with the client over the counter, very often the coalface workers can't fob off the client with a letter of acknowledgement, saying that in due course a longer letter will arrive.

These people can wait to sort you out after work. They can follow you home. They can find your home phone number and make threatening calls to you and your family. There are social security workers by the dozen that have had this experience.

Perhaps you should say to the client that the minister is pretty concerned about the take-up rate of the program which is spinning out of control. My duty is to withhold information to prevent you from knowing about your entitlements. A senior bureaucrat in Finance actually said this to me. This is the kind of world we now inhabit.

Source: "Dilemmas of Ethics," *Directions in Government* (October 1990), p. 59.

---

public service that would encourage a service orientation, allow for flexibility, and attract highly competent professionals to the work of government. Many groups external to the government were involved in the project, but it was led from within the government so that those involved would have a significant stake in its recommendations. Working through ten task forces, the project produced a long list of recommendations, which, if implemented, would change many government structures and practices and establish a strong service culture and a people-oriented approach to public management. "In essence, the task forces called for decentralization with accountability, and a management philosophy based on service to the public and to government, a reiteration and up-dating of public service values, and a major emphasis on people—both clients and employees." The government has now committed itself to a number of these reforms, and hopes of reinvigorating the Canadian public service seem high.

In sum, the public service in Australia, Canada, Great Britain, and the United States endured a variety of attacks during the 1980s. Concerns about the size and scope of government, questions about specific policy initiatives, and doubts about the responsiveness of the bureaucracy to political leadership combined with an especially ideological conservatism to call the notion of public service into question. I should, of course, be clear that managerial reform in public organizations was very much needed during this period, especially efforts to combat the extension of hierarchy and regulation. Indeed, public servants themselves were at the forefront of such activities. But, by giving precedence to economic rather than social and political criteria for public decision making, conservative political leaders in the 1980s, unlike their conservative predecessors, went far beyond the reform of management to encourage a redefinition of the ethics of the public service. In this view, the notion of a public interest was no longer central; there were only private interests, some expressed by government, others expressed by business. By calling into question the moral basis of the public service, critics of the public bureaucracy not only caused severe morale problems but struck at the core of an ethical public service.

PROMOTING ETHICS AND INTEGRITY

What is most important is that, despite these problems, a dedication to the public service has remained an important idea among highly regarded public managers. Although sustained attacks plagued the public service through the eighties, and implicit and explicit efforts to substitute an ethics of private interest for an ethics of public interest were in evidence, the best public managers have held strong in their commitment to public service. Indeed, they have been increasingly sensitive to and active in promoting ethical behavior within their organizations. As we now move through the early nineties, the ethics of public service are not in retreat but, bolstered by the dedicated actions of some very talented public managers, are experiencing a resurgence.

Obviously, the new interest in ethics resulted partly in response to such dramatic public events as allegations of misconduct in Queensland and Western Australia, the Sinclair Stevens and Patricia Starr cases in Canada, the Westland affair in Great Britain, and, of course, the Watergate and Iran-Contra scandals in the United States. A set of *Time* magazine cover stories in 1987 asked the question, "What Ever Happened to Ethics?" The articles commented on ethical dilemmas in business, education, and even religion, but gave special attention to those in government. (Included were the pictures of some hundred Reagan administration officials against whom ethics complaints had been lodged; the fact that almost all of these officials were political appointees rather than career civil servants was probably lost on most people.) In one article, Sissela Bok of Brandeis University argued that moral leadership should come first from those in public office. "Aristotle said that people in government exercise a teaching function. Among other things, we see what they do and think and that is how we should act. Unfortunately, when they do things that are underhanded or dishonest, that teaches too."

Public events have triggered the new interest in ethics, but that interest has also come about because many public managers have recognized the ethical dimension of the attack on the public service and have concluded, quite correctly, that a proper defense of the public service must somehow connect ethics and professionalism. Dick Humphry of the Premier's Department in New South Wales put it succinctly in a recent letter: "I am actively promoting a greater concentration on ethics in relation to professional relationships." Sir Robin Butler, Head of the Home Civil Service, elaborated on the concept of professionalism *in value terms:* "We care about doing our jobs well; we distill our experience into skills and expertise; we work to clearly stated values of service, which are sustained by example and by peer pressures within the profession; and we nurture these skills, expertise and values in those coming along after us." The best public managers know that trust and confidence in the public service will be restored only if the public is convinced that those in public office, whether elected officials or career public servants, seek the public interest (not merely their own) and that they do so with skill and responsibility.

The best public managers are seeking to integrate a concern for ethics into the management of their organizations in a number of ways. Some of their efforts simply try to assure high standards of morality—preventing lying, cheating, or stealing—while others are more directly connected to the special values of public service. Obviously, a number of legal controls bound the work of those in public organizations, and in many agencies, there are offices to investigate violations of these rules. For example, an inspector general's investigation in the U.S. Department of Agriculture disclosed a California couple illegally redeeming food stamps—over $1.8 million worth. Similarly, an audit revealed that more than 75 percent of the vendors for the Women, Infants, and Food (WIC) program were overcharging the government.

Audits and other forms of investigations deal mainly with the "thou shalt nots" of ethics, especially those found in legislation or in internally developed rules and procedures. The best public managers, however, seem to go beyond such regulations to encourage individuals throughout the organization to do those things that are consistent with high standards of service and responsibility. These ideas have been stated in a variety of ways including "codes of ethics" adopted by major public administration organizations such as the American Society for Public Administration or the International City Management Association, some of which have developed enforcement mechanisms to assure that members behave in a manner consistent with their code. Although not a code per se, one well-crafted statement of ethical principles for the public service was developed by the Josephson Institute for the Advancement of Ethics:

I. PUBLIC OFFICE AS A PUBLIC TRUST—Public servants should treat their office as a public trust, only using the powers and resources of public office to advance public interests, and not to attain personal benefits or pursue any other private interest incompatible with the public good.

II. PRINCIPLE OF INDEPENDENT OBJECTIVE JUDGMENT—Public servants should employ independent objective judgment in performing their duties, deciding all matters on the merits, free from avoidable conflicts of interest and both real and apparent improper influences.

III. PRINCIPLE OF ACCOUNTABILITY—Public servants should assure that government is conducted openly, efficiently, equitably and honorably in a manner that permits the citizenry to make informed judgments and hold government officials accountable.

IV. PRINCIPLE OF DEMOCRATIC LEADERSHIP— Public servants should honor and respect the

principles and spirit of representative democracy
and set a positive example of good citizenship by
scrupulously observing the letter and spirit of all
laws and rules.

V. PRINCIPLE OF RESPECTABILITY AND FIT-
NESS FOR PUBLIC OFFICE—Public servants
should safeguard public confidence in the integrity of government by being honest, fair, caring
and respectful and by avoiding conduct creating
the appearance of impropriety or which is otherwise unbefitting a public official.

General principles such as these may be helpful, but
they must be placed in the context of a specific organization. The organizational culture must be one that is attentive to ethical concerns as well as to operational ones. As
we have seen, one way public managers have sought to
change their organizational culture is through development
of statements of values or philosophies, and there are clear
references to ethical issues in many such statements. The
top management team of the Missouri Office of Administration, for example, commented on their organization's role
in "assuring the accountability of government operations"
and committed themselves to "take seriously the special
responsibility that the concept of public service implies."
Similarly, the corporate values statement of the City of
Morgan Hill has, as its first item, "Integrity and fairness are
basic to the accomplishment of the city's mission." Other
organizations have included more specific ethical commitments. Members of the Public Works Department of New
South Wales state, "We implement our programs and projects in a socially and environmentally responsible manner."
Similarly, the British Columbia Housing Management Corporation staff expressed its commitment to "environmental ethics."

Promoting ethical values in a statement of values, as well
as more operational values such as service quality, is a
helpful beginning, but as we have seen, all the values of the
organization need constant attention and reinforcement.

Kathryn G. Denhardt, author of *The Ethics of Public Service*, has written that "managing ethics involves more than making public statements espousing a particular set of values and more than selecting employees with good moral character. Managing ethics also involves careful analysis of the organizational culture, working to develop a cultural environment that places high value on ethical integrity and developing policies and procedures and systems that enable organization members to act with ethical integrity." Unfortunately, most public organizations have not undertaken active efforts to promote ethical behavior, but again, the work of some highly regarded public managers stands out.

Stephen Bonczek, City Manager of Largo, Florida, has been especially attentive to establishing a positive ethical climate in his organization. When Bonczek came to Largo, he spent time getting acquainted with the city and its employees. He found a lot of confusion about the direction of the organization and the values on which it stood. In an effort to clarify the city's direction, Bonczek conducted several early sessions with the executive staff. In these discussions, ethical issues surfaced and were discussed. An employee survey on ethical issues sparked continued dialogue and persuaded top management to develop new programs for communicating the values of the organization to the city's employees and to the public. After Bonczek grasped "the extraordinary power" of discussing ethics and values so openly, there was no turning back. Among other things, he developed and now recommends the following approaches:

- *Making ethics a part of employee orientation and training programs.* In Largo, a promotional video both explains the workings of city government and presents the vision, mission, and values of the organization. Subsequent training . . . increases awareness of the principles that are the foundation of our ethical system.
- *Include ethics in the performance evaluations and regular feedback provided to employees.* The

Largo performance evaluation system has a general required standard, as the following: Ethics, Integrity, and Organization Commitment: Performing all actions in accordance with pertinent laws, rules, and regulations. Setting a good example in situations where discretion is required. Demonstrating commitment to the organization's mission, goals, and values.

- *Publicizing ethical dilemmas and the organization's perceptions of them.* Maintaining open communication with employees on ethics issues and an agreement on how the organization perceives the situation will increase awareness and sensitivity.
- *Reviewing management practices in different parts of the organization* to help identify existing or potential ethics problems. Constant attention on how the administration is managing service areas will reduce the opportunity for ethical dilemmas to occur.
- *Developing a code of ethics.* This action includes not only enforcing the code when violations occur but also continually communicating its meaning and updating its content as new concerns develop.
- *To create an ethical environment, the actions of top officials must be consistent with their expectations for employee conduct.* Leadership by example is an effective tool to establish an ethical perspective among members of the organization.

Bonczek shared with me several lessons he had learned from these activities. First, bringing ethical issues out into the open and then building a consensus around values is very hard work. Bonczek called it "the hardest thing I've ever done," but since he considers ethical issues "the essence of public service," it's worth the effort. Bonczek reminded me that the stakes are high in the area of ethics—ethical judgments can cost people their honor and integrity, to say nothing of their jobs. It's serious business. Second, despite careful efforts to assure an ethical environment, ethical problems can and will occur. However, when those problems are handled in a prompt and open manner, their resolution provides a model for future ethical behaviors. Third, publicly discussing ethics and values causes the manager as well as the organization to spend considerable time reflecting on their own beliefs and values. Beyond the question of figuring out, then "modeling" the right behaviors, the manager needs to demonstrate congruence between his or her personal and professional ethics. Bonczek is pleased when people discover that "he really does believe this stuff!" The best public managers take a concern for the ethics of public service quite seriously and find that concern not peripheral but absolutely essential to the management of public organizations.

A CONCERN FOR
DEMOCRATIC GOVERNANCE

One particularly thorny set of ethical concerns facing those in the public service centers on the manager's role in the governance process, especially the manager's approach to working with political leaders to develop public policies. Again, although political cultures and traditions differ, some of the basic issues for managers are much the same. For instance, public managers constantly wrestle with the question of the proper relationship between elected and career officials. They recognize that the information and expertise they possess is important in the development of policy, but also that issues of democratic accountability must always be addressed. And they understand that their responsiveness to political leaders and to citizens directly may sometimes produce conflict, causing real difficulties. Balancing these issues is a difficult but significant part of their work.

The managers I talked with felt that important differences exist in the various countries; indeed, some asked me to be sure to discuss these differences. Yet I couldn't shake the feeling that in this area, as in so many others, these public managers still shared many common concerns. Let's start with the obvious differences, then move to the more subtle but perhaps more telling similarities. Certainly, the Australian, Canadian, and British approaches to civil service share an important heritage, and for that reason bear many similarities. (However, scholars and practitioners in each of the countries are always eager to point out the subtle differences. More than one Australian pundit has called the somewhat more executive-oriented Australian system "Washminster" rather than "Westminster.") In each of these countries, the civil service is seen as a neutral, professional body accountable to ministers, to parliament, and, through the parliament, to the people (see Box 6.2). The permanent civil service is recruited based on technical merit, and for the most part, its members presume that they will progress through the ranks over a period of years to higher posts.

By tradition, the senior civil service seeks both to advise ministers on the development of policy and to manage implementation of those policies through the executive agencies of government. In their policy role, according to Sir Robert Armstrong, at the time head of the Home Civil Service, "It is the duty of the civil servant(s) to make available to the Minister all the information and experience at his or her disposal which may have a bearing on the policy decisions to which the Minister is committed or which he is preparing to make, and to give the Minister honest and impartial advice, without fear or favour, and whether the advice accords with the Minister's view or not." Although the civil service is considered nonpartisan in the electoral sense, it is presumed to be strongly partisan in behalf of the policies of whatever government has been chosen by the people. As one scholar phrases it, "The professional skill of the senior bureaucrat in Britain lies in being able to perform these functions for any duly constituted government; their professional skill lies in not being politically chaster but in being sufficiently promiscuous to accommodate to changes in the party in power."

What is so interesting is that this traditional role changed significantly in Great Britain in the 1980s, and did so in ways similar to developments in other countries. Some changes had to do with the structure of the career service, others had to do with the relationship between senior executives and ministers. First, there were moves to bring "outsiders" into the civil service at senior managerial levels,

---

BOX 6.2
The Ethic of the Profession

Even if the Cabinet Office did put something on paper . . . on the duties and responsibilities of civil servants . . . the key element would not be that piece of paper. It would be the genetic code of professional expectations transmitted from one generation to another. . . . It's now and always will be more of a personal than a paper phenomenon.

It's now incumbent on me to tell you what I conceive that genetic code to be. Let me rattle off a list in which every item matters and contributes to a sum much greater than its parts.

- *Probity.* We have, by any test, a remarkably incorruptible Civil Service. An honest Civil Service, in which department tills are hand-free zones, is a pearl of great price. Here it's taken for granted. If it could no longer be taken for granted the country would be impoverished in a moral as well as a financial sense.
- *Care for evidence.* The Civil Service is an evidence-driven profession. This can be very inconvenient because politics isn't.
- *A respect for reason.* A civil servant cannot believe political will is all, because politics is the art of mobilising prejudice. Reason is the enemy of prejudice.
- *A willingness to speak truth to power.* If a civil servant can't tell the powerful minister he or she is plumb wrong and why, nobody can. That's part of what you're paid for; that's why you have what amounts to tenure; even though in the end you have to do what the minister says.

---

either to provide ideological consistency or simply to employ better managers. For example, the idea of fixed term contracts, which was examined earlier, flew in the face of continued employment and career progression over time. Second, there were challenges to the notion that civil servants hold allegiance only to ministers and should not act on any independent judgment of their own. Several cases in

- *A capacity not just to live with the consequences of what you believe to be a mistaken course, but to pursue it energetically.* This, however, is the bit of the job Derek Morrell [a senior Home Office Official] found most difficult. "I find it yearly more difficult to reconcile personal integrity with a view of my role which requires the deliberate suppression of part of what I am. It is this tension, and not overwork, which brings me regularly to the point where I am ready to contemplate leaving a service which I care about very deeply."
- *An appreciation of the wider public interest.* This is very difficult. It will always be a dilemma for two reasons: one's definition of the public interest tends to coincide with one's personal views of what is right and proper; and what do you do if the minister acts in a contrary fashion? He or she is elected, after all, and you are only appointed.
- *An awareness at all times of other people's life chances.* Inefficiency in the delivery of benefits which are an individual citizen's entitlement can, at best, be a matter of personal distress to the person deprived and, at worst, a matter of life and death.
- *Equity and fairness.* This has been of great advantage to Britain. It's best looked at in terms of the "pensioner in Orkney" or the "unemployed and angry teenager in Skelmersdale" tests—the requirement being that however remote or "difficult" the recipient of services might be they have the same entitlement to careful, reliable individual treatment as the conveniently located and the personally charming.

Source: Edited from a lecture by Peter Hennessy, historian and journalist. Peter Hennessy, "The Ethic of the Profession," *The Bulletin* (July 1989), pp. 102–105.

which civil servants released information they felt was important to the nation, though damaging to their ministers, were upheld in court. One Canadian official stated the ethical principle in this way: "Surely our responsibility to Canada is greater than any duty we owe to our political masters of the day. We have standards of professional integrity to maintain and a moral position to uphold. The glib, cynical retort, 'Well, you can always resign,' is hopelessly inadequate." Third, there were several efforts to create sources of policy advice other than the civil service, for example, through larger Prime Minister staffs, through the use of independent think tanks or university advisors, or through ministerial consultants. As we have already seen, the use of such groups has varied depending on the particular head of government.

Efforts to supplant the policy role of public servants with an increased emphasis on management were perhaps most significant. The British Next Steps program, for example, suggested that the policy role of top civil servants ill-prepared them to manage the day-to-day affairs of their agencies. Creation of executive agencies was an effort to carve out a much more distinct managerial role. Similarly, in Australia, the managerialist movement represented not only an effort to rely on economic criteria for management decisions but also an effort to give a clearer focus to managerial concerns. At the same time, there were efforts to assert the policy role of ministers, to make the bureaucracy more responsive to political rule. Presumably, managers (as opposed to administrators) would be less tied to particular policy positions and would be more comfortable pursuing whatever political directions their ministers issued.

Similar patterns were developing in the United States. Obviously, in their relation to the executive and the legislature, American civil servants differ from those in Australia, Canada, and Great Britain. At the federal level, senior civil servants report to presidentially appointed agency heads at the cabinet and sub-cabinet level, and, through them, to the president. (At the state and local level the situation is similar, with the exceptions noted below.) The relationship of career officials to the legislative branch, however, is considerably more confused, with few direct reporting relationships but many informal ones that sometimes become quite strong. Indeed, some have described an ongoing contest between the executive, as represented in the presidency, and the legislature, as represented in Congress, for control and supervision of the public bureaucracy.

Despite these differences, in other areas similarities with civil service systems in other countries are readily apparent. For the most part, the civil service is staffed on the basis of merit, and there are prohibitions against political (party) intrusions into the bureaucracy. Although considerably greater possibilities for lateral entry into the public service exist in the United States, a significant portion of American public servants comes into the service at an early age and continues through the course of a career. Like their counterparts in other countries, American public managers, especially those at the top levels, provide advice to political leaders, both in the executive and legislative branches, and at the same time they are expected to manage their organizations efficiently and responsibly.

Perhaps the most interesting and most rapidly evolving aspect of the senior civil servant's role has to do with the development of public policy. For most public servants, the interaction of the top *career* official and a supervisory appointed *political* official is key. This relationship seems to be most comparable to that between the minister and the permanent secretary, deputy minister, departmental secretary, chief administrator, or other civil servant. As elsewhere, early concepts in the United States suggested a distinction between policy and administration—that political leaders should decide issues of policy, and appointed executives should implement those policies through their management of public agencies. If that dichotomy were ever really workable, even in theory, it soon proved quite difficult to sustain in practice. Administrators became experts in their policy fields, knowing as much or more about particular topics as elected political leaders. Their advice became highly valued, and their influence in policy deliberations became significant. In some cases, agency personnel even built political support for their particular views and influenced the policy process in a way rarely seen in the other countries I have discussed.

Over the past couple of decades, the relationship between politically appointed and career officials has changed substantially. During the late 1970s and the early 1980s, newly elected officials expressed serious concerns about whether these career officials would use their expertise to support or to thwart the policy goals of the new administration. At the same time, those suspicious of government generally indicated their concerns about the technical competence of career officials, specifically questioning the ability of these officials to manage public programs effectively. Consequently, efforts were made to exert greater political control over the policy agenda—efforts paralleled by a new emphasis on the managerial skills of top executives. President Nixon quite openly appointed people to executive posts based on partisan considerations rather than their policy expertise, then tried to centralize control in the White House. President Carter sought to institutionalize presidential control of the highest appointed officials (while maintaining the merit principle for most civil service positions) through the passage of the Civil Service Reform Act of 1978. President Reagan continued the politicization of the public bureaucracy by appointing extreme conservative ideologues to major administrative posts and by strengthening the role of central agencies (such as the Office of Management and Budget) in monitoring the bureaucracy "from the outside." As we have noted, the Bush administration continued many of these trends, though basing appointments more frequently on criteria of loyalty and managerial ability than ideological purity.

The challenges to the public service have been both managerial and political. There is no question that the best public managers have responded extraordinarily well to the challenges of improving the quality and productivity of their agencies; indeed, these managers have been most effective in moving their organizations in the right direction. In many different cases and in many different places, these managers have gone beyond expectations. Repeatedly, they have broken the restrictive hold of bureaucratic systems and created new ways of organizing that stand in significant contrast to the traditional approach to public administration. They have revolutionized the practice of public management.

Significantly, they have not given in to the narrow, technical view of organizations suggested by those who see government as just another business. Rather, a high degree of professionalism and integrity has marked their work. The idea of being involved in the process of democratic governance has remained paramount. The best public managers —today, as before—are deeply involved in the policy process. There is no question but that top career officials have substantial expertise in their various policy areas and that their advice continues to be of great value to their political "superiors." Despite the protests of certain politicians, there was absolutely nothing in my conversations with public managers to suggest a desire on their part to *control* the policy process or to impose their views on others, whether politically appointed executives, ministers, or others. Indeed, these managers exhibited a considerable degree of self-restraint in even proposing policy alternatives.

There are, however, at least three reasons these managers occasionally feel an obligation—indeed, an ethical obligation—to present their own views. First, they recognize that the expertise they have developed over the years could improve the quality of public decisions. That being the case, they sometimes feel obligated to voice their concerns. Second, many feel uncomfortable being asked to implement a program they know would damage their clients. "How," one asked, "can you implement a program you know will lead to the death of more homeless infants?" Third, and here only rarely, some managers feel that their understanding of the public interest may be better informed than that of political leaders. When that is the case, their concern for democratic decisions consistent with the public interest may compel them to take a stand. Doing so is not without great pain, for it represents a significant departure from the traditional position—even when it is expressed cynically as in this statement attributed to Lord Vansittart: "The soul of our service is the loyalty with which we execute ordained error."

Most of these managers feel that the new emphasis on effective management, which they not only agree with but applaud because it helps them to do better what they have wanted to do all along, should not exclude an important role in the policy process. Mike Fogdon, for example, argued that the Next Steps program should not be interpreted as once again separating policy and administration, as it might appear on the surface. Rather, in areas such as the Employment Service where there are substantial issues of policy debate, the chief executive should continue to feel comfortable in bringing forward policy suggestions to ministers. For this reason, Fogdon was able to have language to that effect included in his framework document.

A LOCAL GOVERNMENT ILLUSTRATION

I have always found the relationship between American city managers and their elected city councils fascinating because that relationship illustrates so many important issues that arise on the edge between politics (or policy) and administration. It's almost a paradigmatic illustration for all the managers I talked with. Early in this century, the council-manager form of government was conceived as a way to isolate the professional administration of local government from the potentially corrupting influences of politics. The idea was simply that the elected city council would deal with political issues, including deciding matters of public policy, and that a politically neutral city manager would carry out or implement the policies decided upon. In theory, that sounded fine, but in practice it soon became apparent that the line separating policy and administration was not always clear. From time to time, city council members would want to "micro-manage," that is, to involve themselves in the details of administration. On the other hand, city managers (and their staffs) would develop considerable policy expertise, even clear opinions on matters of policy, and feel obligated to bring those views forward. Because of these developments, the code of ethics of the International City Management Association now contains several carefully worded statements about the relationship between the contemporary city manager and the council. For example, the code emphasizes the manager's dedication to "effective and democratic local government *by responsible elected officials*" (emphasis added). On the other hand, recognizing the manager's policy role, the code suggests that managers "submit policy proposals to elected officials; provide them with facts and advice on matters of policy as a basis for making decisions and setting community goals; and uphold and implement municipal policies adopted by elected officials."

Although today's orthodoxy in terms of the manager's role goes considerably beyond what was believed earlier, in practice city managers are not only deeply involved in the policy process (and even the political process) but are becoming more so, and they are becoming much less defensive about their policy role. Phil Penland, City Manager of Altamonte Springs, Florida, was straightforward about his role in policy formation during a recent discussion: "I'm sorry folks," he said, "but I make policy. I make policy every day. That's just what I do."

A part of the city manager's policy role now involves brokering the interests of various segments of the community, both public and private. Such a role puts the manager out front in settling disputes or negotiating various types of partnerships, then bringing the results back to the council. Some managers have even taken this approach to representing certain constituencies within the community before the council. One manager revealed to me that he sees part of his job as being to represent those groups and neighborhoods in the community that are not otherwise represented in the political process. Obviously, this view is a far cry from the traditional separation of politics and administration.

Many managers feel that circumstances around them have created a situation in which they must take a much more proactive role if their cities are to deal successfully with their problems. Council members may be unwilling to stick their necks out on difficult issues—some fearing retribution from the voters, others simply being averse to risk generally. Alan Ehrenhalt, writing in *The United States of Ambition,* suggests that today's political leaders are a far more entrepreneurial breed than their predecessors, running for office based on personal whim or ambition rather than based on previous involvements or a commitment to service. Political leaders of this sort would be expected to be more attentive to "following the opinion polls" rather than taking leadership on sensitive public issues. On the other hand, as Phil Penland told me, "Someone's got to get out in front and take some risks, or the city will be hurt. In lots of situations, it seems like the manager is the only one who can or will do that. For some managers, that is going to mean changing cities pretty often, but somebody's got to take the risks or our cities just won't survive."

MECHANISMS OF ACCOUNTABILITY

For city managers and, indeed, for public managers at all levels, playing such a significant role in the process of democratic governance involves difficult ethical and political issues. In an earlier and simpler time, public administrators were held accountable to the citizens by virtue of their reporting to elected officials. Having public managers assume a more proactive stance with respect to public policy issues, however, raises additional questions about accountability. Obviously, these managers continue to report to elected officials, but is that enough? At least two other devices for assuring that public managers act in the public interest present themselves: public participation and a commitment to the public interest.

I discussed public participation earlier in connection with customer service, the idea being that a strong public service orientation might lead to something more than cosmetic changes in the way organizations approach their own clients as well as the citizenry generally. Participation, however, also has an ethical edge, providing a more direct way for citizens to get closer to the public manager and for the manager to be more responsive to the public. There are many obvious historic examples of public participation, among them open hearings, advisory boards or steering committees, and public opinion polls, but some of the most interesting recent experiences have been British efforts to create and empower area committees, development corporations, tenants' management groups, and local school governing bodies. Michael Clarke of the Local Government Management Board told me that "the very best local government managers are sensitive to the issue of public participation, but I have to admit there's a great iceberg under the water. I think we're still struggling with what participation ultimately is and . . . that the delivery of many public services only makes sense when seen as a partnership between the provider on one hand and the citizen at large on the other."

Clarke's view is that direct participation is helpful in many of the areas local authorities deal with, but he recognizes a number of stumbling blocks along the way. He attributes some of the difficulty to the assumption by many elected political officers that "the ballot box endows the holder of political office with a comprehensive feel for and contact with the people he or she represents. That makes it difficult for . . . a councillor to accept that alternative routes to participation are legitimate or at all necessary." In addition, both the political and administrative cultures in Great Britain seem to provide inhibitions or constraints that make it difficult for the public to play a part. Clarke suggests that those in public agencies look carefully at what they are doing toward facilitating more effective participation, for ultimately it's up to the public manager to make participation work.

Certainly, participation provides one avenue for assuring the responsiveness of the public manager to the citizenry, but the manager's own commitment to public values provides another. While we will discuss this issue in greater detail in the following chapter, for now I will simply note that public managers who commit themselves to the ethics of public service see their work as involving a public trust. Their deeply held professional values require that they be attentive to the public interest (even when the public isn't interested!). This means that when they make decisions about public policies or even about management practices they must take into account the views of citizens and stakeholders; adequate and effective communication is essential. A sense of professional pride and responsibility, including a commitment to serving the public, complements the more structural mechanisms for accountability such as reporting to elected officials. To the extent such a view is held by public managers—whether as a result of their personal values, professional socialization, or work experiences—the public interest will be better served. Obviously, encouraging rather than disparaging the public service pays dividends in terms of democratic accountability, something political leaders around the world would be well-advised to remember.

John Uhr of the Australian National University has elaborated this point eloquently in his discussion of the following three propositions:

> Firstly: public service ethics is really about the political morality of public officials, about how they exercise their power in an office of public trust. Ethics concerns the values which inform the decision-making process, and how officials use and justify their important discretionary powers.
>
> Secondly: public service is intended to serve the public interest, so that public servants must exercise their own political judgements on how best to give effect to public policy. Public servants are partners in government, subordinate but essential colleagues to public officials in the three branches of

government—legislative, executive and judiciary. The public service is not just the play thing of the government of the day, but is instead the common administrative link uniting all their public policy authorities.

Thirdly: public service ethics turn on the quality of public service professionalism. Public trust in the career service of merit depends upon public appreciation of the integrity and impartiality of the service.

Uhr's commentary suggests a connection to the questions raised in the first part of this chapter concerning the image and integrity of the public service. They suggest that only a thoroughly ethical public service will gain and maintain the confidence of the public.

A CONCERN FOR ETHICS IN ALL AREAS, EVEN MANAGEMENT

Public managers operate in a complex world of values, values that are managerial, political, and ethical. As I said before, the best public managers seem to recognize the pervasiveness and importance of being attentive to public service values in all that they do. Consequently, when these managers introduce changes in their organizations, they don't merely ask whether this change or that will be more efficient or even whether it will please more customers and attract more business. They also ask whether the change will enhance the values of democratic governance and whether the organization will be better able to serve the public interest. I think this is a critical distinction. To ask merely about efficiency or pleasing one's customers is quite natural in business where the private interests of the firm are paramount and profit provides the "bottom line." In government, however, there is a different bottom line—that the actions taken by government result in the society being better off or, simply, that the public interest has been served. Ron Christie of New South Wales pointed out that public organizations are concerned with "value maximisation rather than profit maximisation." He continued, "Our profit motive differs from the private sector. We get 'profit' from providing value to clients." This is the democratic bottom line, and it applies to everything that occurs in the public sector.

Even the management advances discussed in this book come under scrutiny. In the private sector, far too often, a new management technique is introduced simply because someone feels it may increase profits, through either improving the quality of the product or service or enhancing the productivity of the organization. In public organizations, the values at play are far more complex. For example, what is done for the sake of efficiency may reduce the responsiveness of the organization to its clientele or to the citizenry generally. Moreover, what might be considered ethical in the private sector may simply be out of bounds in the public sector. These are hard questions, but I am convinced that the fact that questions like these are raised so frequently is indicative of a strong sense of the ways in which the ethics of public service permeate everything that happens.

Let's see how ethics and values affect even the management changes I have been discussing here. First, as you have seen, these outstanding public managers, as a group, tended to be less interested in moving their organizations through changing structures or classic patterns of rewards and punishments than through a careful articulation of values. On the surface, that sounds admirable, certainly less manipulative than the rationalist or managerialist perspectives of earlier times. Is that really the case? One might argue, to the contrary, that manipulating the values of persons in an organization is even more insidious than more overt forms of control. Certainly that's a legitimate argument. On the other hand, if the values of the organization are formulated in a way that involves people throughout the organization and expresses their interests as well as those of management, the charge of manipulation carries far less weight.

A decade ago, in a book titled *In the Shadow of Organization,* I outlined what I called an "educative" approach to leadership in public management, and it was exactly that approach that many of the most highly regarded managers evidenced. This approach suggests a new role for the manager that is less concerned with control or manipulation and more concerned with education. In this view, the manager's chief effort is to stimulate in himself or herself and in others a strong sense of self-awareness and self-reflection, to the point that all will gain both a sense of direction and a measure of autonomy in pursuing that direction. The educative manager trusts that if people in the organization come to know themselves and their organization sufficiently well, they will do the right thing, resulting in an improved organization and an improved environment. The educative manager approaches the outside world, especially clients, in much the same way, helping them to understand their needs as well as the conditions that might aid them in meeting those needs. Again, the role of the educative manager is to create settings in which people are stimulated to learn, settings in which learning is the norm, and settings in which learning is valued above all else. In such places, both people and their organizations can flourish, without manipulation.

Second, I have reported that many of these managers and many throughout their organizations place a high value on serving the public and providing "quality services." In other settings, and even under less sensitive public administrators, such admonitions might simply advise cosmetic changes designed to secure increased support or market share. The intent would be to fool one's customers into a higher regard for the organization. Many public managers, however, are quite willing to move beyond this limited interpretation of customer service to explore ways of actually empowering citizens by providing information and opportunities for choice that would enable customers, clients, and citizens to help in constructing responsive public programs. Here "customer service" means far more than clever techniques to improve the position of one's own agency, although that may be a by-product; rather, service is seen as an essential element of public programs, involving both a political and an ethical commitment to the public interest. As such, it goes to the heart of an ethical public service.

Third, as public managers move toward greater involvement, empowerment, and even shared leadership, they may be asked whether such a move merely represents another management trick to secure compliance, another effort by management to coopt the workers? Or, at the other end of the spectrum, they may be asked whether devolution of power and authority and leadership amount to a shift in responsibility on the part of top management. John Uhr underscores one of the issues: "The trend toward risk management and greater devolution of administrative initiative to line managers means that administrators generally face an increased burden of responsibility. No amount of rhetoric about cost-effective, business-like public management can long disguise the new ethical burdens involved in resource allocation and program administration."

The answer to the first question is, quite honestly, that in many organizations, public and private, ideas such as empowerment have been tried first as devices to improve the position of the organization, to make it more flexible and adaptive. Other managers, however, recognize that empowerment and shared leadership are much more powerful, even liberating, ideas. Public managers are talking about turning hierarchies upside down, literally as well as symbolically. They are talking about devolving real power and real responsibility throughout their organizations and saying that unless devolution occurs the organization can only pretend to real service to the public. These managers also recognize the other side of the equation, that devolution of power involves devolution of responsibility. Frankly, this issue has not been fully resolved, but I am impressed that so many public managers are sensitive to the concern.

Over the years, individual responsibility has been so clouded by the concepts of hierarchy and authority that people throughout public and private organizations have developed a distorted sense of what responsibility is all about. A marked failure to assume personal responsibility, even for one's own actions, is pervasive and has resulted in what I would call "an appeal to hierarchy," an effort to pass one's own responsibility on "up the line." It's a problem that has confounded managers from Nuremburg to General Motors, and one that will continue to confuse for some time. Resolving the question of responsibility is essential to real change in public organizations, but it will take considerable time to work out. Without question, however, the devolution of power and authority in public organizations requires a more significant assumption of responsibility by persons throughout the organization. In this area, perhaps even more than in others, public managers must take an educative stance that helps people throughout the organization recognize their duties and their responsibilities.

Fourth, when we talk about pragmatic incrementalism, are we making a statement about values? The initial answer is easy, "Yes, we are." The follow-up is difficult. Pragmatism doesn't simply mean expediency; it implies both a sense of caution and a sense of movement or change. Similarly, incrementalism doesn't merely suggest making changes at the margins; it suggests that such an approach has positive value, that this is the way change comes about most successfully. Although many, if not most public managers I talked with subscribe to the idea of pragmatic incrementalism, there certainly were skeptics. And even those managers who most clearly follow this approach often add a proviso. I alluded to that reservation in the discussion of organizational culture, commenting that cultures can become too rigid and unresponsive and, when that occurs, much more dramatic change has to take place. Jim Evans of the Canadian Ministry of Revenue sums up this position: "Pragmatic incrementalism has to be complemented by a capacity to evaluate when a trend or progression has reached the limits of its potential, and when a new framework has to be established." A manager's incremental movement in a particular direction may blind him or her to other avenues that might ultimately be more productive.

My own interpretation of this issue is that as long as managers are comfortable working within a particular framework of values they can afford to be both pragmatic and incremental. All managers, however, can be deluded in their pursuit of a vision, even a widely shared vision. Consequently, to resist the conservative tendencies of the incrementalist view, diverse mechanisms for constantly renegotiating programs and processes must be built into the organization. Clarifying a vision of the organization must not lead to rigidity; the entire membership of the organization should be encouraged to contribute regularly to refining both programs and processes.

Fifth, ethical questions may even arise when dealing with ethics. These questions cut in many directions and are extremely complex, but they seem to me to revolve around the question of who sets ethical standards for those in the public sector. Who should decide whether the image of public servants is too positive or too negative? Similarly, with respect to policy issues, how are the standards set—by the people, by their elected representatives, by professional organizations, or by those in the agencies themselves? Certainly, depending on the area under discussion, any of these groups might be the source of ethical deliberation. The question is enormously complex and not easily answered—but at least it's being asked. That much, it seems to me, is a healthy sign, a sign that ethical deliberation in the public sector goes to the most basic of issues.

CONCLUSION

Woodrow Wilson and other early writers in the field of public administration portrayed the field primarily as a managerial concern involving the technical process of implementing public policy and separated from the world of politics. Following this recommendation, over the years, public managers developed considerable skill in the management of public programs, probably more than they are usually given credit for. Others soon realized that public administration is also a political concern, that administrators at all levels are deeply involved in shaping public policy. Indeed, I suspect that those in public organizations will increasingly be called on to do more than simply respond to legislative mandate; they will be asked to identify and to articulate important public interests. Beyond a view of public administration as a managerial concern, beyond a view of public administration as a political concern, we have now seen that public administration today is more and more an ethical concern, that all the "spontaneous" little actions of public managers carry with them important value implications. At the root of every act of every public official, whether in the development or execution of public policy, there is a moral or ethical question.

What does it mean then to recognize public service as a moral and ethical concern and not only a managerial and political concern? It means that public managers must require in their own organizations and demonstrate in their own actions the very highest standards of behavior. They must provide what Mark Twain called "the annoyance of a good example." Beyond that, to see the public service as a moral and ethical concern demands that public managers understand and act always to discover or to clarify the public interest. If the consummate skill of thought is philosophy, then I would say that the consummate skill of practice, at least in the field of public administration, is virtue. For the work of public officials to be free from scandal is important, but that's not enough. The work of public servants, at its best, will indeed be virtuous.

CHAPTER SEVEN

The Pursuit
of
Significance

When the experiences of highly regarded public managers, even public managers in different countries, are brought together, what is striking is the similarity in their work. Although these managers are situated in many different types of organizations and in many different places, they share an approach to the management of public organizations that is revolutionary when placed beside traditional patterns of bureaucratic management. There is no question but that their stories represent managerial successes, efforts heralded as producing important changes in their organizations. These managers represent the "best and the brightest" in the public sector, though most would shy away from that description. In part they are simply more restrained and modest, but in part they genuinely feel that their own efforts are only a small part of what has happened to improve their organizations.

Moreover, these managers recognize that the work continues. This is not to say that they think progress has been slow; rather, they understand that public management is a never-ending process. Many of the managers I talked with expressed this sentiment, although they did so in many different ways. One manager said, "If this were a book of ten chapters, we'd be at about chapter three." Another said, "In a marathon, this would only be a hundred-yard dash." No one felt the job was completed.

In a sense, the continuance of the public manager's work is almost its essence. Occasionally there are milestones, markers, or completion points: a major construction project is completed, a new policy proposed by the agency is approved by the legislature, or the annual budget is put to bed. Despite these milestones, the most effective and most successful managers recognize that their job is best characterized as unending, and indeed that is the fascination. Some achievements are celebrated along the way, but the real issue is not achievements but continuation of the process. Every day a new frustration or, even better, a new challenge or, even better, a new opportunity arises. The most successful public managers are known for their tenacity. The game goes on, and the only winner is the one who is still playing.

PUBLIC AND PRIVATE

We have discussed a variety of management strategies, approaches I have called "revolutionary" in their impact on public organizations and the services they deliver. We have examined a commitment to values, providing quality service to the public, the concept of shared leadership, pragmatic incrementalism, and the ethics of public service. One may be tempted to think of these ideas as merely "techniques" for improving public organizations. Although that would be a natural interpretation in the private sector, for the best public managers, the real story is not about techniques. Nothing that occurs in the public service is *just* about techniques. Everything that occurs is about values and meaning and significance.

Many writers presume that new ideas about management are generated first in the private sector and then transferred to or adopted by the public sector. Consistent with the managerialist view, their recommendation is that government should operate like a business. This presumption is misleading in several ways. First, the view that business leads and government follows implies that what occurs in business is more important than what occurs in government, and that's simply not the case. Admittedly, during the last decade or so, the public sector has been viciously attacked, and its advocates have been few. On the other hand, many businesses have failed to meet international or even local competition and have gone belly up; moreover, scandals of all sorts continue to mount in the private sector, especially in the financial community. Time and time again, the public sector has been called on to "bail out" the private sector. A more discerning view, then, would recognize that the line between fact and fiction with respect to the priority of business is thin indeed. O. Glenn Stahl, a founding member of the American Society for Public Administration, recently summarized some of the myths perpetuated in American political debates about public programs. Stahl wrote, with great skill and conviction, that

1. Public expenditure and taxation are still considered by a majority to be major evils, while the excesses of Wall Street, defense contractors' skullduggery, and other corporate graft . . . get only fleeting criticism. In agonizing over taxes, few make the connection with the much higher cost of paying interest on excessive debts, of selling off America's assets to foreign investors, of bailing out savings institutions, and the like. . . .

2. The pay of higher-level civil servants and judges . . . goes down in flames—while scarcely a ripple of public protest is heard about the unconsionable

multimillion-dollar annual incomes of literally millions of corporate executives, money-market manipulators, media moguls, lawyers, and professional athletes.

3. So much of the American public gets exercised about graft and abuse in government but succumbs meekly to an unregulated, free-booting brand of capitalism in the private sector.

Government is always fair game for attacks by self-serving politicians, cynics from the media, and frustrated (and often floundering) members of the business community. But the record of the private sector, especially with respect to serving the public interest and engaging in ethical behavior, is not always one to be envied or emulated. The assumption that everything that business does is good and everything that government does is bad simply cannot bear up under close scrutiny. Although those in the business community receive better press, those in public organizations around the world can claim great credit for their activities in protecting the environment, eliminating discrimination, providing for the public health, helping those in need, and assisting in thousands of other areas. Unlike those in the private sector, public servants are concerned with increasing good rather than increasing profit; they are concerned with saving lives as well as saving money. Such efforts should be a source of pride to all involved as well as to the public they serve.

Second, despite the popular myth, businesses are *not* always the first to lead in management innovation. Not only does the public sector often excel in improved management systems—for example, in the area of personnel classifications and performance standards—but many of the more strategic ideas discussed here can be traced as easily to their public sector roots as to those elsewhere. Consider, for example, the notion of participation or empowerment that the gurus of contemporary business management have discovered in the last few years. Although many writers suggest that these ideas originated in Japan, then were adopted by managers in Western businesses, then picked up by managers in the public sector, in truth, models of participation and involvement have always been a significant part of public sector management. Participation and involvement are crucial elements in understanding democratic government. They are essential to operating a democratic system. Although both public and private organizations have become more attentive to these concerns in recent times, obviously spurred by the need to adapt and to innovate, public managers, for the most part, actually started out closer to the ideal than did those in the private sector. Indeed, in many cases, public sector managers have now gone farther in the direction of empowering both employees and customers than their counterparts in business.

Over the years, the history, the tradition, and the practice of shared leadership have been far more significant in the public sector than in the private sector. Democratic governance has always meant that public administrators have needed to be attentive to issues of involvement, but very specific efforts at employee participation and public participation were both tested in public sector experiments in the forties and fifties. (Remember, even Deming started as a civil servant.) Certainly, these ideas were absolutely central to discussions of public administration in the late sixties and early seventies. Twenty years ago, one public administration scholar wrote:

> Business organizations must be responsible not only to owners and managers, as in the past, but also to employees located throughout the hierarchy. Public organizations must be responsive not only to high level officials, but also to the clients they serve. This change requires much more than the cooptation of a few. What seems required is a true sharing of power, based on an attitude of mutual trust, especially a trust of the new participants.

It all sounds very contemporary. From this history, we can conclude that public managers seeking to empower their employees or engage their clients in the decision process are not merely employing techniques that seem to work in business. They are instead carrying on a significant tradition of research and practice *in the public service.* Empowerment is not an incidental technique in the public sector; it is an integral part of the *mission* of public institutions. By definition, democratic governments and all of their institutions must seek to empower citizens.

In addition, reviewing the history of these ideas in the public sector, we should note that public managers are often much better attuned to the values and complexities of the management approaches they employ than are their counterparts in business. They simply have to be. Recognizing the importance of service to one's clients or customers has been an essential element of public administration theory and practice for decades.

What is more important to managers in public organizations than their relationships with their constituents and clients? Surely those in public agencies recognize that the issue is not as simple as it is portrayed by those coming from the private sector. Not only do customers vary and even compete for attention but the interests of specific customers must often be overridden by a transcendent public interest. Public managers must necessarily operate with a high degree of sensitivity to the values and concerns of a democratic society—and this is, or at least should be, as much the case in business as in the public sector.

Think about the big picture for a moment. In the last several years, we have witnessed a remarkable movement to conceptualize, design, and build democratic processes throughout the world. Most people think that movement only affects countries in the Eastern bloc, but it's probably fair to say that the move toward democratization has been felt in the West as well, as more and more leaders of major institutions recognize that democracy is not merely "out there"—something that applies only to governments and political systems—but also embodies the belief that all institutions within a democratic society should evidence democratic tendencies. The real anomaly is that most major institutions in democratic societies have been run in a fairly authoritarian fashion, and that includes both public *and* private organizations. In an expansion of democracy throughout society, an expansion potentially embracing all major organizations both public and private, we should expect that public institutions would lead the way, and indeed they have done so. In contrast to the familiar exhortation that government should be run like a business, I would urge that, in their attentiveness to democratic principles, businesses should be run more like public organizations—and there are some excellent models to follow.

No one would pretend that all public organizations should be emulated. Over the years, many public organizations have become far too hierarchical and rule bound, but then, so have many private organizations. On the other hand, models of excellence abound in the public sector. Time after time, as I talked with highly regarded public managers, I discovered new patterns of management being implemented, not simply as imitations of private sector management but as actions better characterized as extensions of the natural concerns of public service. What, for example, could be more consistent with public (rather than private) values than serving the public or shared leadership? What's more important, these public managers were quite aware of the ethical dimensions of what they were about. Rather than trying to dodge those ethical questions that did arise, as we have so often seen in the private sector, these managers confronted them directly and in fact worked hard to make people in their organizations more sensitive and responsive to them. Despite the rhetoric of managerialism, public organizations should not be assumed or constrained to follow what happens in private organizations—perhaps even the opposite.

THE POWER OF PUBLIC SERVICE

These issues come into even greater focus when one considers the power that drives the public service. Certainly most of those managers I talked with consider their work more than just a job. For them it is a calling, even a passion. The reason that their work demands such a fervent commitment is that it involves values; their work is a quest filled with meaning. How else can we explain the fascination of public service but to suggest the moral commitment it involves? How else can we acknowledge the power of a commitment to public service? And, in turn, how can we speak of the image of the public service without also speaking of the integrity of the public service?

Robert Bellah and his colleagues, writing in *Habits of the Heart*, suggest that an occupation is a calling when it is "defined essentially in terms of its contribution to the public good." In their view, an infusion of values into the conduct of government, that is, making public service a calling, is not only essential but has the power to connect both citizens and professionals in the public service.

> The transformation of the state . . . should focus on bringing a sense of citizenship into the operation of government itself. We need to discuss the positive purposes and ends of government, the kind of government appropriate for the citizens we would like to be. Among other things, we need to reappropriate the ethical meaning of professionalism, seeing it in terms not only of technical skill but of the moral contribution that professionals make to a complex society. . . . To change the conception of government from scientific management to a center of ethical obligations and relationships is part of our task.

This change is apparent in the work of the best public managers. An essential moral commitment to the notion of public service distinguishes the work of these managers from that of the "rationalists" or "managerialists." Public service is not just another business, another contractual relationship, it is a calling distinguished by the values it commits to and upholds. As I talked with public managers in many different locations, their dedication to the notion of public service was a recurring theme. Although it is expressed in many different ways, what I have called the "public service motive" almost always includes two elements: a commitment to the ethics and values of public service, and a sense of deep personal satisfaction derived from pursuing the public interest. The two go hand in hand.

Jan Perkins of Morgan Hill remarked that "managing in the public arena . . . requires a commitment to values of providing quality services for all and dealing with all people on an equal basis. It is very important that people who enter the public service do so with a high standard of ethical behavior and an ability to deal honestly and directly with all people." Michael Stahl of EPA wrote, "Democratic government can be a tremendous positive force in society, and in spite of recent political rhetoric and prevailing political ideology, I am convinced that the institutions and programs of government are of vital importance to the nation and that public service is a noble calling. There is great satisfaction in knowing that your work has made an impact on persons who could only have been helped through the intervention of the government." That sentiment was echoed by Pamela Gordon of Sheffield, who told me simply, "I am committed to democratic local government. I like the concept of it. And I've found it very satisfying . . . that I'm giving effect to the result of a democratic process and helping that on its way. I like to feel that what I'm doing somehow fits into the general good." After talking with public managers such as these, I'm convinced that the notion of public service is, despite appearances to the contrary, alive and well.

James Perry and Lois Wise of Indiana University recently reviewed the reasons people are drawn to the public service and the implications of their motives for the conduct of those organizations. They quote Elmer Staats, one-time Comptroller General of the United States, in describing the power and the depth of meaning that the idea of public service holds for these people: "'Public service' is a concept, an attitude, a sense of duty—yes, even a sense of public morality." According to Perry and Wise's review of various studies, certain people evidence a strong attraction to public institutions and public organizations, for reasons that are partly rational, partly norm-based, and partly emotional. For example, people may be drawn to public service in order to participate in the policy process or because they identify with a particular program or interest. They may desire to serve the public interest, or they may have a strong commitment to a concept such as duty or equity. They may believe in the importance of a particular program or, far more generally, be driven by a strong desire to help others.

Several questions flow from Perry and Wise's review, among them questions about the relationship between the motivation for public service and performance on the job: "Individuals who are highly committed are likely to be highly motivated to remain with their organizations and to perform. In addition, because committed employees are likely to engage in spontaneous, innovative behaviors on behalf of the organization, such employees are likely to facilitate an organization's adjustment to contingencies." Although individuals driven by their commitment occasionally may go beyond reasonable bounds, most findings indicate that the public service motive has a positive impact on job performance.

There is really no evidence to indicate what percentage of those entering and remaining in the public service do so based on the public service motive; however, there is every reason to believe that the proportion is high. Given comparatively low salaries, often less than ideal working conditions, and recently, considerable public abuse, one simply would not expect that persons acting solely out of private interests would continue in government employment. Especially among those managers I talked with—people at the middle and upper levels of public organizations for whom other opportunities are frequently available—a commitment to public service *must* be enormously powerful. The evidence is in the remarkable "staying power" of the public service.

That such a compelling idea could survive, even in times when attacks on the public service are frequent, is remarkable, but perhaps understandable if one considers just how important the idea of service to one's community is and always has been. The point could be made in many ways, citing cases and quoting the great philosophers. The issue was distilled for me, however, several years ago as I read the story of Jacqueline Mayer Townsend, who was paralyzed and unable to speak following a massive stroke only eight years after being crowned Miss America. Her muscles drooped, her eyes were downturned, and her mouth was slack. Feeling that others were now seeing her as "deformed, mumbling and, perhaps in their eyes, pathetic," she vowed to battle back. But the road returning to her previous life was a difficult one. With great effort, her muscle movement returned, but regaining speech continued to be very hard. In a world of silence, she told herself: "The ability to fail and bounce back is to turn your problems into challenges. I'll fail and fail until I get it right. Until I put an entire sentence together, until I put an entire speech together."

After an eight-year battle, she was finally able to speak again, and she began doing so regularly on behalf of the American Heart Association, which she now sees as a mission of great value. Indeed, she has remarked that if she hadn't become ill she might never have found a cause to which she could so dedicate herself. Asked why she keeps such a busy schedule on behalf of the Heart Association, even though reminders of her illness such as numbness and occasional slurred speech are still present, she replied, "The pursuit of happiness has nothing to do with joy. It's the pursuit of significance."

In my view, it is exactly the *pursuit of significance*— and the joy it brings—that drives the best public servants, including the best public managers. They are concerned about others, they are concerned about their programs, they are concerned about the public interest, but most of all, they are concerned about *making a difference.* They want their lives and their careers to be meaningful, not just in terms of some lines on a graph of profits and losses but in terms of how worthwhile their efforts have been, how they have changed the world for the better, and how they have helped to meet the democratic bottom line. Very simply, though incredibly powerfully, they are concerned with the *significance* of their lives and their work.

The pursuit of significance is not only a compelling motivation for people entering and remaining in the public service but it also affects almost everything that happens in public organizations. Unfortunately, the way most people conceive of management generally and public management in particular doesn't really take this factor into account. Consider how we think about management and organizations. Most theories of organization in some way follow the rationalist prescription, which suggests that individuals operate out of a concern for their own self-interest. These ideas are reinforced by the ideas of managerialism, which is concerned with extending the notions of business management to the public sector. And what is the central concept of business management? The same pursuit of self-interest. In standard theories of management, the assumption of self-interest is absolutely basic; almost everything else flows from this beginning. Approaches to pay and performance, motivation and control, even communications and conflict—all assume self-interest on the part of the individual.

What if we turned the whole thing upside down and suggested that what is central to the operation of organizations—or, to make it simpler for a moment, public organizations—is not a concern for self-interest but the pursuit of significance. This would change the way we think about public organizations in some very interesting ways. Using this new assumption, for example, wouldn't we want to state more clearly what is significant about the work of the organization so that people could focus their energy and excitement? Wouldn't we want to place the needs of clients and citizens at the forefront of all our activities? Wouldn't we want to give persons throughout our organizations the strength and power and responsibility to be significant? And wouldn't we want everything we do to be touched, indeed propelled by a commitment to public service? In other words, wouldn't we be doing all of those things that the best public managers already seem to be doing?

Obviously, that's exactly the point. The best public managers have grasped intuitively a new theory of public organization that is based on a key assumption about why people work and why they serve. Although this approach has hardly been touched upon by scholars in the field, the best public managers have already begun to do things differently. Some of what they have been doing appears to extend previous practices, even business practices, but when their experience and that of people in their organizations is turned in a slightly different way, and when we assume that people work not only for themselves but for others, the approach of these managers seems to be consistent with a new way of looking at the world. These managers are successful because their approaches appeal to the strong sense of mission that is a part of so many public organizations and the strong sense of commitment that is a part of so many public servants.

Let me cite a couple of examples. Mike Fogdon of the Employment Service told me, "I work from the premise that if you can get people interested in their jobs and satisfied with the work they are doing, the commitment that they give will be greater and you will get an added value from that. In some respects, you get that for free in the public sector. A lot of people come to the public service with a degree of commitment. They know they're not going to make a fortune, but there's something about serving the community around. And what you have to do is build on that." Building on that sense of commitment is exactly what I have just been describing, and it might well provide a new basis for theory and practice in public administration.

Similarly, H. J. Osborne of SaskTel shared with me a view of management quite different from the traditional planning, organizing, staffing, and directing one. "I believe in managing for results *through* people, not managing the people. This is because people usually manage themselves; they decide what they are willing to do, and they usually are best able to determine how they should do it. Managers manage functions, not people. The term 'managing people' for me implies a 'push' approach to management, which is usually counterproductive, whether that counterproductivity is visible or not. Usually it is not. I prefer a 'pull' approach, which implies positive motivation and commitment by the individuals to their jobs and by the managers to their people." Again, the idea of commitment is absolutely central, not something that works at the margins. Note, for example, the commitment of the managers—not to profit but "to their people." How often in these pages have you heard that refrain?

These managers have changed one central premise—they have substituted the pursuit of significance for the pursuit of private interest. Having done so, many other things fall into place. If meaning is important to those in the public service, then providing people with meaningful work is likely to enhance the overall efforts of the organization. If a commitment to values is important, then providing people opportunities to contribute in valuable ways will make a difference. And if the pursuit of significance is important, then providing people with significant roles and responsibilities will move their organizations far beyond mere "excellence."

Recall our early discussion of the two different approaches to the notion of organizational culture. Culture can be conceived in an instrumental way and used as a control mechanism. In this view, what is important is that the analyst or manager understand the appropriate "carrots and sticks" to which individuals respond, then provide whatever combination of rewards and punishments seems consistent with the accumulated self-interests of the organization's members. If the manager is successful in pushing the right buttons, employees will be stimulated to act in the right way, and the quality and productivity of the organization will likely be improved. This older approach has been tried in many settings but is increasingly being called into question. Much evidence suggests that such an approach no longer works, especially in situations in which the real test of the organization is not merely increased production of essentially similar products but rather the creativity and innovativeness with which the organization responds to environmental challenges. Still, organizations of all types cling to this traditional mechanistic view of organization and management and the rationalist/managerialist perspectives upon which it is based.

There is an alternative, however. A second interpretation of organizational culture suggests that culture is concerned with the shared meanings that members of an organization bring to their work. These meanings and values are what Geertz called the "webs of significance" in which we are suspended. If we think of organizational culture in this way, things start to look quite different. The analyst's role or that of the manager is to identify the meanings and values that move people in the organization and stimulate these individuals to think of the world in different ways—to see greater possibilities for their own contributions and those of their organizations—then to provide them the autonomy, the encouragement, and the support for them to act, not in a way that has been dictated to them by an organizational superior but in a way that they choose because it allows them to signify what's most important to them. Rather than leading to instrumental outcomes, this approach can best be characterized as expressive, and the manager's role can best be described as educative.

I imagine a new and different theory of organizations could be built on these premises—and probably will be. But we are concerned here primarily with practice, with the way in which public managers carry out their jobs and their responsibilities. This new approach I have described appears to explain the work of the highly regarded public managers featured here better than that of the older, more traditional, more bureaucratic approach. To build on the pursuit of significance makes it natural to do things in a different way. A focus on meanings and values is clearly consistent with ideas such as a commitment to values, serving the public, shared leadership, and, without a doubt, a dedication to public service.

Several other pieces of the puzzle now begin to fit much better than before. One is the idea of community. In our earlier discussion of community within/cooperation without, I mentioned how surprised I was that so many managers mentioned the idea of community as being important, even though few were able to articulate just what the contribution of community meant to their organizations. Now it becomes obvious. Community deals with the meanings and values that people share; it helps them to establish models for working together or merely being together. A sense of community binds people together around common interests and common purposes. The idea of community is important not because communities are more productive or efficient than other groups but because communities have worked out effective ways of dealing with questions of meaning and significance. The best public managers are engaged in just such an effort. They are trying to work out patterns of meaning and significance in their organizations. To the extent that a sense of community exists in their organizations, these managers have a considerable edge.

Let's be clear. These managers are not seeking some sort of ideological commitment from their members, some special passion perhaps ignited by a charismatic leader or imposed by an authoritarian regime. Just the opposite. The notion of community and the more basic notion of focusing on the meaning and values that individuals bring to the organization suggests the importance of fully involving all members of a community in decisions that affect their work and their being. For example, it suggests that knowing the right values or the correct processes is not the prerogative of a managerial elite but is knowledge and insight that is widely distributed throughout the organization. This view emphasizes the dignity and worth of all persons and builds upon that spirit in every way possible.

So far we have discussed the pursuit of significance as a concept that can transform the internal operations of the organization, but there are important spillover effects with respect to the public as well. I noted earlier that organizations wishing to improve their service to the public need to serve their front-line people better. What you do internally affects the way you interact with those outside as well. Similarly, if you recognize that members of the organization bring important meanings and values with them to their work, perhaps they will also become better attuned to the meanings and values of the public. Under these conditions, I would expect that clients or citizens generally would not be viewed statistically, as numbers to be subjected to some cost-benefit calculus, but as persons of significance—and they would be treated that way.

To this point, I have suggested that those in public organizations, especially those in managerial positions, often view their work as an important part of their pursuit of significance. If this is the case, a model of organization based on premises of rational self-interest and typically played out in notions of hierarchy and control simply won't fit and won't work. Alternatively, an approach that recognizes and supports the meanings and values that people bring with them to the public workplace, including a commitment to public service, may be far more effective. But this still leaves open the question of individual responsibility.

For all of this to work, individuals throughout society and throughout major social institutions must be able and willing to assume far greater responsibility for their own actions than is currently the case. In a world in which decisions are made by a few and transmitted down through a system of organized control, most people don't have to worry much about the choices they make. They don't have to spend time clarifying and refining the values upon which they base their actions and, if something goes wrong, someone up the ladder can shoulder the blame. The fact that we have lived with hierarchical systems of organizations for so long in all segments of our societies has reinforced this very narrow view of responsibility, but it is a view that simply won't work any longer.

Modern organizations, especially public organizations, need creative and innovative solutions. For that to occur, people throughout must shape the vision of the organization, commit themselves to the tasks at hand, be empowered to act, and even take substantial risks. But with risk comes responsibility, and learning that lesson may be the most difficult of all. The individual whose understanding of the world we recognize and value as a source of meaning and integrity bears a reciprocal obligation to act with great responsibility. The public manager, especially the educative public manager, can play an important role in developing such a commitment. The essential charge of the contemporary and future public manager is to help people throughout their organizations and throughout society recognize and accept the responsibility they have for making the world, or at least their little portion of the world, a better place to live. It sounds so simple, yet it is the most difficult task that public managers, and those elsewhere, face.

In this book I have focused on public organizations, but there may be some important lessons here for those in private organizations as well. We tend to think of those in the private sector as driven by private interests, especially the pursuit of profit, and that may essentially be correct. However, in an age featuring new levels of education and awareness, in an age of environmental sensitivity and global complexity, and in an age in which change and turbulence create new and confusing moral dilemmas for all people daily, questions of meaning and significance (not just profit) will become more and more salient. If that's the case, then the approaches now being used by the best public managers—and, even more important, the "right reasons" on which these managers base what they are doing—will hold important lessons for those who seek to manage organizations of all types. To the extent that the best public managers are more attentive to the meanings and values people bring with them to the workplace, to the extent they are able to act upon and indeed to support and facilitate the individual's pursuit of significance—to that extent these public managers will provide models not only for others in the public sector but for those in the private sector as well.

CONCLUSION

In a time of soaring public debt, severe budget cutbacks, and increasing demands for public services, talking of a commitment to values or sharing leadership may appear "soft," even out of touch with the realities of contemporary public programs. But remember that the outstanding public managers recommended to me were not chosen simply because they were nice people; they were recommended because they had succeeded in improving the quality and productivity of their organizations. They were recommended because they had a highly positive impact on their communities, their states, and their nations. They were recommended because they had contributed to the public good in important ways. That they failed to follow the old patterns of hierarchy and authority that have bound government agencies for years, patterns we have long known were limiting progress, is not something that should be held against them. Indeed, it is exactly what makes their contribution most significant.

Managers of public programs today must rid themselves of an easy adherence to the patterns of the past. The rationalist/managerialist perspectives that led to the creation of rule-bound, hierarchically governed systems of organizational control have outlived their usefulness. In their place, the best public managers are experimenting with new approaches based on a better understanding of the meanings and values that people bring with them to the workplace and that not only shape their work but also provide the best hope of developing organizations that are creative, responsive, and imbued with a new spirit of responsibility. Only in this way will the most important work in our society, the work of serving others, be restored to its proper and distinguished standing and a full sense of dignity and worth return to the public service. Both public managers and the public they serve will benefit from this pursuit of significance.

NOTES

Unless otherwise cited, all quotations in the text are from personal interviews or direct correspondence with the author.

CHAPTER 1: A REVOLUTION IN PUBLIC MANAGEMENT

3 He discovered . . . Sandford F. Borins, "Public Management Innovation in Canada," unpublished paper, February 1991.

3 The alternative . . . Thomas J. Peters and Robert H. Waterman, Jr., *In Search of Excellence* (New York: Harper & Row, 1982).

4 For example, prior . . . Kenneth A. Gold, *A Comparative Study of Successful Organizations* (Washington, DC: U.S. Office of Personnel Management, 1981).

4 Later, Barbour, Fletcher, and Sipel . . . George P. Barbour, Jr., Thomas W. Fletcher, and George A. Sipel, *Handbook: Excellence in Local Government Management* (Washington, DC: International City Management Association, 1984).

5 "This mindset . . . " Auditor General of Canada, *Attributes of Well-Performing Organizations* (Ottawa: Minister of Supply and Services, 1989), sec. 4.

6 Weber felt . . . Max Weber, *The Theory of Social and Economic Organizations* (New York: Oxford University Press, 1947), p. 337.

7 In another passage . . . Ibid.

7 It only made sense . . . Luther Gulick, "Notes on the Theory of Organization," in *Papers on the Science of Administration*, edited by L. Gulick and L. Urwick (New York: Institute of Public Administration, 1937), pp. 21–29.

8 Herbert Simon, whose book . . . Herbert Simon, *Administrative Behavior*, 2nd ed. (New York: Free Press, 1957).

10 In Australia . . . Neville Wran, quoted in Mark Considine, "The Corporate Management Framework as Administrative Science: A Critique," *Australian Journal of Public Administration*, vol. 47, no. 1 (March 1988), p. 4.

10 In Great Britain . . . Geoffrey K. Fry, "The Thatcher Government, the Financial Management Initiative, and the New Civil Service," *Public Administration*, vol. 66 (Spring 1988), p. 8.

10 One American writer . . . George C. Edwards, *Implementing Public Policy* (Washington, DC: Congressional Quarterly Press, 1980).

11 For instance, Aaron Wildavsky . . . Aaron Wildavsky, "Administration without Hierarchy? Bureaucracy without Authority?" in *Public Administration: The State of the Discipline*, edited by N. B. Lynn and A. Wildavsky (Chatham, NJ: Chatham House, 1990), p. xiv.

12 In contrast, a variety, . . . Dwight Waldo, *The Administrative State* (New York: Ronald Press, 1948).

12 Pursuing the same point . . . Marshall E. Dimock, "Criteria and Objectives of Public Administration," in *Frontiers of Public Administration*, edited by J. M. Gaus, L. D. White, and M. E. Dimock (Chicago: University of Chicago Press, 1936), p. 133.

12 Perhaps most important . . . Robert B. Denhardt, *Theories of Public Organization* (Pacific Grove, CA: Brooks/Cole, 1984), pp. 69–90.

13 "The capacity for government . . ." Hugh Faulkner, "Looking to Public Management," *Canadian Journal of Public Administration*, vol. 33, no. 3 (Fall 1990), p. 386.

13 But, as Otto Brodtrick points out . . . Auditor General of Canada, sec. 4.42.

14 One student of the Australian public service . . . Mark Considine, "Managerialism Strikes Out," *Australian Journal of Public Administration*, vol. 49 (1990), p. 175.

14 Peter Wilenski . . . Peter Wilenski, "Social Change as a Source of Competing Values in Public Administration," *Australian Journal of Public Administration*, vol. 47, no. 3 (September 1988), p. 217.

14 Wilenski continues . . . Ibid., p. 218.

15 Paul O'Neill . . . Paul O'Neill, *On Public and Private Sector Management* (Washington, DC: Center for Excellence in Government, 1985), part II, p. 5.

CHAPTER 2: A COMMITMENT TO VALUES

22 The Canadian Public Service 2000 . . . *Public Service 2000, Report of the Task Force on Management Category* (Ottawa: Supplies and Services, 1990), p. iv.

23 One writer portrays . . . J. Steven Ott, *The Organizational Culture Perspective* (Pacific Grove, CA: Brooks/Cole, 1989).

24 Jeff Zlonis . . . Jeff Zlonis, quoted in Fred Jordan (with Simpson Lawson), *Innovating America* (New York: The Ford Foundation, 1990), p. 38.

27 "In fact, it is likely that the changes . . ." Linda A. Krefting and Peter J. Frost, "Untangling Webs, Surfing Waves, and Wildcatting: A Multiple-Metaphor Perspective on Managing Organizational Culture," in *Organizational Culture*, edited by P. J. Frost, L. F. Moore, M. R. Louis, C. C. Lundberg, and J. Martin (Beverly Hills: Sage, 1985), p. 157.

28 Instead Schein holds . . . Edgar H. Schein, *Organizational Culture and Leadership* (San Francisco: Jossey-Bass, 1987), p. 6.

29 "It is the most critical element . . ." William P. Belgard, K. Kim Fisher, and Steven R. Rayner, "Vision, Opportunity and Tenacity," in *Corporate Transformation*, edited by R. H. Kilmann, T. J. Covin, and Associates (San Francisco: Jossey-Bass, 1988), p. 135.

30 "Our willingness to take a stand . . ." Peter Block, *The Empowered Manager: Positive Political Skills at Work* (San Francisco: Jossey-Bass, 1987), p. 115.

30 "Because a tenacious culture . . ." Karl E. Weick, "The Significance of Corporate Cultures," in Frost et al., p. 384.

31 "Leaders use the same means . . ." Robert H. Waterman, Jr., *The Renewal Factor* (New York: Bantam Books, 1987), p. 12.

31 For example, two writers on business management . . . Martin and Siehl, quoted in Ott, p. 52.

32 Smircich describes the differences . . . Linda Smircich, "Concepts of Culture and Organizational Analysis," *Administrative Science Quarterly*, vol. 28, no. 3 (1983), pp. 339–358.

32 The anthropologist Clifford Geertz . . . Clifford Geertz, *The Interpretation of Cultures* (New York: Basic Books, 1973), p. 5.

32 For example, a person may be . . . Douglas Sturm, *Community and Alienation* (Notre Dame: University of Notre Dame Press, 1988), p. 143.

35 "It must establish a framework . . ." John L. Manion, *A Management Model* (Ottawa: Canadian Centre for Management Development, 1989), p. 11.

38 "If they could get that under their skin . . ." William G. Ouchi, *Theory Z* (New York: Avon Books, 1982), pp. 33–34.

47 For these reasons . . . Peter Millington, "Implementing Public Policy—Towards a More Efficient Public Service," notes for an address to the Conference on Managing Change in the Public Sector, Sydney, NSW, May 28–29, 1990, p. 4.

48 "That, then, is what staff can expect . . ." NSW Department of Water Resources, "The DWR Way," unpublished statement, Sydney.

49 "Successful implementation will only be achieved . . ." Judy Johnston, *Strategic Management Brief—Number Three* (NSW: Office of Public Management, NSW, 1990), p. 11.

55 Chris Argyris . . . Chris Argyris, *Intervention Theory and Method* (Reading, MA: Addison-Wesley, 1970), pp. 12–13.

56 Based on his familiarity . . . Norman R. King, "Managing Values at City Hall," unpublished paper, 1990.

57 King commented . . . Ibid., p. 22.

58 "Instead of the city council . . ." Norman R. King, "The Palm Springs Project," *Western City* (September 1983), p. 4.

59 "Our rewards . . ." "Palm Springs, Statement of Philosophy," photocopy.

60 "And that, we freely admit . . ." Norman R. King, letter to David N. Ammons, May 25, 1989, p. 2.

62 At a conference . . . Stephen Colloff, "Management Development in British Rail," presentation to the Royal Institute of Public Administration, March 9, 1990, p. 4.

62 *Vision*—Having the image . . . Ibid., p. 5.

65 Over a twelve-month period . . . James E. Stephens, "Turnaround at the Alabama Rehabilitation Agency," *Public Productivity and Management Review*, vol. 11 (Spring 1988), p. 73.

66 Evidence of goal accomplishment . . . Ibid., p. 71.

67 Additionally, instead of continuing . . . Ibid., p. 77.

68 "They often see more value . . ." Waterman, p. 6.

69 In always being aware . . . Belgard, Fisher, and Raynor, p. 137.

CHAPTER 3: SERVING THE PUBLIC

74 "That's it: Other companies . . ." Peters and Waterman, p. 156.

75 "Instead of making . . ." National Commission on the Public Service, *Leadership for America* (Washington, DC: National Commission on the Public Service, 1989), p. 46.

Notes

76 "Those same consumer expectations . . ." Public Service Commission, *APS 2000*, a discussion paper produced by an Interdepartmental Working Party convened by the Public Service Commission, November 1989.

76 "Interaction is strong . . ." Auditor General of Canada, sec. 4.87.

77 "They regard the efficient and helpful performance . . ." Office of the Minister for Civil Service, *Service to the Public* (London: Office of the Minister for Civil Service, 1988), p. 1.

77 "In these circumstances . . ." Ibid., p. 2.

78 The project has just "lifted off" . . . Brian Marson, "Government as a Service Enterprise," presentation to the National Conference of the American Society for Public Administration, Washington, DC, 1991.

78 Joan Barton and Brian Marson . . . Joan Barton and Brian Marson, *Service Quality: An Introduction* (Victoria, BC: Province of British Columbia, 1991), p. 2.

79 "This includes the advice . . ." Ibid., p. 13.

81 "Political processes . . ." Michael Clarke and John Stewart, *Developing Effective Public Service Management* (London: The Local Government Management Board, 1990).

81 Public purposes are distinct . . . Ibid., p. 7.

82 Karl Albrecht and Ron Zemke . . . Karl Albrecht and Ron Zemke, *Service America* (Homewood, IL: Dow Jones-Irwin, 1985), p. 39.

84 "If he gets ketchup . . ." Barton and Marson, p. 41.

85 The commercial work . . . Margaret Lyons, "Works Department Sells Expertise," *Business Review Weekly* (March 15, 1991), p. 64.

86 As one indicator . . . Ibid.

88 Rather than succumbing . . . Fred T. Goldberg, Jr., "Managing the IRS," in *Toward Excellence* (Washington DC: Council for Excellence in Government, January 1991), p. 6.

92 Second, although many efforts . . . Christopher Pollitt, "Bring Consumers into Performance Measurement," *Policy and Politics*, vol. 16, no. 2 (1988), pp. 76–87.

92 Robin Hambleton . . . Robin Hambleton, "Consumerism, Decentralization and Local Democracy," *Public Administration*, vol. 66 (Summer 1988), p. 125.

94 While the Financial Management Initiative . . . David Falcon, "Experiencias Europeas en la Restructuracion del Esatdo Effectos Sobre el Empleo Publico y Medidas Concretas Demodernization el Caso del Reino Unido," paper presented to the Central American Conference, San Jose, Costa Rica, November 1990, p. 7.

95 Most of the concerns . . . Ibid., p. 9.

96 "It is not enough . . ." Peter Kemp, "A View from the Centre," remarks at a seminar organized by the Royal Institute of Public Administration and Ernst and Young, November 26, 1989.

96 "They weren't aware . . ." "Paul Sabin," *Management Week* (June 1991), p. 68.

97 "It was merely a case . . ." Ibid.

97 Under these circumstances . . Paul Sabin. "The Role of the Chief Executive and the Management of County Councils," *New Directions in Public Services* (London: Association of County Councils, 1989), p. 107.

97 "If you can't answer that question . . ." "Paul Sabin," p. 70.

98 "For example, measuring the number . . ." Michael Keating, "Managing for Results in the Public Interest," *Australian Journal of Public Administration,* vol. 49 (December 1990), p. 393.

99 For example, would the number . . . Michael Howard, "Effectiveness and Quality-of-Service Data," working paper of the Public Sector Research Centre, The University of New South Wales (November 1990).

100 "Improved work measurement . . ." Sandra J. Hale and Mary M. Williams, eds., *Managing Change* (Washington, DC: The Urban Institute Press, 1989), p. 17.

100 Working within these guidelines . . . Ibid., pp. 12–21.

102 "The MICE believed . . ." Graham Bashford, "Going Commercial in the Department of Administrative Services," *Australian Journal of Public Administration,* vol. 49 (June 1990), p. 158.

103 TQM has been defined as . . . Office of Management and Budget, "Draft Circular A-132, Improving the Quality of Government Products and Services" (Washington, DC: OMB, 1990), attachment.

103 He also changed the definition . . . David K. Carr and Ian D. Littman, *Excellence in Government* (Arlington, VA: Coopers and Lybrand, 1990), p. 23.

104 In 1990, the U.S. Office of Management and Budget . . . Office of Management and Budget.

107 One such community . . . Joseph Sensenbrenner, "Quality Comes to City Hall," *Harvard Business Review* (March–April 1991), pp. 4–10.

107 "When you look at all the downtime . . ." Ibid., p. 6.

111 "In the long run . . ." Auditor General of Canada, sec. 4.75, italics added.

113 "Investment of self in a community . . ." Rosabeth Moss Kanter, *Commitment and Community* (Cambridge: Harvard University Press, 1972), p. 73.

113 "There is a sense of belonging . . ." John Gardner, *Building Community* (Washington, DC: Independent Sector, 1991), p. 18.

115 "To prevent the diversity from destroying . . ." Ibid., p. 16.

117 "The organizational climate supports . . ." Auditor General of Canada, Exhibit 4.3.

118 "We must adopt a decisionmaking process . . ." USDA Forest Service, *Toward a Multicultural Organization* (Washington, DC: USDA Forest Service, March 1991), p. 2.

119 "This message struck a blow . . ." Sally Reed, *Putting Pride Back in the Workplace with Organizational Transformation* (Paramus, NJ: Prentice-Hall Information Service, 1988), p. 1.

120 "Santa Clara County provides . . ." Ibid., p. 2.

121 Costis Toregas . . . Costis Toregas, "Technology and Our Urban Communities," *Public Management,* vol. 17 (May 1988), p. 3.

121 David Garson . . . G. David Garson, "Human Factors in Information Systems," paper presented to the National Conference of the American Society for Public Administration, Washington, DC, March 23–27, 1991, p. 18.

122 The Australian philosopher . . . Stanley Benn, "Individuality, Autonomy, and Community," in *Community as a Social Ideal*, edited by E. Kamenka (New York: St. Martin's Press, 1983), pp. 51–52.

124 Christopher Pollitt . . . Pollitt, p. 87.

CHAPTER 4: EMPOWERMENT AND SHARED LEADERSHIP

128 "There is more uncertainty . . ." Camille Cates Barnett, "The Ox and Me: A View from Atop an Organization," *Public Administration Review*, vol. 44 (November–December 1984), p. 526.

129 "We must create a vision . . ." Ibid.

130 "It operates, and is vital . . ." *APS 2000*, p. 15.

131 "More and more decisions . . ." Warren Bennis, "The Artform of Leadership," in *Public Administration in Action*, R. B. Denhardt and B. R. Hammond (Pacific Grove, CA: Brooks/Cole, 1992), p. 311.

134 But there is evidence . . ." Sir Robin Butler, "New Challenges or Familiar Prescriptions," The Redcliffe-Maud Memorial Lecture, Royal Institute of Public Administration, London, October 10, 1990, p. 2.

134 Butler especially appreciates the irony . . . Ibid., p. 5.

137 Top managers and those in the legistlature . . . Eileen Shanahan, "The Mysteries of Innovative Government," *Governing*, vol. 5, no. 1 (October 1991), p. 37.

137 William Talley . . . Ibid.

138 Shared Leadership. Material in this section is adapted from Robert B. Denhardt and Kevin Prelgovisk, "Public Leadership: A Developmental Perspective," in *Executive Leadership in the Public Service*, R. B. Denhardt and W. H. Stewart (Tuscaloosa: The University of Alabama Press, 1992), pp. 33–44.

138 John Gardner . . . John W. Gardner, "Remarks to the NASPAA Conference, October 23, 1987," *Enterprise, the Newsletter of NASPAA* (1987), p. 1.

138 James MacGregor Burns . . . James MacGregor Burns, *Leadership* (New York: Harper & Row, 1978), p. 18.

145 "They didn't care . . ." Ron Contino, "Waging Revolution in the Public Sector," unpublished report, June 1989, p. 7.

145 "One only has to envision . . ." Ibid., p. 6.

146 "The union would be kept well aware . . ." Ibid., p. 8.

146 Contino recalls . . . Ron Contino, "The Theory Z Turnaround of a Public Agency," *Public Administration Review*, vol. 42 (January–February 1982), p. 68.

147 Rather, he started with a virtual transfer of power . . . Contino (1989), p. 10.

153 According to the statement . . . HM Customs and Excise, "Management Plan, 1991–92 to 1993–94" (1991), p. 5.

154 After spending hours . . . B.C. Hydro, "Corporate Strategic Plan" (November 1990).

157 Several decades ago, Herbert Kaufman . . . Herbert Kaufman, *The Forest Ranger* (Baltimore: Johns-Hopkins University, 1960).

159 "We knew what was best . . ." John Locke, "Integrating the Regional Office," speech delivered to the National Pilot Symposium, Minneapolis, May 1990, p. 2.

159 "The organization 'boxes' . . ." Ibid.
160 In contrast, the new culture . . . USDA Forest Service, "Restructuring the Work Culture," in *New Thinking for Managing Government* (USDA Forest Service, n.d.), p. 4.
160 In the Eastern Region . . . Eastern Region of the USDA Forest Service, *Fulfilling Our Vision* (Washington, DC: Eastern Region of the USDA Forest Service, February 1990), p. 6.
160 "The Regional Foresters' calendars . . ." Locke, p. 6.
161 "It is within this diverse community . . ." Jeff Sirmon, "Evolving Concepts of Leadership: Towards a Sustainable Future," presentation, n.d., n.p., pp. 4–5.
163 "The two ground rules . . ." USDA Forest Service, "The Evolution of Middle Management," in *New Thinking for Managing Government* (USDA Forest Service, n.d.), p. 3.
165 As Hanna frames the issue . . . Donald G. Hanna, *Police Executive Leadership* (Champaign, IL: Stipes, 1990), p. 31.
166 "A way will be opened . . ." John C. Alderson, "Police and the Social Order," in *Police and Public Order in Europe*, edited by J. Roach and J. Thomaneck (London: Croom Helm, 1985), p. 30.
166 "It is only by first changing . . ." David C. Couper and Sabine H. Lobitz, *Quality Policing: The Madison Experience* (Washington, DC: Police Executive Research Forum, 1991), p. 12.
169 "When power is held at the top . . ." N. L. Grunstad, "The Total Army Leadership Goal," in *Leadership on the Future Battlefield*, edited by J. G. Hunt and J. D. Blair (Washington, DC: Pergamon-Brassey's, 1985), p. 238.
176 Especially under conditions of stress and uncertainty . . . Robert B. Denhardt, "Images of Death and Slavery in Organizational Life," *Journal of Management*, vol. 13 (1987), pp. 123–133.

CHAPTER 5: PRAGMATIC INCREMENTALISM
179 Rather "an excellent manager . . ." Robert D. Behn, "Management by Groping Along," *Journal of Policy and Management Review*, vol. 7, no. 4 (1988), p. 645.
183 "A series of wins . . ." Weick, quoted in Behn, ibid.
186 Without question . . . Alison Crook, "Notes for Performance Improvement Strategies in a Public Sector Corporation," presentation to the SES Seminar, December 4, 1990, p. 5.
187 Ironically, Crook reports . . . Ibid, p. 7.
187 "It's always difficult . . ." Ibid.
188 Similarly, Crook recalls . . . Alison Crook, "Management's Role in the Service Revolution," presentation to the Service Revolution Conference, March 1–2, 1990, p. 3.
188 "Without this, you and your managers . . ." Ibid.
189 Crook, who takes her turn . . . Ibid., p. 6.
189 "For a start . . ." Ibid.
189 Crook describes herself . . . Ibid., p. 8.
190 "But within those parameters . . ." Ibid., p. 9.
191 "Middle management now has to learn . . ." Ibid., p. 11.

198 For example, the framework document . . . Employment Service, "A Framework Document for the Agency," 1990, p. 2.

206 And, third, identify . . . B.C. Housing Management Corporation, "People Power: A Framework for Positive Change in the Workplace," brochure (Victoria, BC: B.C. Housing Management Corporation, February 1991), p. 4.

210 "It survives . . ." Stephen E. Higgins, "An Organizational Approach to Developing People," *The Bureaucrat* (Winter 1990), p. 54.

211 In addition, the executives . . . Ibid., p. 55.

218 "And, they must be willing . . ." Joe Coffee, "Tenacity: Changing the Management Culture of the Bureau of Alcohol, Tobacco, and Firearms," *FMI Journal* (Fall 1988), p. 32.

CHAPTER 6: A DEDICATION TO PUBLIC SERVICE

230 Certainly, the grand tradition . . . John F. Kennedy, "Inaugural Address," in *Speeches of the American Presidents*, edited by J. Podell and S. Anzovin (New York: H. W. Wilson Co., 1988), p. 605.

231 Authors of a Heritage Foundation report . . . See, for example, Donald J. Devine, "Political Administration: The Right Way," in *Steering the Elephant*, edited by R. Rector and M. Sanera (New York: Universe Books, 1987).

232 "In this view, the public service . . ." Robert B. Denhardt and Edward T. Jennings, Jr., "Image and Integrity in the Public Service," *Public Administration Review*, vol. 49 (January–February 1989), p. 77.

233 "It is beginning to look to many of us . . ." quoted in Graham K. Wilson, "Prospects for the Public Service in Britain: Major to the Rescue?" *International Review of Administrative Sciences*, vol. 57 (September 1991), p. 331.

233 Not surprisingly, "the constant reiteration . . ." Ibid., p. 332.

235 These and other agencies . . . Craig McGregor, "Sordid Side of Hard-Core Economics," *Sydney Morning Herald* (October 10, 1990), p. 13.

235 "Public servants were demoralized . . ." Jack Manion, "Career Public Service in Canada: Reflections and Predictions," *International Review of Administrative Sciences*, vol. 57 (September 1991), p. 363.

237 "In essence, the task forces called for . . ." Ibid., p. 366.

239 "Unfortunately, when they do things . . ." *Time*, May 25, 1987.

239 Sir Robin Butler . . . Butler, p. 4.

241 "Public servants should safeguard public confidence . . ." Josephson Institute for the Advancement of Ethics, *Preserving the Public Trust* (Marina del Rey, CA: Josephson Institute for the Advancement of Ethics, 1990), pp. 1, 12, 18, 20, 22.

241 The top management team . . . Missouri Office of Administration, "Statement of Management Philosophy."

241 Similarly, the corporate values statement . . . City of Morgan Hill, "Corporate Values Statement."

241 Members of the Public Works Department . . . Public Works Department, "Statement of Philosophy."

242 "Managing ethics also involves . . ." Kathryn G. Denhardt, "Managing Ethics," unpublished manuscript, 1989, p. 1.

243 "Leadership by example . . ." Stephen J. Bonczek, "Ethics: Challenge of the 1990s," *Public Management* (July 1990), pp. 17–18. Reprinted from the July 1990 issue of *Public Management*, published by the International City/County Management Association (ICMA), Washington, DC.

245 In their policy role . . . Sir Robert Armstrong, *The Duties and Responsibilities of Civil Servants in Relation to Ministers* (Office of the Home Civil Service, 1986), p. 3.

245 As one scholar phrases it . . . Wilson, p. 328.

248 The glib, cynical retort . . . quoted in Kenneth Kernaghan and David Siegel, *Public Administration in Canada*, 2nd ed. (Scarborough, Ontario: Nelson Canada, 1991), p. 331.

252 Doing so is not without great pain . . . Peter Hennessy, "The Ethic of the Profession," *The Bulletin* (July 1989), p. 103.

253 On the other hand, recognizing . . . Elizabeth K. Kellar, *Ethical Insight/Ethical Action* (Washington, DC: ICMA, 1988), pp. 167–177.

254 Alan Ehrenhalt . . . Alan Ehrenhalt, *The United States of Ambition* (New York: Times Books, 1991).

257 "Public trust in the career service . . ." John Uhr, "Ethics and Public Service," *Australian Journal of Public Administration*, vol. 47 (June 1988), p. 109.

259 A decade ago . . . Robert B. Denhardt, *In the Shadow of Organization* (Lawrence: University Press of Kansas, 1981).

260 "No amount of rhetoric . . ." Uhr, p. 117.

CHAPTER 7: THE PURSUIT OF SIGNIFICANCE

268 "So much of the American public . . ." O. Glenn Stahl, in "The Changing Public Service: Looking Back . . . Moving Forward," edited by D. Waldo and J. R. Carr, *Public Administration Review*, vol. 50 (March–April 1990), p. 206.

269 "What seems required is a true sharing of power . . ." Robert B. Denhardt, "Alienation and the Challenge of Participation," *Personnel Administration* (September–October 1971), p. 32.

272 Robert Bellah and his colleagues . . . Robert N. Bellah, Richard Madsen, William M. Sullivan, Ann Swidler, and Steven M. Tipton, *Habits of the Heart* (Berkeley: University of California Press, 1985), p. 211.

272 "To change the conception of government . . ." Ibid.

273 They quote Elmer Staats . . . Quoted in James L. Perry and Lois Recascino Wise, "The Motivational Bases of Public Service," *Public Administration Review*, vol. 50 (May–June 1990), p. 368.

274 Although individuals . . . Ibid., p. 371.

275 The issue was distilled for me . . . "Miss America's Journey Back," *Columbia Tribune*, Columbia, Missouri (October 1982).

INDEX

Index

Index